the *Allure*
of Gnosticism

D1453345

the*Allure*
of Gnosticism

The Gnostic Experience
In Jungian Psychology and Contemporary Culture

Robert A. Segal, Editor
June Singer and Murray Stein, Associate Editors

Open  Court
Chicago and La Salle, Illinois

OPEN COURT and the above logo are registered in the
U.S. Patent and Trademark Office.

© 1995 by Open Court Publishing Company

First printing 1995

Library of Congress Cataloging-in-Publication Data

The allure of Gnosticism : the Gnostic experience in Jungian
    psychology and contemporary culture / Robert A. Segal, editor ; June
    Singer and Murray Stein, associate editors.
        p.   cm.
    Includes bibliographical references and index.
    ISBN 0-8126-9277-2. — ISBN 0-8126-9278-0 (paper)
    1. Psychoanalysis and religion.   2. Gnosticism—Psychology.
3. Jung, C.G. (Carl Gustav), 1875–1961.   I. Segal, Robert Alan.
II. Singer, June.   III. Stein, Murray, 1943–   .
BF175.4.R44A45   1995
299'.932'019—dc20   94-45077
                                                               CIP

CONTENTS

CONTRIBUTORS

GILLES QUISPEL is Professor Emeritus of the History of the Early Church at the University of Utrecht. He has also been a visiting professor at Harvard University and at the Catholic University of Louvain. An eminent scholar of Gnosticism, he is well known for his view that the chief roots of Gnosticism are Jewish. He is equally well known for his lifelong espousal of a Jungian approach to Gnosticism. In 1952 he acquired for the Jung Institute in Zurich the first Nag Hammadi Codex, subsequently known as the "Jung Codex." His many writings include *Gnosis als Weltreligion* (Origo, 1951; 2nd ed., 1972), which originated as lectures at the Zurich Jung Institute; *The Gospel According to Thomas: Coptic Text Established and Translated* (Brill and Harper, 1959); *Makarius, Das Thomasevangelium und das Lied von der Perle* (Brill, 1967); and *Gnostic Studies* (2 vols., Nederlands Historisch-Archaeologisch Instituut, 1974–75), a collection of thirty-two essays, among them several pioneering applications of Jungian psychology. A Festschrift, *Studies in Gnosticism and Hellenistic Religions* (Brill, 1981), was presented to Quispel on his sixty-fifth birthday.

ROBERT SEGAL is Lecturer in the Department of Religious Studies, Lancaster University, England, and Associate North American Editor of *Religion*. He has written *The Poimandres as Myth: Scholarly Theory and Gnostic Meaning* (Mouton de Gruyter, 1986), *Religion and the Social Sciences: Essays on the Confrontation* (Scholars Press, 1989), *Joseph Campbell: An Introduction* (Garland, 1987; 2nd ed., New American Library/Penguin, 1990), and *Explaining and Interpreting Religion: Essays on the Issue* (Peter Lang, 1992). He has edited *In Quest of the Hero* (Princeton University Press, 1990) and *The Gnostic Jung* (Princeton University Press, 1992). His advocacy of a social scientific approach to the study of religion is critically examined in *Religion and Reductionism: Essays on Eliade, Segal, and the Challenge of the Social Sciences for the Study of Religion* (Brill, 1994).

MURRAY STEIN is a Zurich-trained Jungian analyst who received a Ph.D. in Religion and Psychological Studies from the University of Chicago. A training analyst at the Jung Institute of Chicago, he is a founding member of both the Inter-Regional Society of Jungian Analysts and the Chicago Society of Jungian Analysts, where he also served as the first President. He is Honorary Secretary of the International Association for Analytical Psychology. He has written *In Midlife* (Spring Publications, 1984), *Jung's Treatment of Christianity* (Chiron, 1985), and *Solar Conscience/Lunar Conscience* (Chiron, 1993), and has edited or coedited many volumes, including *Jungian Analysis* (Open Court, 1982; 2nd ed., 1995), *Jung's Challenge to Contemporary Religion* (Chiron, 1987), *Psyche's Stories* (2 vols., Chiron, 1991, 1992), *Psyche at Work* (Chiron, 1992), and the Chiron Clinical Series. He is in private practice in Wilmette, Illinois.

JUNE SINGER is a Jungian analyst, trained in Zurich, who received a Ph.D. from Northwestern University in Psychology. She is in private practice in Palo Alto, California, and is a member of the Jung Institute of San Francisco. She was a founder of the Jung Institute of Chicago and of the Inter-Regional Society of Jungian Analysts. Among her widely known books are *Boundaries of the Soul: The Practice of Jung's Psychology* (Doubleday, 1972), *Androgyny: Toward a New Theory of Sexuality* (Doubleday Anchor, 1976; 2nd ed., Sigo, 1987 [subtitled *The Opposites Within*]), *The Unholy Bible: A Psychological Interpretation of William Blake* (Putnam, 1970; Harper Colophon, 1973; Sigo, 1986 [subtitled *Blake, Jung and the Collective Unconscious*]), and *Energies of Love: Sexuality Re-Visioned* (Doubleday Anchor, 1983; 2nd ed., Sigo, 1990 [retitled *Love's Energies*]). Her most recent work focuses on Gnosticism: *Seeing through the Visible World: Jung, Gnosis, and Chaos* (Harper & Row, 1990), and *A Gnostic Book of Hours: Keys to Inner Wisdom* (HarperSanFrancisco, 1992).

SCHUYLER BROWN is Professor in the Faculty of Theology at St. Michael's College, University of Toronto. He also teaches at the University's Centre for the Study of Religion and in the Department of Near Eastern Studies. The author of *Apostasy and Perseverance in the Theology of Luke* (Pontifical Biblical Institute, 1969) and *The Origins of Christianity: A Historical Introduction to the New Testament* (Oxford University Press, 1984), he is currently working on a book entitled *Text and Psyche: The Bible and Religious Experience.* He is the convener of the Jung and Spirituality Group of the Jung Foundation, Toronto, and is also Assistant Priest at the Church of St. Augustine of Canterbury, Toronto.

ELAINE PAGELS is Harrington Spear Paine Foundation Professor of Religion at Princeton University. She was formerly Professor and Chair of the Department of Religion, Barnard College, Columbia University. She is the author of two celebrated books: *The Gnostic Gospels* (Random House, 1979), which won both the National Book Critics Circle Award and the American Book Award, and *Adam, Eve, and the Serpent* (Random House, 1988). She has also written *The Johannine Gospel in Gnostic Exegesis: Heracleon's Commentary on John* (Abingdon, 1973) and *The Gnostic Paul: Gnostic Exegesis of the Pauline Letters* (Fortress, 1975). In 1980 she was awarded a MacArthur Prize Fellowship.

BRADLEY TEPASKE is a Jungian analyst in Santa Barbara, California. He received his training at the Jung Institute in Zurich and also received a Ph.D. in Depth Psychology from the Union Institute. For many years he has investigated the relationship between sexuality and religion in Gnosticism and other religious traditions.

JORUNN JACOBSEN BUCKLEY is a scholar of Gnosticism, particularly of Mandaeanism. She has taught at various universities, including MIT, Emory University, Syracuse University, and Connecticut College. She is the author of *Female Fault and Fulfillment in Gnosticism* (University of North Carolina Press, 1986) and of many essays. She recently translated an esoteric Mandaean scroll, *Diwan Malkuta laita: The Scroll of Exalted Kingship* (American Oriental Society, 1993). In 1992 she began working with Mandaean communities in exile and was invited by the Highest Spiritual Council of Mandaeans of Baghdad to visit Iraq in 1994.

HANS JONAS (1903–93) was born and educated in Germany. He left in 1933, when Hitler came to power, and in 1940 joined the British Army in the Middle East. After World War II he taught at the Hebrew University of Jerusalem and at Carleton University in Ottawa before becoming Professor of Philosophy at the New School for Social Research. He was named Alvin Johnson Professor of Philosophy in 1966 and retired in 1976. An eminent philosopher of existentialism, ethics, and biology as well as a renowned scholar of Gnosticism, he was the author of, among other works, *Augustin und das paulinische Freiheitsproblem: Ein philosophischer Beitrag zur Genesis der christlich-abendländischen Freiheitsidee* (Vandenhoeck & Ruprecht, 1930; 2nd ed., 1965), *Gnosis und spätantiker Geist* (Vandenhoeck & Ruprecht, vol. I, 1934; 2nd ed., 1954; 3rd ed., 1964; vol. II, 1954;

2nd ed., 1966), *The Gnostic Religion: The Message of the Alien God and the Beginnings of Christianity* (Beacon, 1958; 2nd ed., 1963), *The Phenomenon of Life: Towards a Philosophical Biology* (Harper & Row, 1966; Dell, 1968; University of Chicago Press, 1982), *Philosophical Essays: From Ancient Creed to Technological Man* (Prentice-Hall, 1974; University of Chicago Press, 1980), and *The Imperative of Responsibility: In Search of an Ethics for the Technological Age* (University of Chicago Press, 1984). *Gnosis*, a Festschrift for Jonas the scholar of Gnosticism, was published in 1978 (Vandenhoeck & Ruprecht).

STEPHEN MCKNIGHT is Professor of European and Cultural History at the University of Florida. In 1993 he served as Carol Belk Distinguished Professor of the Humanities, University of North Carolina at Asheville. He has written *Sacralizing the Secular: The Renaissance Origins of Modernity* (LSU Press, 1989) and *The Modern Age and the Recovery of Ancient Wisdom: Historical Consciousness, 1450–1650* (University of Missouri Press, 1991), and has edited *Science, Pseudo-Science, and Utopianism in Early Modern Thought* (University of Missouri Press, 1992) and *Eric Voegelin's Search for Order in History* (LSU Press, 1978; 2nd ed., University Press of America, 1987).

WALTER SOKEL is Commonwealth Professor of German and English Literatures at the University of Virginia. He had previously been Professor of German at Columbia University and Stanford University. A distinguished authority on modern German literature, he is the author of, among other works, *The Writer in Extremis: Expressionism in Twentieth-Century German Literature* (Stanford University Press, 1959; German translation, 1960), *Franz Kafka—Tragik und Ironie: zur Strucktur seine Kunst* (Langen-Müller, 1964; Fischer, 1976), and *Franz Kafka* (Columbia University Press, 1966). There have appeared two Festschriften in his honor: *Probleme der Moderne* (Niemeyer, 1983) and *Fictions of Culture* (Peter Lang, 1991). He has also served as President and Honorary President of the Kafka Society of America. He is a member of the American Academy of Arts and Sciences.

DANIEL LINDLEY is a Jungian analyst in private practice in Evanston, Illinois, and a member of the Chicago Society of Jungian Analysts. For twenty years he was Professor and director of the teacher education program in the Department of English, University of

Illinois at Chicago. He is the author of *This Rough Magic: The Life of Teaching* (Bergin & Garvey, 1993).

EDWARD CONZE (1904–79) was born in England to German parents and was educated in Germany. He taught religious studies and Buddhist studies at many universities, including the Universities of London, Oxford, Southampton, Wisconsin, Washington, and Lancaster and the University of California at Berkeley and Santa Barbara. A distinguished authority on Buddhism, he was the author, editor, or translator of many books, including *Buddhism: Its Essence and Development* (Cassirer and Philosophical Library, 1951; Harper Torchbooks, 1959); *Buddhist Texts through the Ages* (Cassirer and Philosophical Library, 1954; Harper Torchbooks, 1964), *Buddhist Scriptures* (Penguin, 1959); *A Short History of Buddhism* (Chetana, 1960; 2nd ed., Allen & Unwin, 1979); *Buddhist Thought in India: Three Phases of Buddhist Philosophy* (Allen & Unwin, 1962; University of Michigan Press, 1967); *Thirty Years of Buddhist Studies: Selected Essays* (Cassirer and University of South Carolina Press, 1968); and *Further Buddhist Studies: Selected Essays* (Cassirer and University of South Carolina Press, 1975), which contains an essay on "Jung's Psychology and the Dharma." His autobiography is entitled *The Memoirs of a Modern Gnostic* (2 vols., Sherborne, England: Samizdat, 1979). A Festschrift, *Prajnaparamita and Related Systems,* was published in 1977 (Berkeley Buddhist Studies Series).

KENNETH O'NEILL is an independent teacher and writer on Buddhism and Gnostic spirituality. He received a master's degree from the Institute of Buddhist Studies, Berkeley, and also received both ordination and a teaching license from Nishi Honganji (1972). In addition, he is a Free Initiator of l'Ordre Martiniste. He is at work on a book to be entitled *Stealing Enlightenment—The Boddhisattva Way.* He founded La Cinta Wisdom School in Tucson in 1993.

ROSAMONDE MILLER is the founder of the Church of Gnosis in Palo Alto, California. Of French origin, she grew up in several cultures. She is an ordained priest and a consecrated bishop in two Gnostic traditions. She bases her work on inner gnosis, left uninterpreted, and has coined the term "wild gnosis" to describe her approach.

RICHARD SMITH teaches in both the religion and the art departments of the Claremont Graduate School. The managing editor of the third edition of *The Nag Hammadi Library in English* (Harper & Row, 1988), he has written extensively in the fields of Coptic language and ancient Gnosticism. Among his publications is "The Modern Relevance of Gnosticism," the afterword to the third edition of *The Nag Hammadi Library in English.* He has recently edited *Ancient Christian Magic* (HarperSanFrancisco, 1994). He also writes on contemporary art.

INTRODUCTION

Robert A. Segal

MANY who have heard of Gnosticism know it as merely an obscure, ancient Christian heresy that died out millennia ago and that remains of interest only to scholars. Gnosticism, however, should be seen much more broadly. Even in the ancient world it was more than a Christian heresy. There were Jewish and pagan as well as Christian Gnostics. Gnosticism likely both antedated Christianity and influenced it. Rather than being relegated to a variant of other religions, Gnosticism might even be regarded as a religion in its own right.

Ancient Gnosticism was the belief in a radical, irreconcilable dualism of immateriality and matter. Immateriality was divine and wholly good. Matter was irredeemably evil. The predicament was the entrapment of pieces, or sparks, of immateriality in matter—the entrapment of human souls in bodies. (In tripartite rather than dualistic varieties of Gnosticism, it was the immaterial spirit which lay trapped in the soul as well as the body.) Because the spark was not merely trapped but hidden, liberation lay above all in knowledge: in the discovery of one's divinity and of the immaterial cosmos and god. Just as the individual Gnostic's goal was to extricate his or her own spark from the body and return it to its immaterial home, so the cosmic goal was to extricate all sparks from the material world and reunite them all with their immaterial home. The aim was to terminate any connection between immateriality and matter. Matter would thereby either still remain, albeit inchoate, or dissolve altogether.

Yet Gnosticism can be understood far more broadly still—as not merely an ancient movement but also a contemporary one. Gnosticism here is alive, not dead. It is the belief in the alienation of human beings either from their true selves or from the world, not usually from any divinity. The true self need not be immaterial, and the place in which it lies lodged need not be the body. Least of all need the true world be immaterial. In fact, there need not be any fixed self or any world beyond, let alone any god. Contemporary Gnosticism need not even involve the cosmos. It can be entirely psychological, political, or social. The dualism can be between parts of the personality, between nations, between classes, or between races.

Contemporary Gnosticism need not even be radically, or antithetically, dualistic. Its dualism can instead be irenic. In radically dualistic Gnosticism, whether ancient or modern, one's old identity is to be rejected for a new one. In irenic Gnosticism, which is an exclusively modern phenomenon, one's new identity is to be harmonized with the prior one.

Among the varieties of contemporary Gnosticism, atheistic existentialism most of all insists on the ineluctability of the alienation of human beings from the world, though certainly not from their true selves. Alienation from the world is exactly the human condition. Conversely, Jungian psychology above all strives to overcome the alienation within human beings, whether or not also that between them and the world. It seeks to reconcile opposing parts of the personality.

This book is scarcely the first attempt to view Gnosticism as a living enterprise. Back in the 1930s the philosopher Hans Jonas first interpreted Gnosticism through the eyes of twentieth-century existentialism, and in a 1952 essay, reprinted in the present book, he juxtaposes the two outlooks. Beginning in the 1950s the political philosopher Eric Voegelin contended that many twentieth-century political movements, including Marxism and Fascism, evince staunchly Gnostic qualities. That contention is assessed by one of the contributors to this volume.

Modernity per se has been called Gnostic by, among others, Martin Buber. Others have identified *post*modernism with Gnosticism. Scores of writers and thinkers of the last two centuries have been labeled Gnostic—Goethe, Schleiermacher, Blake, Hegel, Schelling, Byron, Shelley, Emerson, Marx, Melville, Conrad, Nietzsche, Yeats, Hesse, Schweitzer, Tillich, Toynbee, Heidegger, Sartre, Simone Weil, Wallace Stevens, Doris Lessing, I. B. Singer, Walker Percy, Jack Kerouac, and Thomas Pynchon among them. Harold Bloom has pronounced Romanticism Gnostic and more recently has characterized American religion as Gnostic. One of the contributors to the present book examines Kafka as a modern Gnostic; another, T. S. Eliot.[1]

Doubtless the most influential gaze on Gnosticism through contemporary eyes has been C. G. Jung's. Jung compares the psychological state of many of his patients with that of ancient Gnostics and finds in both the yearning for a hidden self, the discovery and cultivation of which provide the deepest human fulfillment. Jung himself has regularly been called a Gnostic. The first six essays in this book approach Gnosticism from a Jungian point of view.

In the opening essay Gilles Quispel summarizes his lifelong, pioneering effort to tie ancient Gnosticism to Jungian psychology. After describing his purchase for the Jung Institute in Zurich of those Nag Hammadi texts subsequently known as the Jung Codex, Quispel offers his own distinctive Jungian analysis of Gnosticism. For him, Jungian psychology, properly applied, sees the Gnostic cosmos not as the projection of the human psyche but as the parallel to it. The relationship is one of synchronicity, not projection. In taking to task those Jungians who reduce divinity to humanity rather than preserving the autonomy of divinity, Quispel speculates that Gnosticism may be true of the world itself, not merely true to human nature.

In the second essay I try to explain Jung's fascination with ancient Gnosticism. I describe how Jung saw Gnosticism, together with alchemy, as the ancient forerunner of his own psychology and therefore as confirmation of the existence of the collective unconscious. At the same time I question Jung's interpretation of the Gnostic ideal as equivalent to that of individuation. I suggest that from a Jungian point of view the Gnostic aim might more accurately be characterized as inflationary.

In essays three and four Murray Stein and June Singer give psychological translations and interpretations of specific Gnostic myths—Stein focusing on the *Apocryphon of John* and the *Gospel of Truth,* Singer concentrating on the *Exegesis on the Soul.* Following Jung, both Stein and Singer seek to show that ancient Gnostics were dealing with the same psychological conditions as we are today: with the need to advance beyond ego consciousness to the unconscious and to integrate the two to form a cohesive psyche, or self. In the *Gospel of Truth* Error, the creator of the material world, symbolizes the ego that is blind to the collective unconscious; in the *Apocryphon of John* the equally blind creator god is Yaldabaoth. Stein demonstrates how each myth relentlessly exposes the creator god's obliviousness to a higher god, who corresponds to the unconscious. As

Stein interprets the myths, the creator god need cede only his supremacy, not his life, to the higher god. The goal of Gnosticism therefore matches that of Jungian psychology: not the rejection of one side of humanity for another but only the supplementing of one side by the other. The goal is harmony, not conflict. For Stein, the Gnostic castigation of the creator god's arrogance especially befits the modern West, with its vaunted political and technological mastery of the world.

Where the subject of the myths which Stein analyzes is masculine, the subject of the myth which Singer explicates is feminine: the soul. Singer translates her biography of the soul into the biography of the psyche. Interpreting the *Exegesis on the Soul* as a case of tripartite rather than dualistic Gnosticism, Singer parallels the body, the soul, and the spirit to ego consciousness, the ego, and the unconscious. Initially undifferentiated from the unconscious, the psyche emerges as an independent ego, gets cut off from its unconscious roots, and struggles to reconnect itself to those roots and thereby forge a unified self. Like Stein, Singer takes the aim of Gnosticism to be the reconciliation rather than the severance of opposites. Because all human beings must harmonize the disparate parts of their nature, Gnosticism for Singer can teach persons even today.

In the fifth essay Schuyler Brown boldly interprets ancient Gnostic texts not as statements of metaphysical doctrines but as expressions of archetypal images. For him, the ancient antagonism between orthodoxy and Gnosticism was not simply a disagreement, however severe, over conceptions of divinity, humanity, and the cosmos. It was, more deeply, a clash between a conceptual approach to religion and an experiential one. Inspired by Jung's writings on not only Gnosticism but also modern Christianity, Brown sees the Gnostics as using their religion to tend to their unconscious rather than, like their orthodox adversaries, to flee from it. Where orthodoxy employed secondary process thinking, Gnosticism touted primary process thinking. Without claiming that Gnosticism itself continues to exist today, Brown maintains that its concern with psychological necessities is of significance for any age.

In the next essay Bradley TePaske singles out the figure of Mary Magdalene, who appears in all four Gospels within the New Testament but appears far more fully in several Gnostic Gospels, including one named for her. As TePaske shows, the Gnostic Mary enjoys a more elevated status than the canonical one. She is closer to Jesus than any of the Apostles, has an outright erotic bond to Jesus, and is granted by him an extraordinary vision of the ascent of the soul.

Without claiming that Gnosticism itself is a present-day phenomenon, TePaske suggests that Mary in Gnosticism, if also to a much lesser extent in the New Testament, exemplifies that rare figure in any period who dares to confront the unconscious. Mary is both feared and envied by the Apostles exactly because they themselves would never undertake that confrontation.

In the seventh essay Jorunn Buckley enumerates the range of views that Gnosticism holds of the feminine. Where, says Buckley, mainstream Christianity has typically viewed female figures either entirely negatively or entirely positively—Eve and Mary epitomizing the extremes—Gnosticism offers a spectrum of views. Female gods and feminine attributes are often associated with a complex blend of positive and negative qualities. While Buckley restricts herself to ancient Gnosticism, she suggests that its balanced outlook offers a more realistic option for women in the contemporary world.

In the eighth essay Elaine Pagels sifts out the meaning of some of the main issues considered by the Gnostic *Gospel of Philip:* the mystery of marriage, the relationship of opposites, and the source of evil. Understood psychologically, the parts joined in marriage are the parts of the psyche, which have become isolated from each other and must be reconnected. Yet Pagels proceeds to argue that the Gospel actually refuses to endorse marriage over celibacy or, alternatively, to oppose it. Rather than taking a stand, the Gospel beckons adherents to decide for themselves this and all other questions of morality. In refusing to define morality in terms of prescribed practices, the Gospel espouses a strikingly up-to-date stance, concerned as it is more with attitude than with action and with the array of individual convictions. Still, the Gospel for Pagels is not preaching any easy moral relativism and on the contrary is insisting that the capacity for evil—a capacity too often unconscious—be both recognized and contained. Pagels is not asserting that Gnosticism, as represented by *Philip,* is itself a contemporary phenomenon, but she is asserting that ancient Gnostics were confronting the same fundamental issues as human beings today.

In an essay that has become a classic, Hans Jonas parallels the ancient Gnostic outlook to the modern existentialist one, which he traces all the way back to Pascal and which is best represented in the twentieth century by the early Heidegger and Sartre. For Jonas, the central tenet of both Gnosticism and existentialism is the radical alienation of human beings from the world. Human beings find themselves trapped in a world that is at odds with their true nature. Jonas stresses that the two outlooks are far from identical. In

Gnosticism the world is demonic and hostile; in existentialism it is impersonal and indifferent. In Gnosticism one is presently separated from one's true self; in existentialism one has no fixed nature. In Gnosticism the alienation is surmountable; in existentialism it is not. Still, Jonas emphasizes the overarching similarity of radical alienation from the surrounding world. While not claiming that Gnosticism itself is modern, he does claim that it expresses the same unremittingly dour world view as that of modern existentialism.

Stephen McKnight, in the tenth essay, evaluates the kindred claim by Eric Voegelin: the claim not that Gnosticism is modern but that modernity is Gnostic. Like many other thinkers, Voegelin deems confidence in its mastery of the world the key trait of modernity. Unlike others, however, Voegelin ascribes that confidence not to the rise of science and of seculardom but to the resurfacing of an ancient, esoteric religion: Gnosticism, which boasts knowledge of the true nature of the world. McKnight praises Voegelin for identifying the transformative power of knowledge as the central link between Gnosticism and modernity, but he observes that Voegelin's labeling Gnostic the use of knowledge to perfect the material world oddly gives Gnosticism a world-affirming rather than world-rejecting character. McKnight argues that a more fitting source of the modern outlook is the Renaissance Hermeticism of Ficino, who interprets optimistically even the most pessimistic of the Hermetic texts, the *Poimandres* (or *Pimander*). McKnight does note that Voegelin himself came to recognize the Hermetic as well as, for him, the Gnostic roots of modernity. In any case Voegelin's optimistic reading of Gnosticism parallels Jung's—and contrasts conspicuously to Jonas's pessimistic reading.

In the first of two essays on Gnosticism in literature Walter Sokel delineates the Gnostic side of Franz Kafka's life and thought. In traditional Judaism, according to Sokel, God's relationship to the world is ambivalent: God is at once near and distant. Kafka carries God's distance to its logical finale, removing God altogether from the world. For Kafka, the material world is a godless, fallen prison into which humanity, itself ultimately divine, has fallen. Death alone offers escape to an immaterial haven occupied by a divinity higher than the hostile, tyrannical ruler of the everyday world. In Gnostic fashion, knowledge of the world beyond this one entails acting accordingly. Hence Kafka rejected family, career, sex, and other worldly endeavors in order to concentrate, chiefly through writing, on the beckoning higher world. Yet Sokel emphasizes that, for all Kafka's Gnostic proclivity, he never abandoned traditional Judaism.

And it was the tension between the two rather than the Gnosticism itself which caused Kafka his keenest suffering.

In the following essay Daniel Lindley compares Jung's extraordinary encounter with the unconscious after his break with Freud to several of T. S. Eliot's "peak" experiences. Taking as autobiographical the writings that immediately followed these episodes—Jung's "Seven Sermons to the Dead" and Eliot's early poems—Lindley suggests that both figures were struggling to liberate themselves from confining, conventional, respectable lives. The breakdowns that both suffered were in fact encounters with another reality—encounters that provided the impetus for their lifelong quests. Lindley broadly terms Gnostic not so much their beliefs as their adventurousness, their willingness to "leave home" for a strange, new world.

In the first of a pair of essays on Gnosticism in Buddhism Edward Conze catalogues eight main similarities and no fewer than twenty-three similarities of detail between Gnosticism and the Mahayana form of Buddhism. Many chief tenets of Gnosticism find their counterparts in Mahayana Buddhism—among them, the emphasis on knowledge as both necessary and sufficient for salvation, the attribution of one's present state to ignorance, the hierarchical hiatus between those with knowledge and those without it, and a division between the highest god and the creator god. Conze briefly considers the possible explanations for these similarities. Perhaps because he comes to Gnosticism through Mahayana Buddhism, he challenges Jonas's characterization of the Gnostic world view as pessimistic.

In contrast to Conze, Kenneth O'Neill allows for pessimistic as well as optimistic strands of both Gnosticism and Buddhism. Indeed, he parallels Hinayana, or Theravada, Buddhism to pessimistic Gnosticism and parallels Mahayana Buddhism to optimistic Gnosticism. In Theravada one is emancipated from the everyday world. In Mahayana one continues to live in this world, simply with a new understanding of it. Yet O'Neill, like Conze, concentrates on the optimistic strand of Gnosticism and so devotes most of his essay to its Mahayana counterpart.

In the penultimate essay Rosamonde Miller provides a heartfelt autobiographical sketch of her coming to the Gnostic fold. Now bishop of her own Gnostic church in Palo Alto, California, Miller was raised to believe the world to be fundamentally good. Suddenly, at the age of nineteen, she found herself imprisoned, tortured, and raped in Castro's Cuba. Nearly despairing of finding any good amidst so much evil, she happened to overhear her jailer's expression of love for his daughter. Miller then recognized that even he was a mix of good and evil and, more, that she herself must be a mix of evil as well as good. The whole world must be accepted as a combination of good and evil rather than embraced only if exclusively good or rejected as wholly evil. This balanced outlook, while contrary to the world-rejecting ancient Gnostic one, exemplifies the optimistic strand of present-day Gnosticism.

In the final essay Richard Smith examines two contemporary Gnostic churches in Los Angeles: the Ecclesia Gnostica, founded by Stephan Hoeller, and the Gnostic Association, the English-language branch of a worldwide movement founded by Samael Aun Weor. Smith compares the two groups not only with each other but even more with their forebears. He shows that the world-affirming, nondualistic outlook of the Ecclesia Gnostica stems from nineteenth-century Theosophy rather than from second-century Gnosticism and that its psychological interpretation of Gnosticism derives from Jung, its patron guru. Where the Ecclesia Gnostica is at least familiar with ancient Gnosticism, the Gnostic Association is not. Yet its beliefs, while likewise rooted in Theosophy and other modern occult sources, are somewhat closer to those of ancient Gnosticism.

NOTES

1. On the vaunted scope of modern Gnosticism see, for example, Susan Anima Taubes, "The Gnostic Foundations of Heidegger's Nihilism," *Journal of Religion,* 34 (1954), 155–72; Thomas J. J. Altizer, "The Challenge of Modern Gnosticism," *Journal of Bible and Religion,* 30 (1962), 18–25; John E. Burkhart, "Gnosis and Contemporary Theology," *McCormick Quarterly,* 18 (1965), 43–49; Gilles Quispel, "Faust: Symbol of Western Man," *Eranos-Jahrbüch,* 35 (1967), 241–65; Quispel, "Hermann Hesse and Gnosis," in *Gnosis,* ed. Barbara Aland (Göttingen: Vandenhoeck & Ruprecht, 1978), 492–507; Ihab Hassan, *Paracriticisms* (Urbana: University of Illinois Press, 1975), ch. 6; Harold Bloom, *Poetry and Repression* (New Haven: Yale University Press, 1976); Bloom, *Agon* (New York: Oxford University Press, 1982); Bloom, *The American Religion* (New York: Simon & Schuster, 1992); Cleanth Brooks, "Walker Percy and Modern Gnosticism," *Southern Review,* n.s., 13 (1977), 677–87; Bruce Henricksen, *"Heart of Darkness* and the Gnostic Myth," *Mosaic,* 11 (1978), 35–44; Carl A. Raschke, *The Interruption of Eternity* (Chicago: Nelson-Hall, 1980); Pheme Perkins, *The Gnostic Dialogue* (New York: Paulist Press, 1980), 205–17; Gerald Hanratty, "Gnosticism and Modern Thought," *Irish Theological Quarterly,* 47 (1980), 3–23, 119–32; 48 (1981), 80–92; Robert Galbreath, "Problematic Gnosis: Hesse, Singer, Lessing, and the Limitations of Modern Gnosticism," *Journal of Religion,* 61 (1981), 20–36; Philip J. Lee, *Against the Protestant Gnostics*

(New York: Oxford University Press, 1987); Richard Smith, "The Modern Relevance of Gnosticism," in *The Nag Hammadi Library in English,* ed. James M. Robinson, 3rd ed. (San Francisco: Harper & Row, 1988), 532–49; Dwight Eddins, *The Gnostic Pynchon* (Bloomington: Indiana University Press, 1990); Giovanni Filoramo, *A History of Gnosticism,* tr. Anthony Alcock (Oxford: Blackwell, 1990), xiii–xxi, 12–13; Ioan P. Couliano, *The Tree of Gnosis,* trs. Hillary S. Wiesner and Ioan P. Couliano (San Francisco: HarperSanFrancisco, 1992), ch. 11; and my introduction to *The Gnostic Jung* (Princeton, NJ: Princeton University Press, 1992), 3–7.

[1]

GNOSIS AND PSYCHOLOGY

Gilles Quispel

DURING the war we had plenty of time: you could not go out, or eat, or resist, or participate in public life. It so happened that I was a teacher of Greek and Latin in a small provincial town of the Netherlands and was working on my dissertation. For this I had to read Christian Fathers of the second century, heresy hunters like Irenaeus and Tertullian. And then, in the particular constellation of that time and that moment in my life, I found that the heretics were right. Especially the poetic imagery of a certain Valentinus, a second-century Gnostic, the greatest Gnostic that ever lived, made a deep and lasting impression upon me. Only a few fragments of his writings remained, but the reports about the views of his pupils were so numerous that it was tantalizing to try and reconstruct the original doctrine of the Master himself. This I did from 1941 till 1945—I told you I had nothing to do—and after the war I published an article about it. You know what happens in such circumstances. You are young; when you have laid an egg, you think it is the world egg; in short I sent an offprint of this article to Aldous Huxley in California, Karl Barth in Basel and Carl Gustav Jung in Zurich. At that time I was disappointed that the first two mentioned did not answer; now I am rather astonished that Jung, at that time already a world celebrity of seventy-one, replied with a personal and encouraging letter. This led to an invitation for a conference in Ascona, Switzerland, one of the so-called Eranos Conferences, which Jung and his followers used to visit every year. Of course I lectured about my Valentinus, Jung said a few words of appreciation and then everybody liked me. This was in 1947.

Soon afterwards the news spread that Gnostic manuscripts in Coptic had been discovered in Egypt. It was said that among them there was the so-called *Gospel of Truth,* which according to a Father of the Church was in use among the Valentinians. And there was more.

One day the French professor Henri-Charles Puech, when sitting in the underground railway of Paris, was turning over the leaves of transcriptions from Nag Hammadi which a young Frenchman, Jean Doresse, had given to him. His attention was drawn to the beginning of one writing, which runs as follows: "These are the secret words which the Living Jesus spoke and Didymus Judas Thomas wrote."

In a flash it occurred to him that he had read that before. When the train stopped, he ran home and took a book from the shelf of his bookcase. It was so: the famous fragments of the sayings of Jesus in Greek, found at Oxyrhynchus in 1897 and 1903, began with the same words and turned out to belong to one specific writing, the *Gospel of Thomas.* For the first time in history a collection of sayings of our Lord, independent of the New Testament and in some cases completely new, had come to light. Puech had discovered this. And he had no possibility to get access to the manuscript. He wrote to me, I wrote to Jung, and in 1951 we had the opportunity to discuss certain matters in Ascona with Jung and his associate C. A. Meier. Why was this?

At that time the whole collection of Coptic writings known as the Nag Hammadi Library and discovered in 1945 could have been published completely. The Director of Egyptian Antiquities, the French priest Etienne Drioton, would have surveyed the whole enterprise and distributed the writings to French scholars exclusively. A start had already been made: Jean Doresse and Pahor Labib made an edition and translation of the very important *Apocryphon of John,* printed at the Imprimerie Nationale of Paris, which I have seen with my own eyes, but which was never published. But there occurred a revolution in Egypt, Drioton had to leave the country, Doresse could no longer get a passport, not even from his own government, and this precious treasure of mankind fell into the hands of a people not really interested in it. The legal owner of most of these manuscripts, Egyptian antiquities dealer Phocion J. Tano, was persuaded to bring them to a place and later to the Coptic Museum for expertise, where they were seized (the reason for which remains unknown) and left in Tano's suitcase, where I found them in 1955. No contacts with other scholars were made; at a later date it was even stipulated that the greatest experts, Puech and Walter Till, were not to participate in the edition, for reasons unknown. How little some people cared is obvious from the fact that the whole file with correspondence on Nag Hammadi had gotten lost in the Coptic

Museum. And yet experts urged the authorities to proceed. Prominent scholars of Harvard, among them Arthur Darby Nock, wrote in this sense to Mustafa Amr, the successor to Drioton, unselfishly adding that they themselves did not know Coptic. In these circumstances Jung and Meier have rendered an invaluable service to impatient students of Gnosticism. The old man had considered what he could do and had come to the conclusion that he would help these manuscripts to be put at the disposal of the qualified scholars who had already waited so long (in his own words: "den zuständigen Gelehrten zur Verfügung gestellt werden sollten" [so put them to the disposition of the competent scholars]). Therefore one codex which had left Egypt was to be acquired and after publication given back to the Egyptian government on the condition that the other manuscripts would be released for serious study. So I acquired the Jung Codex on May 10, 1952. Now imagine what it is for a scholar to study Valentinus during a whole war and afterwards to acquire a whole manuscript with five authentic and completely new writings of Valentinus and his school. Is not that an act of God?

So in 1955 the lacking pages of the Jung Codex were found in the Coptic Museum and an arrangement was made which was accepted at a meeting of an international committee in Cairo in 1956: (1) the Jung Codex was to return to Egypt and an international committee of experts was to publish all the writings of Nag Hammadi; (2) the firm Brill at Leiden (and not the French Institute at Cairo) was to publish them; (3) the Rask Oersted Foundation at Copenhagen was to finance the photographic edition of the manuscripts; (4) the Bollingen Foundation at New York was to pay all the expenses of the committee, including the travel of some Egyptian members to Paris. Of course, everybody concerned signed the convention that only members of the committee would have access to the manuscripts. This solemn pledge was broken and pirated editions were published in Germany.

And then the decline of classical studies became only too obvious. All these writings have been translated into Coptic from the Greek. Knowledge of Greek is a must for everybody who wants to study these documents, if only because so many Greek words still occur in the text. The mistakes made against the Greek in these pirated editions are appalling. In these texts the spouse of God, a female symbol of wholeness, is sometimes called Metro-pator, Mother-father, because she has synthetized the male and the female principle. This extremely profound imagery is completely obscured by the unspeakable translation: "Grandfather" ("Grannie is now in heaven"). Moreover, these editors proved too prudish for Gnosis; they translated *métra* as "mother," and *physis* as "nature," whereas *physis* means in this context "uterus."

And even those who translated the Coptic correctly did not establish and fix a text, but printed manuscripts, sometimes even three. There has been, however, since antiquity, a technique of edition. The first rule of it is that you have to establish a text of your own choice, based upon the manuscripts available, but with the necessary conjectures and emendations, of which account is given in the critical apparatus under the text. I'm sorry to say that quite a few editions are completely deficient in these respects. Therefore it was right that Antoine Guillaumont, of the Collège de France in Paris, urged UNESCO to publish photographic editions. This desire has been implemented at last. Moreover, we may trust that our American friends, under the inspiring leadership of James Robinson, will see to it that the Coptic, the Greek, and the art of editing will be adequately dealt with in their future editions. It will be only then that Jung's wish that these texts might be put at the disposal of the qualified scholars available will be realized.

What was the reason that Jung, already an old man, had a hunch of the importance of this discovery, whereas so many prominent theologians and philosophers at that time disparaged the perennial religion of Gnosis as "nihilism" and "metaphysical anti-Semitism"? That was because Jung was one of the few outsiders who had really read the fragments of this faith forgotten and was keenly aware of its relevance for scholarship. He had written his doctoral dissertation "On the Psychology of So-called Occult Phenomena" (1902): in this he had interpreted the fancies of a medium, who was none other than his niece Helly Preiswerk, and had rightly called them Gnostic. And yet the youth and mentality of the patient precluded the possibility that she knew the reports of the anti-heretical Church Fathers. Hence the conclusion arises that Gnosis lives unconsciously in the soul even of a modern woman.

Jung was already on the right track at that time, but the rising sun of the "Religionsgeschichtliche Schule" helped him to continue in the right direction. German theology at that period was dominated by the political theology of Ritschl and Harnack, who were very much against Rome, mysticism, and pietism, and all for Luther, justification by faith alone, and the nation. Jung, the doubting son of a clergyman, was as a student already an outspoken opponent of Ritschl.

On the contrary, people like Hermann Usener, Albrecht Dieterich, and Wilhelm Bousset loved popular religion, mysteries, syncretism, and Gnosis. They found that God very often had been experienced as a Woman, Mother Earth, that "rebirth" is found also in the Hellenistic cults of the beginning of our era, etc. Dieterich even wrote a book about a cosmic God of good and evil, represented as an officer with the head of a cock and serpentine legs, called Abraxas. They explored what they called "die Grundformen religiösen Denkens," the fundamental patterns (or archetypes) of religious thought. Jung knew this literature. It should be observed that at that time studies had already been made of symbols that were held to be typically Aryan or Indo-Germanic. And others already divided humanity into classes with different patterns of thought. Against these, men like Dieterich found basic forms of religious symbolism that are characteristic for all human beings. The implications of their work are thoroughly liberal and humanistic.

When working in an asylum, Jung one day was told by a patient that the sun had a tail, which caused the wind. Later on he read in a book by Dieterich, *Eine Mithrasliturgie,* that a magical papyrus of antiquity contained the same view. The hallucinations of a mad clerk in Zurich showed affinity with Gnostic lore. This fact led Jung to suppose that our collective unconscious contains basic patterns which he called archetypes.

Jung studied the then available Gnostic literature, especially after his rupture with Freud, when he had terrible experiences and the Gnostics were his only friends. He even made a Gnostic painting reflecting his own state of mind. The stream of Eros starts with dark Abraxas, a world creator of contradictory nature, and leads up to the figure of a youth within a winged egg, called Phanes and symbolising rebirth and the true Self. At the same time he wrote a Gnostic apocryphon called *The Seven Sermons to the Dead by Basilides of Alexandria,* in which he proclaimed a new God beyond good and evil, called Abraxas. The German author Hermann Hesse took over these ideas in his book *Demian.* As a matter of fact, the impressive image of individuation, the young bird who picks its way out of the eggshell, comes from Jung. So a whole generation in Europe found the expression of its deepest aspirations in a Gnostic symbol. As Fred Haynes remarked, Jung had renewed and revitalized Gnosticism in Europe after the First World War. And Jung really thought that familiarity with Gnostic imagery and Gnostic experiences helped uprooted modern man to solve his psychological problems. Starting from his own experiences and their parallels in ancient lore Jung tried during a long life to prove that these patterns were to be found in all religions and recur in dreams of modern men (in fact, his theory is also liberal and humanistic). He considered the archetypes as the language of life itself, universal symbols of all men, black, white, yellow, or red, and of all times. He discovered sense in nonsense and thought he could perceive in the soul an inbuilt tendency toward self-realization, the process of individuation.

When man comes to himself, he is, according to Jung, in the first place faced with his shadow of deficiency; then he starts to explore his female side, the *anima,* often accompanied by the wise old man, who incarnates the cumulative wisdom of mankind, until the Self announces itself in dreams and visions, symbolized by the child or the square, heralding the healing of the split between reason and instincts. All these archetypes are and were already then to be found in Gnostic texts: the Demiurge as shadow, Sophia as *anima,* Simon Magus as the wise old man, the Logos as child, the *tetraktys* or four fundamental aeons as *quaternio.*

It did not take long for students of Gnosis to realize that this theory and this terminology were useful tools for the interpretation of Gnostic texts. Especially Henri-Charles Puech, once a teacher of Simone Weil, later professor at the Sorbonne and the Collège de France, pointed out that the center of every Gnostic myth is man, not God. These confused and confusing images of monstrous and terrifying beings should be explained according to Puech in terms of the predicament of man in search of himself. The discovery of the Self is the core of both Gnosticism and Manicheism. Even before Nag Hammadi this psychological approach was already a necessary supplement to the purely historical or unilaterally existentialistic interpretation of Gnosis which prevailed in other quarters. There is no question that psychology in general is of great help, an auxiliary science, for history in general, which otherwise tends to become arid and pedantic. And more specifically the Jungian approach to Gnosticism, once decried as a soul-shaking spectacle concocted by decadent psychologists and vain students of Judaic mysticism, turned out to be adequate when the *Gospel of Truth* was discovered. For then it became clear to everybody that Gnosis is an experience, inspired by vivid and profound emotions, that in short Gnosis is the mythic expression of Self experience.

This is the state of unconscious man without Gnosis:

> Thus men were in ignorance concerning the Father, Him Whom they saw not. When [this ignorance] inspired [in] them fear and confusion, left

them uncertain and hesitant, divided and torn into shreds, there were many vain illusions and empty and absurd fictions which tormented them, like sleepers who are a prey to nightmares. One flees one knows not where or one remains at the same spot when endeavoring to go forward, in the pursuit of one knows not whom. One is in a battle, one gives blows, one receives blows. Or one falls from a great height or one flies through the air without having wings. At other times it is as if one met death at the hands of an invisible murderer, without being pursued by anyone. Or it seems as if one were murdering one's neighbors: one's hands are full of blood. Down to the moment when those who have passed through all this wake up. Then they see nothing, those who have passed through all this, for all those dreams were . . . nought. Thus they have cast their ignorance far away from them, like the dream which they account as nought.

And this is how man discovers his unconscious Self:

Therefore he who knows is a being from above. When he is called, he hears; he answers; he directs himself to Him Who calls him and returns to Him; he apprehends how he is called. By possessing Gnosis, he carries out the will of Him Who called him and seeks to do what pleases Him. He receives the repose. . . . He who thus possesses knowledge knows whence he comes and whither he goes. He understands as someone who makes himself free and awakes from the drunkenness wherein he lived and returns to himself.

How gratifying it was to visit the old man in his lonely tower at the border of the lake, where he had cooked the meal himself, and to read these and similar passages from the newly discovered codex which was to be named after him Codex Jung. He is quoted as having said on this occasion: "All my life I have been working and studying to find these things, and these people knew already." And it is true that the best confirmation of a Jungian interpretation of Gnosis is the Codex Jung. On the other hand, Jungian psychology makes us understand that Gnostic imagery is not nonsensical nor a purely historical phenomenon, but is ever recurrent in history—in Manicheism, in Medieval Catharism, in the theosophy of Jacob Boehme and the poetry of William Blake—because it is deeply rooted in the soul of man.

So Jungian psychology has already had a considerable impact on Gnostic research. The term Self is used by practically everyone; the insight that Gnosis in the last analysis expresses the union of the conscious Ego and the unconscious Self is commonly accepted; nobody, not even the fiercest existentialist, can deny that Jung is helpful in discerning the real meaning of myth.

But students of Gnosis seem not to have observed that among the

Jungians certain new views have been formulated which are relevant for our field. That is, the concept of synchronicity. Because these developments are not generally known, some examples should be given in this context.

Adolf Portmann is a famous biologist and a reputed humanist, who lectured every year at the Eranos Conferences which took place in Ascona in Italian Switzerland. He always extemporized, but, of course, prepared his talks. Once upon a time he had in mind to end his lecture with a story about the praying mantis, not only because it was important for his scholarly aims, but also because it sounded so well in a peroration. Just when he had in mind to broach this subject and felt somehow moved by the insect's beautiful name, *Gottesanbeterin,* through the open window of the lecture hall a praying mantis flew into the room, made a numinous and ominous circle around the head of the professor, then sat down upon the lectern just under the lamp which threw its light upon the lecturer's notes, to the effect that two enormous dark wings, the arms of a praying man, were projected upon the white wall behind Portmann.

Sheer coincidence, of course, and it would be blasphemous and magical to suppose that the state of mind of the lecturer provoked the insect. Such a causal connection is absolutely impossible. But it is true that it would cost the famous biologist several weeks to find a praying mantis in Italian Switzerland. In fact he had never seen one there, though he came there every year. In any case, it is remarkable that the mantis appeared at the moment that the man was emotionally involved in the insect with the telling name. Such happenings Jung calls "synchronicity."

In his old age Jung was fascinated by the symbolism of the fish. He held that mankind was passing in our days from a period of dualism, characterized by the constellation of Pisces, to a long period of unification, indicated by Aquarius. This is what he wrote in his notebook on April 1, 1949:

> Today is Friday. We ate fish for lunch. Somebody casually makes a remark about the April-fish. In the morning I noted an inscription: Est homo totus medius piscis ab imo. In the afternoon a former patient shows me some very impressive paintings of fishes which she made herself. In the evening I am shown an embroidery of fish monsters. In the early morning a former patient tells me a dream of her standing on the beach of the sea and a *big fish* landing at her feet.

When some months later he wrote this down again, he found before his house a foot-long fish on the wall of the lake. There certainly is something fishy about this. These coincidences receive a religious dimension when we remember that the fish is the symbol of Christ. *Ichthus* in Greek stands for: Jesus Christ Son of God Savior. But the whole story became uncanny after the publication of the *Gospel of Thomas* found at Nag Hammadi. There we find a very peculiar parable attributed to Jesus:

> And he said: Man is like a wise fisherman, who cast his net into the sea. He drew it up from the sea full of small fish: among them he found a *large* and good fish; that wise fisherman, he threw all the small fish down into the sea. He chose the large fish without regret.

Compare this with a dream of a modern man, written down long before the publication of the *Gospel of Thomas:*

> I came to the bank of a broad streaming river. At first I could not see very much, only water, earth and rock. I threw the page with my notes into the water and felt that I had given back something to the water. Immediately afterwards I had a fishing rod in my hand. I sat down upon the rock and started fishing. Still I do not see anything but water, earth and rock. All of a sudden I get a rise and have a bite: *a large fish* got hooked. He had a silver belly and a golden back. When I drew the fish ashore, the whole landscape was illuminated.

This dream should be interpreted in terms of self-realization. Without knowing it, that man had a bite, a manifestation from the deepest Self, the very center of his personality: he is developing in the right direction, and this is not possible without religious experience. But what really matters about this is that obviously the outside world is in full sympathy with our inner emotions, without any causal connections. Obviously the rationalistic approach towards reality is one-sided: the principles of time, space, and causality should be supplemented by the principle of synchronicity. And this means that both the absurd world of the unconscious within and the absurd nonsense of the world outside is pervaded by a mysterious and awe-inspiring Sense. Old-fashioned people would call it the hand of God.

Jung had collected such stories of meaningful nonsense during a long life. And it seems that synchronistic happenings do occur very often in the life of medical doctors. But he never dared to publish his views, until an American, J. B. Rhine, had proved him to be right by complicated statistics and impressive calculations. And even then Jung found the courage to make his views known only when his friend Pauli, the Nobel prize-winner for theoretical physics, had consented to publish a study about the mechanization of our world picture in the same book. A preview was given by Jung in Ascona in 1951, in the same place and year that it was decided to acquire the Coptic Gnostic codex.

One cannot imagine what impression this lecture made upon his followers. And even Jung himself seemed quite relieved and unusually good humored. All his life he had rummaged in the collective unconscious, but now he had forced a breakthrough from the soul to the cosmos. He beamed when he told me: "Es geht um die Erfahrung der Fülle des Seins"; it is the experience of the fullness, the pleroma, of Being that matters. And he said to me on another occasion that now the concept of projection should be revised completely. Up till that moment Jung had simply taken over from Freud the naive and unphilosophical view of projection, that man is just projecting his own illusions on the patient screen of eternity. Freud in his turn had borrowed it from Feuerbach, and it is already there in the Latin poem of Lucretius. That solution is so simple that it cannot be true.

It is, however, the main associates of Jung who have drawn the consequences from "synchronicity" and who have thoroughly modified the old-time view of projection. Among those present at the conference of 1951 in Ascona, where Jung launched his theory of synchronicity, Erich Neumann, the well-known author of *The Origins of Consciousness* and *The Great Mother,* was most deeply moved. He had returned to the land promised to his fathers, but could not come to terms with the God of his people. Erich Neumann was a sweet soul, but he had a ruthless mind. His logic was as prosaic and rectilinear as a certain Berlin avenue called the "Kurfürstendam": the world is a projection, your wife is a projection, the neighbor is a projection, God is a projection. And now Jung left the limitations of the psyche and found in the cosmos meaningful correspondences, which made sense and seemed to convey a message. This played havoc with Erich's views. And perhaps he had premonitions of his premature death which was to follow soon afterwards. He became more open to reality and disciplined the fancies of his reason. With great emotional relief he told a fascinated audience in 1952 that there was a "Self field" outside the psyche, which created and directed the world and the psyche, and manifests itself to the Ego in the shape of the Self. And this Self in man is the image of the creator. Erich Neumann had found peace with himself, with the world, and with God.

C.A. Meier, Jung's associate and successor, the same who did so much to acquire the Codex, went a different way. He always had had his doubts about the vulgar concept of projection and focused his special attention on Eros, a specifically Jungian theme, ever since the rupture with Freud caused by a different concept of libido. In fact, from the very beginning Jung had conceived this in a sense that was broader than the merely sexual, as a vital energy which can take different forms. And Jung had seen long before the war that his ideas on the subject agreed with the Orphic and Neoplatonic lore on Eros.

Meier has amplified this theory. In his recent book *Personality,* the fourth volume of a systematic textbook on psychology, he conceives Eros as a more than personal force, a stream of love that is a principle of wholeness which reconciles creatively all opposites and tensions. In this Meier claims to agree with one of the greatest men of the Italian Renaissance, which was not an anticipation of pragmatism and positivism but in reality the revival and discovery of Jewish Gnosis. Meier quotes extensively the *Dialogues on Love* of Leone Ebreo, a Portuguese doctor living in Italy, who taught his gentile fellows about Kabbalism and androgynous Adam. This man wrote about the circle of Love which originates in God, pervades the universe and descends to matter and Chaos, but returns in human Eros to its source. Meier agrees, and observes: "This renaissance-platonic imagery leads us far from the soul into the cosmos, and yet we would rather not call this a simple projection, but an authentic symbol." And obviously this symbol manifests the truth about reality. Symbolic, imaginative thinking can be true. And Leone Ebreo, who found this key symbol, was right.

I always wonder how it happens that so often Jews are the ones who show us the truth of the image. In our century it was Henri Bergson who warned us that reason is a useful instrument for making tools and machines and cars, but that discursive, intellectual reasoning is neither meant nor authorized to uncover the truth: he thought that truth could only be grasped by intuition and only expressed by poetical images. Ernst Cassirer, so influential in the United States, differed from him insofar as he preferred mathematical, conceptual symbols to imaginitive, mythological symbols; but he brought home the unfamiliar truth that both intellect and intuition produce symbols, and he certainly took myth very seriously. In this general perspective of European Judaism Wolfgang Pauli certainly was no exception to the rule, but it made all the difference that he was a nuclear physicist, and secondly that he was thoroughly familiar with Jungian psychology.

What a man!

Bald, fat, ironic, with bulging eyes. As a student he already frequented nightclubs, then studied, slept the whole morning and arrived towards midday at the seminar. A typical metropolitan, born in Vienna in 1900, known to all as the man of the Pauli embargo, a man who created embarrassment around him wherever he went. He and his friends Niels Bohr and Werner Heisenberg are the founding fathers of our modern world picture and our atomic age. And this man was passionately interested in everything religious and Gnostic. He could listen attentively to a lecture about the *memoria* in St. Augustine. And when on November 15, 1953, the discovery of the Jung Codex was made public, he was among the audience. I will never forget what he then said to me: "This negative theology, that is what we need. As Schopenhauer said, he cannot be personal, for then he could not bear the suffering of mankind. This is it, the Unknown God of Gnosis."

He was interested in this material, because the difference between conceptual, analytic, discursive thinking and magical, symbolic, mythical thinking to him was a vexing problem. In his book on Kepler of 1952 he studied the transition from the earlier magical-symbolic description of nature to the modern, quantitative, mathematical description of nature. A representative of the former organic view is the alchemist Robert Fludd (1547–1637), a representative of the latter is Isaac Newton (1642–1727). Kepler (1571–1630) is just in between. Of course, Pauli does not deny that this development was necessary. But he deplores that in the course of this evolution the sense of the whole got lost. And he underlines that the analytical, quantitative approach is not the only true method, but needs to be supplemented by symbolic, intuitive thinking. Newton was right, but Fludd too.

Pauli says,

Modern quantum physics again stresses the factor of the disturbance of phenomena through measurement, and modern psychology again utilizes symbolical images as raw material (especially those that have originated spontaneously in dreams and fantasies) in order to recognize processes in the collective ("objective") psyche. Thus physics and psychology reflect again for modern man the old contrast between the quantitative and the qualitative. Since the time of Kepler and Fludd, however, the possibility of bridging these antithetical poles has become less remote. On the one hand, the idea of complementarity in modern physics has demonstrated to us, in a new kind of synthesis, that the contradiction in the applications of old contrasting conceptions (such as particle and wave) is only apparent; on the other hand, the employability of old alchemical ideas in the psychology of Jung points to a deeper unity of psychical and physical occurrences. To us, unlike Kepler and Fludd, the only acceptable point of view appears to be the one that recognizes *both* sides of reality—the quantitative and the qualitative, the physical and the psychical—as compatible with each other, and can embrace them simultaneously. . . . Among scientists in particular, the universal desire for a greater unification of our world view is greatly intensified by the fact that, though we now have natural sciences, we no longer have a total scientific picture of the world. Since the discovery of the quantum of action, physics has gradually been forced to relinquish its proud claim to be able to understand, in principle, the *whole* world. This very circumstance, however, as a correction of earlier one-sidedness, could contain the germ of progress toward a unified conception of the entire cosmos of which the natural sciences are only a part.[1]

When I consider these theories of Pauli I think it is permitted to summarize his views in the following parable: an authentic symbol is like a pane of glass, a millinery shop window in one of our big cities. Sometimes it mirrors your own image, sometimes it gives you an insight into the display behind the glass. It all depends upon your own point of view.

In the newly discovered writings of Nag Hammadi, it is said again and again that the world and man are projections. The first Idea, God's Wisdom, looks down on the Chaos below, and the primeval waters mirror her shadowy image: that is, the Demiurge, who orders unorganized matter. So the world originates from the projecting activity of the great Goddess Barbelo. Even today we find the same among the Mandaeans, the only Gnostics in this world who can boast an uninterrupted continuity of the ancient Gnostics; according to them the Holy Spirit (Ruha d'Qodša) produces a dragon, Light (Ur, from Hebrew *'ôr* = "light") from the black water of Chaos. According to another version, at the commandment of God ("Life") the heavenly weighmaster, Abatur, looks down from above into that black water; at the same moment his image was formed in the black water, the Demiurge, Gabriel or Ptahil, took shape and ascended to the borderland (on high near heaven, near the realm of light).

Or, again, this holy Motherfather reveals herself to the demonic powers of this world through her luminous image in the primordial waters: then these archons, rulers, create a "golem," a robot, the material frame of man, Adam, according to that image. And so, in a way, man too is a projection of Barbelo.

If we could trace the origin of this fascinating and appalling poetry, then the much-debated origins of Gnosticism would be discovered. And I think this possible, if only you allow me to tell a few stories which you may know, but perhaps not precisely:

1. There was a beautiful youth in Greece, called Narcissus, who scorned love and so offended the god Eros. One day he fell in love with his own image, mirrored in the water when he looked down. He saw his *eidolon,* his reflection, hovering on the water. Therefore he faded away or, according to another tradition, drowned in the water. The story goes to show that the beauty of the body is not real. If you are engrossed in it, you are like this man, who wanted to seize his own reflection upon the water, dived into the deep, and drowned. So your soul dives into the abyss, where you live blind with the phantoms of Hell. Or again in another version: they tell that he, when looking in the water, saw his own shadow, fell in love with it, jumped into the water to embrace his own shadow and so was suffocated. *This is not true* (cf. the *Apocryphon of John:* "not as Moses said"). For he was not suffocated in the water, but he contemplated the transient and passing nature of his material body, namely life in the body, which is the basest *eidolon* of the real soul. Desiring to embrace this, he became enamored with life according to that shadow. Therefore he drowned and was suffocated, as it were perverting his own soul and a really decent life. Therefore the proverb says, "Fear your own shadow." This story teaches you to fear the inclination to prize inferior things as the highest, because that leads man to the loss of his soul and the annihilation of the true Gnosis of reality.

2. The young god Dionysus was set upon a throne as soon as he had been born in a cave on the isle of Crete. But titanic monsters, who wanted to kill the child, gave him a mirror to distract his attention; and while the child gazed in the mirror and was fascinated by his own image, the Titans tore the child into pieces and devoured him. Only the heart of the god was saved. This means that Dionysus, when he saw his *eidolon,* his reflection in the mirror, in a sense was duplicated and vanished into the mirror and so was dispersed in the universe. But Apollo gathers him and brings him back to the spiritual world above, truly the savior of Dionysus. According to the Orphic sages, this means that the worldsoul is divided and dispersed through matter. But the worldspirit remains undivided and pure from every contact with matter.

3. About this distinction between the soul and its image, its *eidolon,* which makes contact with matter, there is still another story.

Helen is said to have eloped with Paris and to have been the cause of the war between Greeks and Trojans. But it is not true that Helen was ever in Troy: she remained in Egypt and the Greeks and Trojans fought only about her idol, a "doll" which resembled her. The Pythagoreans say that this refers to the soul, which does not become incarnate in the body proper, but makes contact with it through its *eidolon,* its lower part, properly speaking its image reflected in a mirror or in water, but here meant to indicate the subtle or astral body.

It was after the pattern of these stories that the oldest Gnostics known to us, Simon Magus of Samaria and his followers, told that the tragic fate of divine Wisdom, raped by hostile powers and at last saved from dispersion, was symbolized by the myth of Helen of Troy and her *eidolon.* And this, I think, throws an unexpected light upon Gnostic origins.

But more important, these myths enabled the Gnostics to give a new and original solution to a vexed problem. They knew that such a thing as projection exists. In fact projection is the literal and adequate translation of the Gnostic technical term *probolé.* But they did not agree that God is a projection of man. They rather expressed in their imaginative thinking that the world and man are a projection of God.

It all depends on whether you agree that a window can have a double function: from a certain angle you see yourself in it, from a different angle you can also look through it and see reality and the truth. For the ancients a mirror is more mysterious than it is for us. You could see your own reflection in it. But when you used it for "katoptromancy," i.e., for magic soothsaying, then the gods would manifest themselves in the mirror and the future could be discerned in it. The mirror could be a magic mirror, reflecting darkly the outlines of your face on its bronze surface and yet allowing an insight into an unknown dimension, which later on will be seen clearly. "Now we see only through a glass darkly, but then we shall see face to face to face, eye to eye," says Paul in 1 Corinthians 13.

I suggest that this is a correct definition of the truth of imaginative thinking as revealed by the Gnostic symbols. The world and man are a projection of God. And the consummation of the historical process will consist in this: that man and the universe are taken back and reintegrated into their divine origin. That is eternal life; that is the Kingdom of God. Certainly this is a plausible, spirited, and provocative hypothesis concerning the nature and end of the psyche, the universe, and ultimate reality.*

NOTE

1. W. Pauli, "The Influence of Archetypal Ideas on the Scientific Theories of Kepler," in C. G. Jung and W. Pauli, *The Interpretation of Nature and the Psyche* (London: Routledge & Kegan Paul, 1955), pp. 207–9.

---

*This essay was originally published in *The Rediscovery of Gnosticism: Proceedings of the International Conference on Gnosticism at Yale University, March 28–31, 1978,* ed. Bentley Layton, vol. I (Leiden: Brill, 1980), pp. 18–31, and is reprinted here with permission.

[2]

JUNG'S FASCINATION WITH GNOSTICISM

Robert A. Segal

I N his autobiography, *Memories, Dreams, Reflections,* C. G. Jung describes his search for objective evidence of the collective unconscious—evidence beyond his own experience of it:

> As my life entered its second half, I was already embarked on the confrontation with the contents of the unconscious. . . . First I had to find evidence for the historical prefiguration of my inner experiences. That is to say, I had to ask myself, "Where have my particular premises already occurred in history?" If I had not succeeded in finding such evidence, I would never have been able to substantiate my ideas. (1963, p. 200)

Jung found that evidence in two sources: alchemy and Gnosticism. Interpreted psychologically, both served as hoary forerunners of analytical psychology and therefore as evidence of its objectivity:

> The experiences of the alchemists were, in a sense, my experiences, and their world was my world. This was, of course, a momentous discovery: I had stumbled upon the historical counterpart of my psychology of the unconscious. The possibility of a comparison with alchemy, and the uninterrupted intellectual chain back to Gnosticism, gave substance to my psychology. (1963, p. 205)

Jung interprets alchemy and Gnosticism identically. Indeed, he sees medieval alchemy as not only the link to ancient Gnosticism but the outright continuation of it: "In spite of the suppression of the Gnostic heresy, it [the heresy] continued to flourish throughout the Middle Ages under the guise of alchemy" (1938/1940, p. 97). For Jung, the alchemical process of extracting gold from base metals is a continuation of the Gnostic process of liberating fallen souls, or sparks, from matter. Both processes are seemingly outward, physical or metaphysical ones which in fact are inner, psychological ones. Both represent a progression from sheer ego consciousness to the ego's rediscovery of the unconscious and reintegration with it to forge the self.

In alchemy the progression is from base metals to the distillation of vapor out of them and the return of that vapor to the metals to form gold. In Gnosticism the progression is from the Gnostic's sheer bodily existence to the release of the immaterial spark within the Gnostic's body and the reunion of that spark with the godhead. In both cases the state truly sought is between the ego and the unconscious rather than between the vapor and the metals or between the spark and the godhead. The external state is simply the projection of the internal one.

JUNG'S HISTORY OF THE PSYCHE

Tracing Jung's history of the psyche helps pinpoint the significance of Gnosticism for him. Jung divides the psychological history of humanity into four stages: primitive, ancient, modern, and contemporary. (Some of these terms are mine, not Jung's.)

At birth, according to Jung, humans are entirely unconscious. Only slowly does consciousness emerge. Because the initial human state is unconscious, unconsciousness is natural rather than, as for Freud, artificial.

By "consciousness" Jung means awareness of oneself as a subject, or "I," distinct from both the external world and the unconscious. The first center of consciousness is the ego, so that the development of consciousness means at first the development of the ego.

Because the consciousness of humanity has developed slowly, the ego of primitives is weak.[1] Rather than differentiating themselves from their unconscious and the world, primitives project themselves onto the world and thereby encounter their unconscious rather than the world. In projecting themselves, as personalities, onto the world, they create a religious world—a world ruled not by impersonal forces like atoms but by gods. Events in the world are not merely caused but willed.

So weak is the primitive ego that primitives not only project themselves onto the world but also identify themselves with it. Like infants, primitives have scant sense of themselves "over against" the world. They do not distinguish between subjectivity and objectivity. They experience themselves objectively, as part of the world itself. In identifying themselves with the world, primitives consequently identify themselves with the gods they have projected onto it. Humans and gods are taken as one.

The difference for Jung between ancients and primitives is that ancients have sturdier egos.[2] Because even their egos are shaky, ancients, too, project themselves onto the world in the form of gods. But they do not identify themselves with the world and therefore with those gods. They worship gods distinct from themselves. Like primitives, ancients experience the world through the unconscious and thus are not truly separated from either, but they nevertheless possess a budding sense of themselves vis-à-vis both.

By "ancients"—my term, not Jung's—I refer to all humans between the primitive stage and the modern one. Ancients include Egyptians, Mesopotamians, Greeks, Romans, Jews, Christians, and Muslims.

To the extent that ancients forge egos, they create a split within themselves between the ego and the unconscious, from which the ego has emerged. That split is not, however, antagonistic. In developing their egos, ancients do not forsake the unconscious. Like primitives, they continue to tend to it through religion.

The difference between moderns and ancients is that moderns possess fully independent egos.[3] By withdrawing their projections from the world, they have substantially demythicized it. They thereby experience the world itself, largely unfiltered by the unconscious, and thus are differentiated from both.

Invariably, moderns do not merely separate themselves from the unconscious but reject it altogether. They thereby pit themselves—their egos—against the unconscious. Moderns consider themselves wholly rational, unemotional, scientific, and atheistic. Religion, through which earlier humanity had realized its unconscious, gets dismissed as a prescientific delusion. Where primitives identify themselves with the world, moderns identify themselves with their egos, which *deal with* the world but are distinct from it.

The difference between "contemporaries"—again, my term—and moderns is that contemporaries are conscious of their nonrational side, whether or not of its unconscious source.[4] Like moderns, who correspond crudely to nineteenth-century intellectuals, contemporaries—twentieth-century intellectuals—reject religion as a prescientific relic. Unlike moderns, however, they are not satisfied with the scrupulously rational life that they have inherited from moderns and yearn instead for the kind of fulfillment that religion once provided. They seek new, nonprojective outlets to replace the dead, projective ones of religion. They do not, like moderns, boast of having transcended the need that religion once fulfilled.

In identifying contemporaries with twentieth-century persons, Jung is deeming them not average but distinctive. Psychologically, most persons today are either moderns, and so oblivious to any nonrational needs, or ancients, and so satisfied with traditional means of fulfilling them. Because contemporaries are sensitive both to the existence of nonrational inclinations and to the demise of past means of fulfilling them, they comprise a select minority.

Because contemporaries, unlike moderns, consciously experience rather than ignore their nonrational beckonings, they do not suffer from ordinary neurosis, or threats to the ego from a spurned unconscious. Rather, they suffer from emptiness, or malaise. Like moderns, contemporaries are severed from their unconscious, but unlike moderns they are striving to overcome the severance. For the most part they remain severed not because they, like moderns, deny their nonrational side but because they, as the heirs of moderns, do not know how to reconnect themselves to it. Distinctively Jungian patients are contemporaries rather than, like Freudian patients, moderns.

GNOSTICS AND CONTEMPORARIES

The connection between this history of the psyche and Gnosticism is that for Jung Gnostics are the ancient counterparts to contemporaries and therefore to distinctively Jungian patients. In turn, Jungian patients are the contemporary counterparts to ancient Gnostics:

> The spiritual currents of our time have, in fact, a deep affinity with Gnosticism. . . . The most impressive movement numerically is undoubtedly Theosophy, together with its continental sister, Anthroposophy; these are pure Gnosticism in Hindu dress. . . . What is striking about these Gnostic systems is that they are based exclusively on the manifestations of the unconscious. . . . The passionate interest in these movements undoubtedly arises from psychic energy which can no longer be invested in obsolete religious forms. (1928/1931, pp. 83–84)

Like Gnostics, contemporaries feel alienated from their roots and are seeking to overcome the alienation. They are seeking new outlets for their unconscious. Where Gnostics feel cut off from the outer world, contemporaries feel cut off from the inner one. Contemporaries do not, like Gnostics, project their alienation onto the cosmos. They seek to discover their true selves nonprojectively, within rather than outside themselves.

Gnosticism for Jung is an ancient, not a contemporary, phenomenon. Jung thus pegs his psychology not as the contemporary *version* of Gnosticism but as the contemporary *counterpart* to it. At the same time he considers Gnosticism the ancient version of something that itself is recurrent: alienation from the unconscious, which in Gnosticism is expressed in alienation from the immaterial essence.

Jung is not saying that this recurrent alienation is constant or widespread. It still characterizes only a few periods and persons. For by alienation Jung means the awareness, not merely the fact, of severance from the unconscious. He therefore excludes moderns from the camp of the alienated. Likewise neither primitives nor ancients are alienated, for religion links both to their unconscious, even if it does so indirectly through projection. Only Gnostics and contemporaries, together with alchemists, qualify, for they alone are both severed from their unconscious and aware of the fact.

A JUNGIAN INTERPRETATION OF GNOSTIC MYTHS

The chief Gnostic myths are creation myths. Other Gnostic myths presuppose them. Understood in Jungian terms, Gnostic creation myths describe the development not of the world or even of human beings but of the human psyche. The literal account of the creation of the world must be made not merely human but, even more, psychological. Cosmic terms must be translated into human ones and physical terms into mental ones.

The godhead symbolizes the unconscious. As a symbol of the unconscious, it is primordial. It is the source or agent of everything else. Prior to its emanating anything, it lacks nothing. It is whole, self-sufficient, perfect. The godhead thus symbolizes the unconscious before the emergence of the ego out of it.

The emergence of matter alongside the immaterial godhead symbolizes the beginning, but only the beginning, of the emergence of the ego out of the unconscious. Inert matter itself does not symbolize the ego, which requires a reflective entity conscious of itself as a subject distinct from the external world. The ego emerges not with the creation of either the Demiurge or Primal Man but only with the creation of individual human beings.

The ego is symbolized not by the spark but by the thinking part of the human body, the unspecified center of human thoughts and actions vis-à-vis the external world. The spark, as the link to the forgotten godhead, symbolizes the unconscious. As long as one remains unaware of the spark, one remains an unrealized self. As long as one's values are material, one is merely an ego.

Insofar as a Jungian interpretation of myth is psychological, it conflates the literal distinction between the outer world and humanity. Both matter and the body symbolize the development of the ego—raw matter symbolizing the beginning of the process and the thinking portion of the body the end. Similarly, both the immaterial godhead and the spark symbolize the unconscious, if also at opposite stages of development.

The ego in Jungian psychology develops not just alongside the unconscious but also out of it. Those Gnostic myths in which matter originates out of the godhead thus express the dependence of the ego on the unconscious. Those myths in which matter is preexistent and merely comes into contact with the godhead express dissociation of the unconscious from the ego and thereby foreshadow the problems that dissociation spells.

The emergence of the ego is a gradual process. The long chains of emanations found in many Gnostic myths capture the gradualness of the task. The emergence of the ego is a difficult process as well. If on the one hand the unconscious creates spontaneously, on the other hand it clings possessively to its progeny. The ego for its part wants at once to be independent of the unconscious and to be sheltered by it. In Gnostic myths the godhead freely and knowingly emanates parts of itself yet then strives to reclaim those parts. In turn, those parts commonly yearn both to create themselves and to be reabsorbed by the godhead. This mutually ambivalent relationship between the godhead and its emanations fits the relationship between the unconscious and the ego. Yet for all its ambivalence, the ego, once independent, inevitably forgets, if not repudiates, its origins.

Non-Gnostics, who for Jung ideally also possess a divine spark, are not only ignorant of their origin and the origin of the world but also smugly satisfied with the false, material nature of both. Their complacency makes them apt counterparts to moderns. Gnostics have also forgotten the true nature of themselves and the world, but they are nevertheless dissatisfied with the existing nature of both. Their dissatisfaction makes them suitable counterparts to contemporaries.

If ignorance alone, according to Gnostic tenets, keeps humans tied to the material world, knowledge frees them from it. Because humans are ignorant, that knowledge must come from outside them. Because the powers of the material world are ignorant, too, that knowledge must come from beyond them as well: it can come from only the godhead. The dependence of humanity on the godhead matches the dependence of the ego on the unconscious to reveal itself.

The response of Gnostics to the revelation parallels that of contemporaries to their own discovery: gratitude. The disclosure of a heretofore unknown dimension of oneself and, for Gnostics, of a heretofore unknown world provides a fulfillment that amounts to salvation. As Jung says of contemporaries, "I do not believe that I am going too far when I say that modern [i.e., contemporary] man, in contrast to his nineteenth-century brother, turns to the psyche with very great expectations, and does so without reference to any traditional creed but rather with a view to Gnostic experience" (1928/1931, p. 84).

The response of non-Gnostics to the revelation parallels that of moderns to their own discovery: fear. The disclosure, which applies to non-Gnostics as well as to Gnostics, shatters the non-Gnostics' vaunted image of both themselves and the world.

Gnostic and Jungian Goals

Gnostic myths preach total identification with one's newly discovered divinity. Because that identification symbolizes the Gnostic's identification with the unconscious, Jungian psychology would regard it as no less lopsided and dangerous than the non-Gnostic's identification with the ego—more precisely, with ego consciousness, or consciousness of the external world. Jungian psychology would regard both attitudes as unbalanced. It would say that non-Gnostics, like moderns, suffer from an exaggerated persona: their ego identifies itself wholly with the conscious, public personality. But Jungian psychology would equally say that Gnostics, whether or not contemporaries, suffer from an exaggerated, or inflated, ego, which, conversely, identifies itself wholly with the rediscovered unconscious. Minimally, the consequence of inflation is excessive pride in the presumed uniqueness of one's unconscious. Maximally, the consequence is outright psychosis, or the dissolution of any consciousness of the external world. The Jungian goal is no more to reject ego consciousness for the unconscious than, like the modern aim, to reject the unconscious for ego consciousness. Rather, the goal is to balance the two. This point will prove decisive.

In Gnosticism knowledge itself is liberating: the revelation of the existence of a higher reality automatically diminishes the hold of the lower one. Recognizing matter for what it is, Gnostics cease to grant it the status they had till now, even when they had been discontented with it. The freedom from matter given them by the revelation symbolizes freedom from ego consciousness and parallels that given contemporaries by their self-discovery. With the revelation Gnostics are at last free, not to say obliged, to forsake the material world altogether. By contrast, with their discovery contemporaries are hardly similarly free, let alone obliged, to forsake ego consciousness: doing so would constitute inflation. This continuing difference will, again, prove central.

In Jungian psychology the cultivation of the unconscious does involve a break with ego consciousness and a return to the unconscious. That break, however, is only temporary. The goal is not reversion to the original state of sheer unconsciousness but, on the contrary, the elevation of the unconscious—better, the symbols of it—to consciousness. One returns to the unconscious to raise it to consciousness:

> Man's worst sin is unconsciousness, but it is indulged in with the greatest piety even by those who should serve mankind as teachers and examples. When shall we stop taking man for granted in this barbarous manner and in all seriousness seek ways and means to exorcize him, to rescue him from possession and unconsciousness, and make this the most vital task of civilization? (1945/1948, pp. 253–54)

Humans should seek a unified state, as they possessed at birth, but now they should seek the integration of the unconscious with ego consciousness, not the restoration of pristine unconsciousness. The aim now is to make the unconscious conscious, not the reverse.

The Gnostic aim, however, is the opposite: reversion to the incipient state of both humanity and the cosmos, not the transformation of either. The aim is a return to the state prior to the emergence of both the material world and humanity itself. The aim is the dissolution of all creation and a reversion to the original state of a unified godhead. In Jungian terms, that aim is sheer unconsciousness. It parallels the state not of contemporaries but of primitives—and, even earlier, the "uroboric" state before birth. In shedding both the body and material values, the Gnostic is shedding ego consciousness altogether.

Accordingly, Gnostic myths do not urge humans to alter either their sparks or the godhead. The myths do not urge the enlightened to fuse their sparks with their bodies or the godhead with the material world. Rather, they urge the escape of the spark from both the body and the material world and the restoration of both it and the godhead to their pristine state. That state *is* one of unity, but the unity is of all divinity, not of divinity with matter. In preaching both a return to the original state and a rejection of the present one, Gnosticism advocates the opposite of Jungian psychology.

What for Jung is only a means to an end—return to the unconscious—is for Gnosticism equivalent to the end itself. What for Jung is the end—the integration of the unconscious with ego consciousness—is for Gnosticism equivalent to the present predicament itself: the association of divinity with matter. Conversely, what for Gnosticism is the end—the severance of the link between divinity and matter—is in Jungian terms the predicament: the dissociation of the unconscious from ego consciousness.

Perhaps Jung interprets Gnosticism the way he does because he views it through alchemical eyes. As noted, he parallels the Gnostic process of liberating the immaterial sparks from matter to the alchemical process of extracting gold from base metals. Where, however, gold is produced *out of* the metals, the sparks are scarcely produced out of matter. Where gold lies latent in the metals, the sparks lie imprisoned in matter. Far from originating in matter, they have fallen into it and await not realization but release. Saying, then, that gold, like the sparks, is produced by extraction is most misleading. Gold is produced not by shedding but by transforming the metals.

Indeed, gold is produced not merely by the distillation of vapor out of the metals but by the return of that vapor to the metals. Rather than escaping from them, the vapor is fused with them. By contrast, the sparks, once liberated from matter, flee from it. They return not to matter but to the immaterial godhead, their true origin. A severance, not a fusion, occurs.

For Jung, the base metals, like the thinking side of the Gnostic's body, symbolize ego consciousness. Similarly, the vapor, like the sparks, symbolizes the unconscious. Where, however, the fusion of the vapor with the metals symbolizes the forging of the self, the reunion of the sparks with the godhead symbolizes, or should symbolize, reversion to primordial unconsciousness. The reunion of the Gnostic with the godhead does mean reunification, but of a piece of divinity with the rest of divinity, not of divinity with matter.

To say that Gnosticism, interpreted psychologically, breaks with the Jungian ideal is hardly to say that Jungian psychology cannot still interpret it. Gnosticism should simply be interpreted differently—as evincing inflation rather than individuation, as espousing the ego's rediscovery of the unconscious as an end in itself, not as a means to a different end.

Interpreting the Gnostic's permanent return to the godhead as inflationary would enable Jungian psychology to make sense of the key Gnostic paradox: why an omniscient and omnipotent divinity creates a world that he then seeks to destroy. Jungian psychology would make not the creation but the dissolution of the world the mistake. Though it would admittedly thereby be evaluating Gnosticism by its own world-affirming rather than world-rejecting ideal, it would at least be able to make sense of creation. The unconscious, as symbolized by the godhead, would not be erring in creating the ego, as symbolized by the material side of humanity. The unconscious would truly be both omniscient and omnipotent. It is the ego which would be neither: lacking both the knowledge and the will to resist the spell of the unconscious, it would be returning of its own accord to the unconscious, which, to be sure, would be enticing it.

Whatever the exact fit between the Jungian ideal and the Gnostic one—a fit that the Jungian contributors to the present volume find much tauter than I—the kinship that Jung deciphers between Gnosticism and analytical psychology is remarkable. Both movements, he sees, stress the inevitable severance of human beings from their true nature, the hidden state of that nature, the necessity of rediscovering it, the difficulty of rediscovering it, and the pride at rediscovering it. Put summarily, Jung deems the Gnostic quest for salvation a form of therapy: a process of discovering and exploring who one really is.

THE GNOSTICS AS PSYCHOLOGISTS

On the one hand Jung concedes that the Gnostics were probably unaware of the psychological meaning of their beliefs: "It seems to be highly unlikely that they [Gnostics] had a psychological conception of [archetypal images]" (1963, p. 201). Gnostics thought that they were dealing with the cosmos as well as with themselves: "The Gnostics projected their subjective inner perception . . . into a cosmogonic system and believed in the [metaphysical] reality of its psychological figures" (1921, p. 19).

On the other hand Jung says that his "enthusiasm" for the Gnostics "arose from the discovery that they were apparently the first thinkers to concern themselves (after their fashion) with the contents of the collective unconscious" (1952, p. 664). Jung declares that "Gnosis is undoubtedly a psychological knowledge whose contents derive from the unconscious" (1968, p. 223) and that "it is clear beyond a doubt that many of the Gnostics were nothing other than psychologists" (1968, p. 222).

It is not easy to reconcile these two sets of statements. Despite Jung's tribute to Gnostics for their psychological precocity, presumably he is not saying that they recognized the psychological meaning of their myths. His qualifying phrase "after their fashion" suggests that for him Gnostics were tending to the unconscious without knowing it. They *were* more psychologically savvy than other ancients, but not because they realized that they were projecting their psyches onto the cosmos. Rather, they felt unfulfilled and, so like their contemporary descendants, consciously sought new myths to provide the fulfillment that traditional ones no longer yielded:

> The psychological interest of the present time is an indication that modern [i.e., contemporary] man expects something from the psyche which the outer world has not given him: doubtless something which our religion ought to contain, but no longer does contain, at least for modern man. . . . That there is a general interest in these matters cannot be denied. . . . The world has seen nothing like it since the end of the seventeenth century. We can compare it only to the flowering of Gnostic thought in the first and second centuries after Christ. . . . What is striking about these Gnostic systems is that they are based exclusively on the manifestations of the unconscious. . . . The passionate interest in these movements undoubtedly arises from psychic energy which can no longer be invested in obsolete religious forms. (1928/1931, pp. 83–84)

JUNG AS GNOSTIC

It is one thing to maintain that Jung was entranced by Gnosticism. It is another to say that he was a Gnostic himself. Jung himself makes this distinction and bitterly rejects the epithet "Gnostic"—not on the grounds that he disagrees with any Gnostic tenets but on the grounds that he is an empirical scientist rather than a metaphysician: "The designation of my 'system' as 'Gnostic' is an invention of my theological critics. . . . I am not a philosopher, merely an empiricist" (1958, p. 727). Despite Jung's disclaimer, he has regularly been labeled a Gnostic. Sometimes the term is bestowed in praise, other times in condemnation. What the designation means varies from designator to designator.

Is Jung a Gnostic? If he is, he is surely a psychological, not metaphysical, one. Like ancient Gnostics, he seeks reconnection with the lost essence of human nature and treats reconnection as tantamount to salvation. The rediscovered essence is equivalent to latent divinity within oneself. For Jung, as for ancient Gnostics, reconnection is a lifelong process and typically requires the guidance of one who has already undertaken it: the Jungian therapist, if not Jung himself. Knowledge for both Jung and ancient Gnostics is the key to the effort, and knowledge for both means above all self-knowledge. In these respects Jung can legitimately be typed a Gnostic. Still, Jung's chief contribution to the understanding of Gnosticism is conceptual, not biographical. Jungian psychology elucidates Gnosticism, whatever its founder's personal outlook.*

NOTES

1. On primitives see, above all, Jung 1931.
2. Jung devotes no single work to ancients, whom he discusses throughout his writings.
3. On moderns see, above all, Jung 1938/1941.
4. On contemporaries see, above all, Jung 1928/1931. Despite the title, this essay concerns those whom I call "contemporaries," not "moderns."

REFERENCES

Jung, C. G. 1921. *Psychological Types. Collected Works,* vol. 6. Princeton, NJ: Princeton University Press, 1971.

———. 1928/1931. "The Spiritual Problem of Modern Man." In *Collected Works* 10:74–94. Princeton, NJ: Princeton University Press, 1970.

———. 1931. "Archaic Man." In *Collected Works* 10:50–73. Princeton, NJ: Princeton University Press, 1970.

———. 1938/1940. "Psychology and Religion." In *Collected Works* 11:3–105. Princeton, NJ: Princeton University Press, 1969.

———. 1945/1948. "The Phenomenology of the Spirit in Fairytales." In *Collected Works* 9.1:207–54. Princeton, NJ: Princeton University Press, 1968.

———. 1952. "Religion and Psychology: A Reply to Martin Buber." In *Collected Works* 18:663–70. Princeton, NJ: Princeton University Press, 1976.

---

*This essay is an abridgment and revision of pages 8 to 35 and 43 to 48 of Robert Segal's introduction to *The Gnostic Jung,* ed. Segal (Princeton, NJ: Princeton University Press; London: Routledge, 1992), and is reprinted with permission.

———. 1958. "Jung and Religious Belief." In *Collected Works* 18:702–44. Princeton, NJ: Princeton University Press, 1976.

———. 1963 [1961]. *Memories, Dreams, Reflections,* ed. Aniela Jaffé, trs. Richard and Clara Winston. New York: Vintage Books.

———. 1968. "The Structure and Dynamics of the Self." In *Collected Works* 9.2:222–65. Princeton, NJ: Princeton University Press, 1968.

[3]

THE GNOSTIC CRITIQUE, PAST AND PRESENT

Murray Stein

THE EGO, YALDABAOTH, AND THE PROBLEM OF EVIL

When the spiritual history of our times is written, the Holocaust will go down as the major religious event of the twentieth century. I believe it will be seen, in the long view of Western spiritual history, as a defining moment, as decisive as the Crucifixion and, like the Crucifixion, a tragic historical event that becomes a symbol of transformation.

Any future Western theological thinker in the broad biblical and Judeo-Christian tradition who does not place the Holocaust at the center of theological reflection on human and divine natures will, in my judgment, be seen as missing the mark. After the Holocaust we cannot possibly think clearly or truly about the spiritual condition of the West and the West's God-image without devoting a major portion of our reflection to this crucial moment in history. It is an event whose very darkness illuminates the radical (and evil) one-sidedness of conscious development in the West and whose critical mass of intense suffering places the implacable obligation for deep change, for transformation of consciousness, upon each of us. It also raises questions about a one-sided God-image that has overemphasized the attributes of love and goodness and underestimated God's capacity for absence and evil.

Like a bolt of dark lightning, the Holocaust illuminates an invisible demonic god of our past and present culture, Yaldabaoth, the Gnostic archon whose intransigent quest for power and domination over every creature on the face of this earth has been the hallmark of Western ego development. The Holocaust forces us to repudiate the notion, now obviously false but so fundamental to Western cultural attitudes, that spiritual and material progress has been the dominant force driving our history. While this restlessly Yaldabaothian ego has managed to produce a great deal of technical and material advancement, although at great human cost and suffering, it has simultaneously attacked and destroyed the spiritually gifted for millennia. The ancient Gnostics were among its victims.

On a cultural collective level, there has been no moral or psychological progress during the past two or more millennia. The notion of spiritual and moral progress is an idol that was toppled decisively by the cataclysmic events in Europe during this century. The Holocaust has shown, among other things, the moral and spiritual hollowness at the core of Western civilization and has confirmed our darkest suspicions about human nature.

As children in Sunday school, we played the imagination game of asking ourselves what we would have done in Jesus's time: would we have been disciples? Would I have given up all I had and followed him? Would I have denied him thrice like Peter, or would I have been steadfast and loyal to our Lord? Naturally, in my heroic fantasies, I usually imagined myself as doing the noble thing. Never was I Judas, rarely even Peter. Later, in high school and college, after reading books like *The Diary of Anne Frank,* I asked myself a similar question: if I had been living in Germany in the 1930s and 1940s, would I have stood up against the evil of Nazism, risked my life to help the persecuted, hidden an Anne Frank in my attic or basement, even gone before the firing squad like Dietrich Bonhoeffer? Or would I have looked the other way, contributed anonymously to the reign of terror, denied my knowledge of what was going on, and tried to preserve my own possessions and life?

The Nazi years defined a moment of truth in the West, and for the most part the Christian church and Western civilization failed the test. What a glorious moment in Christian history it would have been if the Catholic Church had come to the unqualified defense of Edith Stein, who, even though a Catholic convert and a Carmelite nun, was sent to Auschwitz as a Jew and burned in the Holocaust. Is it not an irony that she has been beatified by the very Church that could not find the means in 1942 to remove her and her sister to safety in Switzerland?

I do not want to fix Yaldabaoth altogether in Europe, however. Americans have worshiped at the same egoistic shrine and, in the name of this golden calf, have decimated numerous tribes of native peoples, raped the land, and spoiled countless possible futures. What

I speak of is an ego attitude that holds as sacred the value of control and the subjugation or elimination of differences above all else. It is an attitude endemic in our nationalisms, each claiming superiority; in our hundreds of fundamentalist religious sects, each claiming ultimate truth and excoriating all unbelievers; in our politics of prowess and preening and ambition for rank. It is an attitude that cannot accept difference without polarizing it and that attempts only to reform, convert, or eliminate those who differ. This is precisely the attitude imaged as Yaldabaoth by the Gnostics of two thousand years ago.

THE STORY OF YALDABAOTH

Where does this ego attitude come from? Before resorting too quickly to biopsychological explanations that might appeal to the possible evolutionary advantages in such an ego attitude, we will look to myth for a clue. According to the *Apocryphon of John,* Yaldabaoth is the offspring of Sophia, the last in a long line of archons descended from "The Monad," "a monarchy with nothing above it. . . . [the invisible] One who is above [everything, who exists as] incorruption, which is [in the] pure light into which no [eye] can look" (Robinson 1988, p. 106). The Monad represents what Jung in his psychological writings calls the human being's pre-conscious original state of wholeness. The Monad is the Self before it has begun to "de-integrate" (Fordham 1969) and to unpack itself into emergent psychic structures.

As the chain of archons proceeds and development gets underway, the generations advance by couples, and each couple unites to produce the next rung in the chain of being. Each generation is produced by a cooperative effort of two archons in the preceding generation. This pattern changes, however, in Sophia's generation when she decides to create on her own, without consultation and without a mate. The result is a son whom she names "Yaldabaoth." Her reaction to the monstrosity she has wrought is reminiscent of Hera's response to her parthenogenetic creation, Hephaestus:

> And when she saw (the consequences of) her desire, it changed into a form of a lion-faced serpent. And its eyes were like lightning fires which flash. She cast it away from her, outside that place, that no one of the immortal ones might see it, for she had created it in ignorance. And she surrounded it with a luminous cloud, and she placed a throne in the middle of the cloud that no one might see it except the Holy Spirit who is called the mother of the living. And she called his name Yaltabaoth. This

is the first archon who took a great power from his mother. (Robinson 1988, p. 110)

Yaldabaoth (or "Yaltabaoth") then empowers himself with power stolen from his mother, and with this derivative might he gets busy and creates a whole crowd of other, lesser beings whose principal duty it is to serve him and do his bidding. In this first act of creation, he shows the most fundamental trait of his character: the wish for power and domination. When he finishes fashioning his 365 minions, he looks around with satisfaction and declares himself to be the only real god. Thus he exalts himself above the lesser powers he has created and also, perhaps in ignorance or perhaps in defiance, denies the powers that preceded him: his own mother, Sophia, and beyond her the source of her being, of whom he is surely ignorant, the Monad and the Pleroma.

To interpret Yaldabaoth psychologically, he represents a radically egoistic and anti-relational attitude, which in its inflation pridefully severs its connection to its own source, the mother unconscious out of which it comes, and the collective unconscious from which she comes. What the brilliant Gnostic author of the *Apocryphon of John* did was to penetrate behind this deceptive mask of ego self-sufficiency and narcissistic hubris to elucidate the depths and layers of being from which it is descended and to which it owes its being. This "knower" (for *gnostic* literally means "knower") saw through the delusional screen of individual and collective consciousness of his day and, glimpsing the depths, must have realized that this vision would radically relativize the given dogmatic assumptions of the times. This made the Gnostic, of course, a heretic.

The myth answers the question of how and why Yaldabaoth came into being differently from the Darwinian evolutionary-biological stance that we have come to assume. Yaldabaoth does not represent a valuable adaptation to the environment but rather an accident, an inadvertent result of experimentation, a bad mistake. Yaldabaoth is not a sound product of evolutionary process but rather a miscreation, an anomalous experiment that went wrong and now needs to be corrected.

Taken in its own terms, the Gnostic critique was a radical revision of religious assumptions that had become accepted commonplaces in the ancient biblical world. Just as the ordinary person in our time might say, unreflectively, that people are in charge of their lives, that they control their actions rationally and therefore are accountable for all of their behavior, so the ancient biblical conformist would unreflectively say that the creator was good and only good, that all the fault for suffering was to be placed at the feet of humanity, and that any notions of "other gods" or "goddesses" was illusion or, worse still, idolatry punishable by whatever means might be necessary. Pluralism, wholeness, completeness, the fullness of being, God as Mother-Father were denied. The fullness of being was divided into segments and arranged in a strict hierarchy of values, and difference was demonized. What we call borderline splitting and narcissistic self-aggrandizement today are the psychological heritage of Yaldabaoth.

In Yaldabaoth, the Gnostics identified a pattern of conscious attitudes that were endemic to their cultures, and today we can see an identical pattern in ourselves and in our fellow citizens. Yaldabaoth represents the ground plan of the individualistic, controlling, narcissistic ego so familiar in Western culture. What the Gnostics identified and named in Yaldabaoth is still with us, perhaps even more so.

JUNG AND THE GNOSTICS

Jung placed himself and his depth psychology directly in line with the tradition of the Gnostics (Jung 1957). Having produced an original Gnostic text himself in "The Seven Sermons to the Dead" (1963), he knew about the Gnostic experience of the unconscious psyche firsthand. In this text, Jung describes a Gnostic revelation much like those of his ancient colleagues. Analytical psychology, based as it is so strongly on Jung's own inner experiences, is a Gnostic-like psychology that sees beyond the ego dominants of the individual, the society, and the age to the deeper historical and archetypal layers. In doing so, it relativizes the claims to ultimacy made on behalf of the separated, divided and dividing, repressive ego attitudes.

At the same time, it should be noted, Jung's psychological theory does not demonize the ego itself, the central core of a person's identity. Rather, in practice, it attempts to connect the ego to its ultimate source and the ground of its own being: the Self and the pleromatic collective unconscious. Like the Gnostics' challenge to traditional religion, in which they discovered the god Yaldabaoth to be a less-than-ultimate power, Jung challenges the inflated ego that would say, "I am the master of the psyche, the only god within the psychological universe." Both Jung and the Gnostics challenge the ego's supremacy by pointing out that it is not the ground of its own being, that it owes its existence to another who is greater. For the Gnostics, this was Sophia, the mother of Yaldabaoth, and behind her there were many other archons and powers and ultimately the Mother-Father Monad, the Pleroma. In Jung's more modern language of psychological abstraction, the ego owes its existence to the psyche ("Sophia"), of which it is a part (it is a complex), and ultimately to the Self (the "Monad" or "Pleroma"), which supersedes the ego and even the psyche itself in an even larger framework of totality and wholeness.

It was inspired of Jung to detect such profound connections between modern depth psychology and what was then the very obscure, disregarded Gnostic movement of the ancient world; to recognize in the Gnostics' nearly impenetrable writings experiences that paralleled his own; and to perceive in their spiritual explorations the equivalent of his research of the depths of the collective unconscious.

This hermeneutical leap between ancient myth and religion and modern analytical psychology became a hallmark of Jung's methodology, and it opened the way both for understanding the unconscious of modern human beings and for rendering the ancient texts more intelligible to the modern sensibility.

THE *GOSPEL OF TRUTH* "IN JUNGIAN TRANSLATION"

Using Jung's hermeneutic, I will now attempt to translate an ancient Gnostic text, the *Gospel of Truth* (Robinson 1988, pp. 38–51), into the language of modern analytical psychology. I hope this will serve several purposes. The first is to demonstrate some of the surprising psychological wisdom contained in this ancient text. A second is simply to offer a sample of such translation. A third and deeper purpose is to show how much in agreement are the critiques of ancient Gnosis and modern analytical psychology regarding the naivete of an ego-bound (Yaldabaothian) consciousness.

It is especially fitting to consider this particular text from the Nag Hammadi collection because it was found in what has come to be called the Jung Codex, the first of the documents to be opened to the eyes of Western scholars through the ingenious detective work of Gilles Quispel and the financial assistance of one of Jung's students. This Codex was presented to Jung at the Zurich Institute in a ceremony in 1953 in recognition of his long and enduring interest in the Gnostic materials. Jung, it should be noted, was highly instrumental in putting Gnosis back in the center of religious interest and reflection in our time. Similar to what he did for alchemy, Jung resurrected Gnosticism as a legitimate religious philosophical movement, with a wealth of valuable materials for the modern psychologist to study in the pursuit of plumbing the depths of the human soul. Using Jung's psychological hermeneutic, we can grasp something of the deep perceptions of the ancient author. The Jungian translation:

> The ego lives in the Self but is ignorant of this fact. So the ego searches for the Self, not realizing that it is actually contained in it. Now it becomes confused and terrified, and in this confusion and terror it creates a substitute for the truth, which is a false image of the Self. This, of course, has no effect on the Self.
>
> When the ego fell into this fog of illusion, it created further terror and confusion and sought to find company with others. Soon many lived together in a collective fog. The Self, on the other hand, had no part in this and remained opposed to all of them.
>
> Now this is the story of the coming of the symbol that clears the fog of illusion and provides true information about the Self. This symbol [the "Savior," named Jesus Christ in this text of a Christian Gnostic] is a true representation of the Self, and it brings enlightenment to the ego, true consciousness.
>
> Yet the ego remains committed to its own illusory ideas and identifications. It becomes defensive and angry at this new symbol of the Truth and tries to repress it. But the message gets through anyway, that the Self contains the ego and the ego contains something of the Self, and that this is good.
>
> This symbol is the teacher, a guide to the truth of the Self.
>
> It should be said that children are naturally closer to the Self than adults. But only the symbol can reveal the Self to adult egos, because adults do not recognize this same truth in children and cannot learn from them.
>
> The latent knowledge of the Self lies within a person, but only a symbol can bring this out into the open and show it convincingly.
>
> Now, the ego that is open to this knowledge of the Self is the one that had a better connection to the Self in the first place. The knowledge of the Self was already latent in this ego; this ego was already a part of the ego-Self axis, but this had not yet become conscious. The savior symbol, this inner guide and teacher, reveals this hidden connection to the Self but does not create it.
>
> The ego that receives and integrates the knowledge of the Self, therefore, is already solid and has an identity; it already knows who it is and who its parents are, and it has formed an inner core of identity.
>
> The Self reaches out to the ego through the symbol, and in this way it draws the ego to itself. The symbol is the means by which the connection to the Self is made conscious. The symbol is a "complete thought," like a

complete book, and the ego that reads this thought reaches the Self by intuition. This complete symbolic thought, the symbol, unites the ego and the Self. The Self is both a mother and a father.

By itself the ego is deficient, riddled with envy, strife, and confusion. But when the ego is united with the Self, its deficiency ceases. Now the ego becomes filled with the Self. When the Self is known, envy and strife come to an end.

The ego must be silent and must make space for the Self. This means that the ego must break and abandon its schemes and defenses against the Self. For when the Self comes near to the ego, the ego defenses become upset and a crisis ensues. Now the ego must make some hard decisions.

The truth-loving part of the ego welcomes the symbol of the Self and feels itself to be already part of it. The false-self part of the ego becomes upset and is thrown into turmoil. In fact, the truth of the matter is that a part of the ego is actually an emanation of the Self.

The Self has a lot of potential, that is, possibilities for being, which are not yet shaped or formed. These potentials are contained within the Self, and they become conscious, receiving a form and a name, when the Self decides the time is right.

There are psychic phantoms and shadows, which are illusory features of the psyche, which have no real existence and are not rooted in the Self. They are derivatives of the ego, not aspects of the Self. When the ego connects to the Self [i.e., experiences "gnosis"], these illusory shadows are shown to be the unrealities they in truth are. But when the ego is caught up in these miscreations, life is a nightmare. The ego is constantly defensive: it is in flight, it is being chased, it falls into conflicts over and over again, it falls down, it fights. When knowledge of the Self comes, the ego wakes up from this nightmare and sees through these illusions. Now they look like an unreal dream.

The Self awakens the ego, and a new consciousness is aroused. The Self performs this awakening function by incarnating in a tangible symbol.

The symbol brings knowledge of the Self. It brings light; it frees the ego from guilt and bondage to the former complexes. One such symbol of the Self is the shepherd.

The ego that is enlightened and connected to the Self should relate to others similar to itself and should help those who want to be similarly enlightened. One should leave the narcissistic and egocentric ones to their own devices. Do not bother with them. Bother with those who want insight and knowledge.

The Self is fragrant and warm. The ego is cold. The ego without the Self is sick and deficient. The Self is like a doctor who comes to heal: when the Self comes, the ego should not hide its deficiency. The doctoring Self will apply an "ointment," which is empathy and understanding. Feeling accepted, the ego will be healed.

The true symbol comes from the Self at the instigation and according to the will of the Self. The goal of the ego is to realize the meaning of the symbol and to integrate it. The symbol is a true representation of the Self; it is not deceptive. The Self possesses consciousness and offers this to the ego. The symbol offers the ego the awareness of the Self's fullness, and it brings this reality to the ego. The ego that is filled by the symbol and instructed by it about the Self also becomes full and is united with the Self. The ego that is so united to the Self, through the symbol, comes to a place of repose in fullness and knowledge.

This is my Jungian psychological rendition of this ancient Gnostic masterpiece, the *Gospel of Truth* (Robinson 1988, pp. 40–51). The text itself, graced with evocative images, is infinitely more poetic than my rather schematic and abstract modern translation, but I think the simple change of terms—which is about all this translation amounts to—provides us with a better purchase on the profundity of the experience and insight represented in the text.

THE EGO AS YALDABAOTH

What this Gnostic text exposes, and what Jung's analytical psychology also affirms, is the illusory nature of our usual perceptions regarding ego autonomy, independence, and control. This is the ego's characteristic illusion: it lives in a fog of self-deception about its independence and about its lack of origin or need of anything outside of itself. The text points out the ego's fierce resistance to insight into its deeper dependencies upon extra-ego structures. Like Jung, this text diagnoses the malaise (a "nightmare") of this type of ego existence; in this delusional state, the ego suffers massive anxiety and becomes aggressive; it lives in envy and despair. This text recommends as treatment for this malaise, much like Jung, the experience of a symbol that will connect ego-consciousness to the Self. At bottom, every neurosis is a religious problem, Jung was fond of saying, and the solution for a religious problem is an experience of the pleromatic wholeness of one's own being and its solidarity with Being itself.

In contrast to the "messenger" or "savior," that true symbol of the Self, Yaldabaoth is an image of the unconscious factor (an archon or archetype) that creates and backs up the deluded ego's lust for radical independence, control, separateness, and supremacy. Yaldabaoth must be seen as a universal principle of human psychological life, an archetypal image, but one that stands in contradiction to the unity and wholeness of the Self. Yaldabaoth is the principle of individuation (the ego), as opposed to the principle of comprehensive unity (the Self), and as such it is the force also behind such social imperatives as territoriality, blind nationalism, and "ethnic cleansing"; behind an individual's narcissistic insistence on specialness and entitlement, grandiosity; and behind the ego's intrapsychic heroic quest for power and domination of other parts of the psyche. Yaldabaoth is also the psychic factor that turns others into objects to be manipulated rather than relating to them as subjects to be loved. Yaldabaoth is the rigorous perfectionist in us that wishes to eliminate anything foreign, alien, or even just different. He is the psychic archon that creates in order to control and controls in order to feel and be seen as supreme. He is familiar indeed.

The Gnostics who fixed their attention on the biblical tradition identified Yaldabaothian attributes in Yahweh, who would have "no other gods" before him and who was a "jealous God" who promised his chosen people specialness in exchange for ethnic purity and obedience to tribal laws. This is an attitude that we can see in every kind of provincialism, in every instance of nationalism, and in all forms of sexism. It was precisely this archetype, and not only or primarily Wotan, as Jung thought, that was behind the fanaticism and purism of Nazi Aryanism.

Yaldabaoth is certainly not the God of the prophets, who calls out for justice to the widow, the orphan, and the stranger and who insists on decency in economic dealings "in the gate," nor is he to be identified with the Logos of the New Testament or the God of love of the Christian faith. And yet within even these familiar traditions Yaldabaoth shows his face: in the splintering of the biblical tradition into groups and factions—Jews and Christians, Catholics and Protestants, orthodox and reformed and fundamentalists of every stripe and doctrinal nuance, each insisting with absolute conviction on its own views and ideas and condemning all others to eternal damnation. From the pleromatic point of view, all of these certainties are tragic illusions, and all they amount to is people without gnosis banding together and reinforcing one another in common delusional systems. The Yaldabaothian splitting attitude in these groups teaches that where there are differences, there must be enemies, opposites who must battle for dominance and the right to claim all truth for themselves. There can be only one god, and he is ours, he is us. Here Yaldabaoth is ruler.

The Gnostics held that Yaldabaoth is the Lord of this world and dominates the human condition. Yaldabaoth in some sense defines human psychological existence on this planet. As a species, humanity is bound to the law of individuation by virtue of having inherited an individual consciousness, an ego, rather than a group or race consciousness, a consciousness of the whole. This seems to be written into the genetic code. Humans are of necessity ego-bound, in the sense of being bound to develop an individual ego, and especially in the Occident this "deficiency" has been deemed a virtue and cultivated like a rare and precious flower. We have now reached the point where we can speak of cultures of narcissism, that is, human societies in which this type of psychic state is nurtured by a supportive culture. A Gnostic critique would condemn this type of culture as demonic and perverse, a mirror of Yaldabaoth.

While many scholars and commentators have seen Gnosticism as world-denying and one-sidedly anti-materialist and spiritual, the Gnostic perception of the human condition as an accurate psychological assessment and critique of commonly experienced human behavior in all times and places, and especially so in the West in our century, is also apparent. The Gnostic explanation for the universal human experience of evil and tragedy is arguably a sound one if one interprets the figure of Yaldabaoth as the principle of individuation that results in unrelated human egohood and sees Yaldabaoth's creation as common human ego-consciousness with its now familiar anxieties and defenses. Psychoanalysis has uncovered and described Yaldabaoth in exquisite detail. It is the twentieth-century's version of Gnosticism without the fantasy of salvation. Jung supplied the missing piece—a doctrine of the saving symbol—in his revision of psychoanalytic reductionism.

Jung and the Gnostics would agree on a point that essentially sets both of them apart from atheistic materialism and pessimistic biological reductionism—in short, from the psychoanalytic *Weltanschauung*. This point is that although Yaldabaoth is an archon, an archetype, which creates and sustains an inevitable development within human consciousness (the focal narcissistic ego), there is also a piece of the ego that, at its deepest core, is "divine," of the Self, from the Pleroma. There is a spark of light in the darkness of matter, a redemptive possibility. When the author of the *Apocryphon of John* writes about the creation of humanity (i.e., ego-consciousness), a complicated story is elaborated in order to make this subtle point. Yaldabaoth, like Yahweh, creates a primal man (Adam), but according to the Gnostic text he does not create man in his own image but rather in the image of the Pleromatic One whom he had seen in a revelation:

And the whole aeon of the chief archon trembled, and the foundations of the abyss shook. And of the waters which are above matter, the underside was illuminated by the appearance of his image which had been revealed. And when all the authorities and the chief archon looked, they saw the whole region of the underside which was illuminated. And through the light they saw the form of the image in the water. And he said to the authorities which attend him, "Come, let us create a man according to the image of God and according to our likeness, that his image may become a light for us." And they created by means of their respective powers in correspondence with the characteristics which were given. And each authority supplied a characteristic in the form of the image which he had seen in its natural (form). He created a being according to the likeness of the first, perfect Man. And they said, "Let us call him Adam, that his name may become a power of light for us." (*Apocryphon of John,* Robinson 1988, p. 113)

At the core of the human ego, according to this text, resides the image of Pleromatic wholeness, which Yaldabaoth and his minions themselves look to for guidance and inspiration. And Adam does turn out to be a most magnificent creature indeed—in fact, so superior to Yaldabaoth and his 365 "authorities" that they become wildly jealous of him. The Blessed One, called "Mother-Father," gives Adam some protection against the powers of Yaldabaoth, although Adam is, of course, still under the sway of the Lord of this world, and eventually falls victim to temptation and forgets his divine origin. Yet this fact of Adam's inherent likeness to and indeed identity with the divine Pleroma remains latent in ego-consciousness. This, in Jungian terms, is the point of contact between ego and Self.

Jung's similar view of the ego, as he reflects upon it in his late work *Mysterium Coniunctionis* (see especially pars. 130–32), makes him, like the Gnostic author, a guarded optimist about human nature, although in both cases this is severely tempered by a critical awareness of the force and power of Yaldabaoth, the principal agency behind ego-illusion and the architect of the nightmare of deficient ego existence in humankind. According to the Gnostics, humanity cannot escape the power and wiles of Yaldabaoth without a convincing revelation of previous and original oneness and wholeness in the Pleroma. This knowledge is what the "messenger" brings in Gnosticism, and it is what symbols of wholeness—the Tibetan mandala, the alchemical lapis, the mystic Christ—bring in Jung's experience and in his theory of analytical psychology. Both Gnosticism and Jung's psychology offer a tempered optimism about human potential—or, put another way, a hopeful realism. Yaldabaoth cannot be ignored or overcome, but his power is not ultimately in control of human destiny.

Beyond Yaldabaoth

If we ask what can replace the Yaldabaothian ideology of narcissistic ego development that has been rampant in Western societies from time immemorial, we may catch a hint from Gnostic texts, from Jung, and from modern psychological experience. What all of these propose as an option for post-Yaldabaothian consciousness is a "myth of connectedness." One can only hope that this will be supported by at least a trace of evolutionary movement at the genetic level of our existence—our creatureliness—as well.

Western culture stands now at the conclusion of a development that began among the antecedents of the ancient Greeks and Hebrews. This tradition forms a late chapter in the evolution of human consciousness on earth. Its grand culmination is represented in the complexity of the twentieth century, in our politics, in our technology, in our economics, in our religions, and in our conscious attitudes. Its crown jewels appear to be enlightened rationality and individualism, which have led to the modern scientific laboratory, the several technological revolutions of the last centuries, and the many voyages of exploration and efforts at domination over the past millennia. The ideas of History and of Progress, which are thematic in Greek and Hebrew thought, have come to mean for many that increasing control over nature and even over history are perhaps inevitable, that bigger is usually better, that ego control is a measure of success, that expansion is always a positive sign of growth, that one god is better than many gods. This is the work of Yaldabaoth, the expansive and controlling dominant of consciousness that underlies the Western ego. Now the time has come to see through this dominant and to align ourselves with the unconscious, which is calling for a transformation. The Holocaust is the gravestone of this archetypal dominant.

The unconscious is calling for change. Modern depth psychology has mounted a powerful critique on the technological ego. As never before, we can see its relativity and its slender archetypal support. Modern depth psychology and its derivative therapies stand prepared to act as midwife to a new constellation. The new dominant arriving is a myth of connectedness rather than one of separation and control; it is based on a perception of the network of relations that

ties the earth and all peoples together into one pluralistic unity; it
requires almost unimaginable tolerance of differences and acute
consciousness of interdependence among all the parts.

Progress, the false god of the past centuries, gloried in the voyages
of exploration and discovery and reveled in the West's dominion
over the known world. In the wondrous rise of science and the
technological juggernaut also resides Yaldabaoth, that dark and evil
god who is ignorant of others and even of his own condition and does
not care, who grinds on without consideration and rages with envy
and greed. He must be transcended. This version of progress—a
serpent with the head of a lion—is a terrible mistake.

Is the contemporary ego wise enough to analyze and counteract
the force of Yaldabaoth effectively? Our great advantage is that we
can learn from the painful spiritual lesson of the Holocaust and that
we have been given a vision of gnosis and of the greater psyche out
there beyond the dominant of contemporary ego structure and
striving. This greater psyche, we now know, is grounded in the
Pleroma, the All, the collective unconscious that reaches out to the
infinite and to the ultimate mystery of life and creation.

Freud, then Jung, heard the uncanny whisper of the unconscious,
and Jung noted its demand for transformation and wholeness. Jung
interpreted the message of the unconscious "Gnostically," as meaningful and prospective and symbolic. Thus Jung has come, in our
time, to function as a kind of harbinger, introducing the new content,
the savior, who will come to humanity as an inner conviction that
Yaldabaothian ego separateness and control are evil and that the
myth of relatedness must now take root as the master attitude of the
coming age.

This new revelation of connectedness does not come without a
price. In the extreme darkness of the Nazi years, there were brilliant
bursts of light that disclosed this attitude at its brightest intensity,
and these I believe will inspire and orient us for centuries to come.
When Edith Stein was torn from her Carmelite convent in Echt,
Holland, and taken by police escort to the trains that would carry her
with hundreds of other baptized Jews to Auschwitz, she landed for a
time in the camp at Westerbork. There a Dutch official named
Wielek interviewed her, and ten years later he reported the following
scene:

> Once it became apparent that in a matter of hours she was going to be
> transported with the rest of the baptized Jews, I tried to find out whom I
> should notify. I wanted to know if there was some way I could be of

service. Would it help, I asked, if I had a reliable policeman telephone Utrecht? With a smile, she asked me not to do anything. Why should there be an exception made in the case of a particular group? Wasn't it fair that baptism not be allowed to become an advantage? If somebody intervened at this point and took away her chance to share in the fate of her brothers and sisters, that would be utter humiliation. But not what was going to happen now. Then I saw her go off to the train with her sister, praying as she went, and smiling the smile of unbroken resolve that accompanied her to Auschwitz. (Herbstrith 1971, pp. 107–8)

In this exemplary figure, Edith Stein, we have an icon for the age of relatedness.*

REFERENCES

Fordham, Michael. 1969. *Children as Individuals.* New York: C. G. Jung Foundation.

Herbstrith, Waltraud. 1971. *Edith Stein.* San Francisco: Harper & Row.

Jung, C. G. 1955–56. *Mysterium Coniunctionis. Collected Works,* vol. 14. Princeton, NJ: Princeton University Press, 1970.

———.1957. Foreword to the second German edition, Commentary on "The Secret of the Golden Flower." In *Collected Works* vol. 13, pp. 1–56. Princeton, NJ: Princeton University Press, 1968.

———.1963. "Septem Sermones ad Mortuos." In *Memories, Dreams, Reflections,* Appendix 5 (New York: Vintage Books, 1963), pp. 378–90.

Robinson, James M., ed. 1988. *The Nag Hammadi Library in English.* 3rd ed. San Francisco: Harper & Row.

---

*This essay was originally published in the *San Francisco Jung Institute Library Journal,* 12 (1994), pp. 47–59, and is reprinted here, in revised form, with permission.

[4]

THE EVOLUTION OF THE SOUL

June Singer

A Prophecy Realized

In 1945, three Egyptian brothers looking for birdlime to fertilize their crops came upon a huge earthenware jar at the foot of some high cliffs near the town of Nag Hammadi. Breaking open the jar, they found a cache of ancient Coptic books. Muhammad Ali, being the eldest, assumed responsibility for dealing with the discovery. Unable to read Coptic, he regarded the find as of no importance unless he could make some money by selling some of the volumes. Little did he know what momentous words were contained in this, the largest body of *original* Gnostic material from the first and second centuries ever to come to light. But what he could not have guessed, the books themselves proclaimed, "I shall give you what no eye has seen and what no ear has heard and what no hand has touched and what has never occurred to the human mind" (*Gospel of Thomas,* saying 17, Robinson 1988, p. 128).

Before this discovery, most of what was known about Gnosticism had come from its detractors, the early Church Fathers. Struggling to establish the new religion, Christianity, they represented themselves as the hierarchy of this religion, "the elect," whose task it was to define the new faith with creeds and doctrines, and to determine which books would be included in its sacred canon and which would be excluded.

The Gnostic books were contemporaneous with the New Testament writings, but the Gnostic works were excluded from the canon and pronounced heretical. It is not difficult to see why. The Gnostics had no faith in the many gods who were said to rule over this world, the gods of the nations, but discerned instead "a higher God, an unknown God," whose nature was undescribable, yet who was intimately accessible to those who sought after truth. This God was everywhere: "Split a piece of wood, and I am there. Lift up the stone, and you will find me there" (*Gospel of Thomas,* saying 77, Robinson 1988, p. 135). And: "The kingdom of the father is spread out upon the earth, and men do not see it" (*Gospel of Thomas,* saying 113, Robinson 1988, p. 138). For the Gnostics, no churchly authority was needed to intercede between people and God. The path to God lay within the human soul.

If everyone felt this way, there would be little impetus for building great cathedrals or for supporting an expensive Church hierarchy. For these and other reasons, the ideas of the Gnostics were not approved by the nascent Church. Nor were many of the ideas of the nascent Church approved of by the Gnostics. Declared heretical, the original Gnostic documents disappeared, and only the critical commentaries were left to stand; thus almost all that we knew about Gnosticism came from the established Church position toward it.

It is said that an ancient prophecy foretold that the books of the Gnostics would again see the light of day when the world arrived at a state of readiness to hear their messages. What a coincidence, what a meaningful coincidence, that those Egyptian peasants stumbled upon that jar just at the end of the Second World War, after the Holocaust and after the dropping of the atomic bombs on Hiroshima and Nagasaki—a time when we human beings had reached a new low in our capacity for unleashing horror upon our fellows! These writings only now begin to seep into mainstream literature. We must have needed some distance, like abused and violated children, before we could look psychologically and with some objectivity upon what the unspeakable assaults of war and degradation have done to our souls.

After much intrigue and dickering, scholars finally managed to bring these documents together. They were translated into English and first published as a whole in 1977 through the efforts of Professor James M. Robinson and his team of scholars, members of the Gnostic Library Project of the Institute for Antiquity and Christianity, Claremont, California. It is from *The Nag Hammadi Library in English* that I have taken my texts for what follows.

MATTER, SOUL, AND SPIRIT

My theme comes from one of the fifty-six volumes of that Library, the *Exegesis on the Soul.* In my book titled *A Gnostic Book of Hours,* I have rephrased parts of the *Exegesis* to reveal the poetry hidden in the document. This is a short tale, narrating the Gnostic myth of the soul from her fall into the visible world to her return to heaven. People in antiquity understood the "soul" not so very differently from the way we understand her. She is the nonmaterial essence of our beings—what C. G. Jung called the *anima,* or the animating principle. She thrives in inwardness and lives in our deeply felt sensibilities.

The Gnostics had a way of explaining the soul that I find meaningful. It follows the Neoplatonic tradition, which posits a tripartite character for every person: body, soul, and spirit. These three aspects live in each of us, but we do not necessarily accord them the same degree of prominence.

The *body,* sometimes called the "hylic" aspect of being (from the Greek word *hyle,* meaning "matter"), is associated with everything material. The body concerns itself with the realities of *this world:* making a living, eating, drinking, sex and other pleasures, greed and other vices, politics and public service, institutions and corporations, facts and figures, and so on. We need the hylic part of ourselves in order to carry on our lives in the material world.

The *spirit,* for the Gnostic, is the spark of the divine concealed in us from our beginning. We may not even know that it exists. Yet the spirit feels its affinity to the divine mystery which is its source, and reaches out toward it. In biblical terms, "spirit" is the breath that God breathed into Adam, inspiring him and transforming him from a modeled lump of clay into a man. Some speak of spirit as the longing in each of us for the eternal mystery, the source and ground of being. Spirit partakes of two realms, the human and the divine.

The *soul* lies somewhere between body and spirit. The soul is our essential nature. Soul inhabits the truth of our own being, the part that seeks to express itself and to live its own life, the part so often repressed or disregarded as we go about our practical lives making our practical decisions for the sake of expediency. The soul is that part of us which we most often betray, yet she never ceases in her struggle to be heard, to be attended to, to be redeemed. Soul is a very personal aspect of the human being. The ancient Gnostics identified her with *psyche.*

I do not believe that the Gnostic writer(s) of the *Exegesis on the*

Soul were any less sophisticated about matters of body, soul, and spirit than we are today. The Gnostics of the third century of the common era were a very urbane people. Most of them lived in Alexandria, a cosmopolitan city at the Delta of the Nile where the intellectual currents of Judaism, Christianity, Hellenism and other Middle Eastern religions mingled to create an exciting and stimulating ferment of ideas. The unknown author of the *Exegesis on the Soul* uses Greek, Christian, and Jewish quotations in the text, which suggests the desire to expound a certain doctrine in a way that would be comprehensible to all who would listen. Some scholars have suggested that the author was a woman because she speaks from the deepest feeling about experiences that are specifically available to women. She would have intended the story symbolically. The soul's journeys and travails evoke the pain and passion that many people experience in the course of their lives as they search for something from which they feel separated and which, if pressed, they might not be able to identify.

THE HOLY PROSTITUTE

The story begins:

> Wise men of old gave the soul a feminine name.
> Indeed, she is female in her nature as well; she even has a womb.
> As long as she was alone with the father, she was virgin and, in form, androgynous.
> But when she fell down into a body and came to this life, she fell into the hands of many robbers.
> The wanton creatures passed her from one to another; some took her by force, others seduced her with a gift.
> They defiled her and she lost her innocence.
> She prostituted herself, giving her body to one and all; each one she embraced, she considered to be her husband.
> Even when she turned her face from those adulterers, she ran toward others.
> They compelled her to live with them and render service to them upon their beds, as if they were her masters.
> Out of shame she no longer dared to leave them, while they deceived her, pretending to be faithful as if they greatly respected her.
> After this, they abandoned her, and went away. *(Exegesis on the Soul,* Robinson 1988, p. 192)

In this text, the soul is described as feminine: she even has a womb. But when she was with her father in *heaven,* she was androgynous.

What can this possibly mean for us? Heaven is the metaphor for Wholeness, for the Unity of all things. It is the dwelling place of the divine and in a certain sense *is* the divine. Jung understood this when he spoke of the archetype of the Self as the inner image of wholeness or completeness, in which everything exists along with its opposite: good and evil, light and dark, and all the rest, including the masculine and the feminine. Even the ego is embedded in the Self, just as the earth is contained in the heavens.

When life begins, even before we are actually born, we exist in a condition of undifferentiated wholeness with the mother. This condition continues on in the psyche as a kind of relative unconsciousness for as long as the infant remains unaware of the distinction between self and mother. The infant is imbedded in the "all" as a seed is immersed in the ground without ever knowing what the earth is. No sword of discrimination has yet cut through the wholeness of the psyche and divided it into its parts. If we are halfway fortunate, we begin life protected, innocent, and trusting. But sooner or later, experience jolts us into the reality of *this world.*

The Gnostic myth tells that the soul fell down into a body and came to *this* life. When we are born, we take on the burden of gender. But when the Gnostics speak of soul, they speak in metaphor. The soul is not really female. The soul has qualities which liken it to a female, regardless of the sex of the actual person in whom the soul dwells. The soul is feminine because she is vulnerable in a particular way. She can be not only misused and abandoned but also entered into, raped, and contaminated.

THE REPENTANT WIDOW

The continuation of the text makes this point clear:

> The soul becomes a poor desolate widow, without help; nor is even any food left from the time of her affliction.
> From the adulterers she gained nothing except the defilements they gave her while they had sexual intercourse with her,
> And her offspring by them are dumb, blind, sickly, and stupid.
> But when the Father who is above looks down upon her and sees her sighing, with her sufferings and disgrace, and repenting of the prostitution in which she engaged,
> And when she begins to call upon him, that he might help her, crying out with all her heart: "Save me, Father! I will repay you for abandoning my home. Restore me to yourself again!"
> When he sees her in such a state, he will have mercy upon her, for

many are the afflictions that have come upon her, because she abandoned her home. (*Exegesis on the Soul,* Robinson 1988, pp. 192–93)

It is evident from this why scholars have suggested that a woman probably wrote this text. They based their conjecture on the powerfully evocative feelings expressed that, in their minds, could *only* have been experienced by a woman. Such intensity wells up from woman's awareness of the sanctity of her own body and the outrage, shame, and humiliation she feels when her body is abused and defiled or even when she is used and abandoned. The pain is least of all physical; the wound to the soul causes far more suffering. The soul is, after all, *psyche,* composed of both mind and emotion. Mind, or intellect, deals with the visible world in a practical way, solving problems, considering issues, and accomplishing what needs to be done to sustain life and to enjoy it. Emotions temper the mind—they come unbidden and exert tremendous power over individuals, even when they are unaware of their presence.

Even though the soul, in her dejected state of "widowhood," does not remember that the spark of the godhead is present within her, yet it is through the glimmering of that spark that she becomes vaguely aware of the other world, of what in my book *Seeing through the Visible World* (Singer 1990) I have called "the invisible world." This invisible world is where the "one whom we call 'Father' " lives. This is to be understood metaphorically: the Gnostics did not mean, literally, a patriarchal father-god, not at all. They thought of the One whom we call "God" as utterly unknowable and mysterious, one whom we cannot really say anything about because our words are limited and the *mysterium tremendum* which we would like to describe is beyond description. So "Father" here means the invisible world of "otherness," the world of the unknowable. Jung, trying to put this into psychological terms, called it the archetypal world of the collective unconscious.

This is where the soul comes from, but she has forgotten her true home. *Home* has a particular meaning for the Gnostics. They assert that we know where we have come from, we know who we are, we know why we are here on this earth, this visible world, and we know where we are going—but the soul tends to forget all this. Up to this point in the myth, the soul does not yet know that she will be called upon to redeem the holy spark which is in her by bringing it fully into consciousness. In pain and anguish she cries out for help. But she does know, as we all know at times, that what she has been doing is out of character. It is not her true essence that is being expressed in her life. She has tolerated this inauthentic situation for too long, and she can no longer endure it.

Many individuals confront similar painful conditions. They know the terrible feeling of coming face to face with those dark corners where guilt and shame lurk, deadening any zest for life. The soul knows that she must regain her capacity to act, even if, in the past, she has been paralyzed by fear or feelings of powerlessness. She must do something about it. And so she does. She repents what she has done and vows to make amends for what she has brought to pass. She begs the "Father" to restore her to himself—that is, to her place in the original unity. We can see this as a prayer, or as the expression of an ego that becomes aware of its subordination to the Self. The soul does not ask anything simple of the Self, but the task of a lifetime, perhaps of many lifetimes: to help her to bring together fragments of the eternal light that were scattered abroad in the visible world.

The terrifying state of the lost soul calling out to God in fear and trembling is a precondition for becoming whole again. She realizes, as we all realize at one time or another: I *absolutely* do not know who I am, yet he *absolutely* knows. It is the sunken feeling of wanting with all your heart not to exist at all. Having descended into the darkest depths of the shadow, the soul returns, not so much to experience the mercy of God as to find out who she *now* is.

It is not enough for us to be conscious of the divine presence; it is also necessary that we confront our own selves and our errors due to ignorance. Gnosticism does not speak of sin; it speaks of ignorance. If we ignore our true identity and live according to false values, we feel at odds with ourselves, as though we were wandering about without direction. We may be outraged that we must repent of our ignorance, for how could we know that we should have known what we did not know? But repent we must nevertheless. The soul must repudiate her unwholesome involvement with the experiences of her former life before she can embark on her ascent to the Father.

TURNING THE WOMB INWARD

The text continues:

> As long as the soul keeps running about everywhere, copulating with whomever she meets and defiling herself, she exists in suffering, and justly so.

But when she perceives the straits she is in and weeps before the Father and repents, the Father will have mercy upon her.

He will make her womb turn from the external domain and will turn it again inward, so that the soul will regain her proper character. (*Exegesis on the Soul*, Robinson 1988, p. 194)

The task of the soul is to complete the divine program that is established for those who live in the world. It is a sort of life plan—an archetypal pattern, Jung would say: to find the lost fragments of Spirit, to know them for what they are, to liberate them and thereby to regain a state of wholeness with them. To do this the soul reaches out to her brother, the Logos. If the Logos, which appears in masculine form, represents an expression of the word or the light, then Sophia, the soul in its feminine form, represents that which receives the word or the light.

For the Gnostic, the soul is the archetypal vessel that is given form in order to be able to carry the holy seed, or spark. Perhaps there is something in each of us, whether we are women or men, that holds this potential, but she (or we) can fall upon bad times and be defiled. Then the soul must be purified and renewed before she can be restored to the condition of wholeness. In sacred myths, this is called the condition of "virginity." It refers to a person who is one with herself, and not dependent upon the approval of others for identity or support. The process of the soul's descent into the depths of the unconscious, its awakening into awareness, and its emergence into the light of consciousness is what I believe Jung meant when he spoke of the "individuation process." Though such a process can never be adequately described in words, the metaphor of the soul's journey reveals the agony and the glory that attend the experience.

For transformation to take place it is necessary to turn the womb inward. This is surely a strange metaphor! The text reads:

When the womb of the soul, by the will of the Father, turns itself inward,

It is baptized, and cleansed of the external pollution which was pressed upon it, like dirty garments which, when put into water and turned about until their dirt is removed, become clean.

In this way, the cleansing of the soul is to regain the newness of her former nature, and to turn herself back again. (*Exegesis on the Soul*, Robinson 1988, p. 194)

When we are ignorant of her presence, the soul runs about aimlessly like an orphan child to whom no one pays attention. She explores all sorts of places. Since there is no longer a connection with the inner Self to warn her where danger lurks, she knows neither fear nor caution. She solicits affection from any likely source. Easily deceived by flattery, she goes to whoever offers her the appearance of pleasure; yet she finds no pleasure in intimacy with strangers. Since she does not know where she belongs, she looks everywhere for a place to call home, not knowing that "home" is not a place but a manner of existence.

Isn't this the picture of the person who does everything for some imagined immediate gain, who cosies up to people who might give him or her certain favors—the social climber, the fair-weather friend? After a while such people no longer know who they are or where they live, in the deepest sense. Sometimes they are sufficiently unhappy to turn inward.

The Gnostic soul of our myth knows this feeling only too well. In her suffering she weeps and repents of her ignorance. Her prayer is heard. The spark of the divine glows brighter within her, and grace is given. She is chosen for the task of redemption, not because of her error but because of the spark in her which desires to return to the Father. The work of redemption is long and hard. It is a psychological work. The soul prepares herself to perform it. This is according to the will of the Father whom she no longer remembers. We can understand this as a natural tendency to seek wholeness, or integrity in depth, which is somewhere in us whether or not we are aware of it.

The myth tells us that the first part of the soul's work is to turn inward. The place of interiority is the womb of the soul. When she was occupied with the attractions of the visible world, she became enchanted into obliviousness concerning her past and her future. Turning inward, she begins to regain her proper character. She recognizes the charms of the visible world as illusions that enticed her from her true nature. By the will of the Father, the soul is baptized and cleansed of the pollution that was pressed upon her.

When we feel guilt or shame over what we have done or what we have allowed to be done to us, the first step toward healing is to turn inward. The womb turned outward suggests turning ourselves inside out to please others, to adapt to situations which are not right for us, to relinquish our autonomy for the sake of peace and quiet, to relinquish our deeply held beliefs for the sake of an immediate gain. To turn the womb inward is to give up the psychological prostitution that makes us feel compromised.

As long as we are fully outer-directed, we are unconscious of our own motivations. Driven by our fears, by loneliness, greed, willfulness, and desperation, we see only the objects of our desires and not the mechanisms behind our efforts to satisfy them. Before the soul can emerge from her state of degradation, we must remove thoughts born of ignorance or willfulness and the actions resulting from them through something like ritual washing, until we are no longer contaminated. Only then will renewal be possible.

Waiting for the Bridegroom

The text tells us what this process is like in a totally feminine expression:

> The soul will begin to rage at herself like a woman in labor, who writhes and rages in the hour of delivery.
> But being female, she is powerless to beget a child by herself.
> The Father sends her man to her, her brother, the firstborn; the bridegroom comes down to the bride.
> She has given up her former ways and cleansed herself; she is renewed so as to be a bride.
> She adorns herself in the bridal chamber; she fills it with perfume.
> She sits in waiting for the true bridegroom. (*Exegesis on the Soul,* Robinson 1988, p. 195)

The desire for renewal is not easily fulfilled. Once the soul has recognized her faithlessness and repented, she feels her anger and self-hatred with full force because of what she has done to herself. She wants to be worthy of the grace that has been given to her, but she is terrified that she will be found lacking and that no amount of cleansing and purifying will remove the stains of her transgression. As to a woman in labor, the hour of delivery comes whether she is prepared for it or not, and she cannot complete the process alone.

> No longer does she run about the marketplace, copulating with whomever she desires.
> She continues to wait for him, saying, "When will he come?"
> She fears him, for she does not know what he looks like.
> She no longer remembers, since she fell from her Father's house.
> But by the will of the Father, she dreams of him like a woman in love with a man. (*Exegesis on the Soul,* Robinson 1988, p. 195)

He descends to meet her, he who is that other aspect of her wholeness which she had forsaken, the one who is her brother, the first-born, the archetypal Man. Indeed, this first-born son of the alien and unknown God has been known by many names in diverse cultures. In human experience he appears in the psyche as the counterpart of the soul. Sometimes he is called "the Logos," sometimes "the Christ." In this context, Jung has called him "the symbol of the Self." In our Gnostic narrative, he appears as the true bridegroom, with the soul as his bride.

The soul as bride is cleansed, renewed, and restored to her virginity; all that she had suffered is like a horrific dream that vanishes in the light of dawn. She prepares the bridal chamber for herself and her bridegroom, making herself as lovely as possible. Who does not know the excitement of anticipating the lover who is the first true love of one's life? The soul waits with such an impatient patience, longing for him yet wishing for the torturous rapture of her desire to be prolonged. She waits in delicious fear, savoring her curiosity about the unknown mate who will fulfill her and make her complete. She knew him once, when she was in the realm of the Father, but she no longer remembers him. And so she dreams, as we all dream, of the lost paradise, of the lost innocence, of the time that never was.

THE SACRED MARRIAGE

The bridegroom, according to the Father's will, came down to her, into the bridal chamber which was prepared.

He decorated the bridal chamber.

And since that marriage is not like the carnal marriage, those who are to have intercourse with one another will be satisfied with that intercourse.

As if it were a burden, they leave behind them physical desire, and they turn their faces from each other.

But once they unite with one another, they become a single life.

Wherefore the prophet said of the first man and first woman: "They will become a single flesh."

For they were originally joined to one another when they were with the Father before the woman led astray the man, who is her brother.

This marriage brings them back together again and the soul is joined to her true love, her real master. (*Exegesis on the Soul,* Robinson 1988, p. 195)

The ritual of the Sacred Marriage speaks to the archetypal union of heart to heart that surpasses every individual act. Entering the bridal chamber means to take that step into the hidden place and to lay aside all that belongs to the rational world. Here the opposites may join together in the most tender of relationships. Here boundaries dissolve, or we break through boundaries. Aspects of ourselves that were unknown to one another now become known in the fullest sense. All feelings of separateness vanish.

Marriage, the universal image of sexual union, also symbolizes in many cultures the union of opposites that are other than sexual. Sacred Marriage in mystery cults may represent the union of the human being with the god. Sacred Marriage may also represent the union of a community with its celestial deity. For many, it is a sacrament in which the holy place is entered and where, through a communal meal, the substance of the One enters into the substance of the many. The Sacred Marriage described in the Gnostic text is not celebrated in remembrance of an event in the past, nor is it even the reenactment of an event. It does not come to pass because of knowing *about* the union of woman with man or the union of person with divinity. The Gnostic rite is actually taking place within the consciousness of the person who participates—at the very moment of partaking. All barriers dissolve, like the bread and wine in the mouths of the bridal pair. Because this is done according to the will of the Father, or according to the nature of the fabric of the universe, the Spirit is contained in the act. All that pertains to the physical world is left outside this bridal chamber, including all carnal desire. The statement that "those who are to have intercourse with one another will be satisfied with that intercourse" strikes deeply into the sensibility of the soul, for she has known the carnal marriage and every perversion of it and was not satisfied, but now she *will* be satisfied. She will no longer strive to separate herself from an other but will unite with him as her lover, and they will become one. The two who were unbegotten, the soul and the logos, yet who emanated from the Father-Mother, had been lost to each other for many aeons. During this time the soul wandered over the lower worlds and came to know the ultimate in pain and suffering. Now the soul and the Self are rejoined as sister and brother and become one, a single flesh.

But this happy reunion is not the end. So often when we attain a level of spiritual or psychological development, we feel a new peace, a new energy, a sense of fulfillment. This is a very dangerous time, because we are tempted to fall back into the delicious sleep of unconsciousness. Were we to give way to the temptations that taunt us from every side, we could easily lapse into the former state. This would be all the more painful because now we have had a glimpse of what we could be, or what we might have been.

So now we find ourselves face to face with the greatest test of the soul's evolution: the necessity of sustaining our new level of consciousness. We cannot get away with simply accepting a new state of

being and putting the past away. We must look carefully at where we
have gone astray and take personal responsibility for our part in
bringing about what has happened to us.

RECOGNIZING THE BELOVED

The text presents just the image we need when we reflect on this:

> Gradually the soul recognizes her beloved and she rejoices once more, yet
> weeping before him as she remembers the disgrace of her former
> widowhood.
> She adorns herself still more, so that he might be pleased to stay with her.
> He requires her to turn her face from her people and the multitude of her
> adulterers in whose midst she once was,
> To devote herself only to her king, her real lord, and to forget the house of
> the earthly father where things went so badly with her,
> But to remember her Father who is in heaven.
> And the prophet said in the Psalms [45:10-11]: "Hear, my daughter, and
> see, and incline your ear: forget your people and your father's house,
> for the king has desired your beauty; he is your lord." (*Exegesis on the
> Soul,* Robinson 1988, pp. 195–96)

In the very moment when the soul is joined to her beloved, she
weeps before him. Why, we wonder, was she ever allowed to fall or to
descend into the world of form? When she was with the Father, they
were one and she was at peace. That was the original state of
innocence—or of unconsciousness, as we might say. But she separated herself by a thought, and the primal unity was broken. Why
must the soul in this life undergo shame and humiliation over and
over again at the hands of the powers of this world? Why must she be
deceived and seduced, raped, and ravished? These are legitimate
questions.

We might as well ask why the innocence of an infant is not
permitted to endure throughout its entire life. The infant's first
awareness of its separation from its mother was the catastrophe that
all children must undergo. It did not know when she walked away
from its crib whether she would ever return. So the infant began to
perceive the world with its own eyes, no longer trusting in the same
way as before that its mother would always take care of it. This is the
painful beginning of consciousness. Gradually, as the child develops,
it grows further away from its parents and begins to make its own way
in the world. It stumbles and falls many times. It meets with trials
and temptations, it makes its own mistakes, and it comes upon

difficult times. It experiences pain and loss, grief and desire. It becomes entangled in sensual experience, as represented by the worldly powers that the Gnostics called the "archons."* Perhaps it vaguely remembers that there was once a place of joy and peace. Memory traces surface from time to time, casting doubt upon what the person is doing in the world. Like the wandering soul, memories may become torture, and sometimes there is no rest.

The individual soul is not unlike the soul imago that is the subject of our story. She does not know that her suffering comes about through the will of the Father. He subjects her to ordeal after ordeal, not out of anger because she has acted without his agreement but out of his wish to recover the sparks of his glory that have been lost in the world and to return them to the Light. Those darker aspects of ourselves represented by the archons also desire to take possession of the sparks concealed in us, hoping thereby to take possession of our higher potentials and subvert them to their own ends. The myth tells us that this does not have to happen. The Father sends his messenger to enter into the struggle for the liberation of the sparks. If we listen, we will hear the voice of the messenger speaking from a place within us. Then a furious struggle takes place in the human soul, where the archons do their work, and there the hapless soul must strive to protect the holy spark.

How much suffering must we endure before we can begin to know our true selves? The allegory suggests that life requires that we submit to many kinds of experiences so that we may come to know what kind of stuff we are made of. In order to gauge our strength, we have to be tempered by fire. It is an easy thing to praise the gods when they shower us with blessings. But when we have lost everything, our virtue, our pride, even our sense of who we are, it is not so easy to cry out for help to an alien God. The unknown God, like the absent mother, is far away from us and we are not even sure that God exists. Yet the very act of calling out to God leads us toward an awakening of consciousness.

---

*The term "archon" originally referred to the magistrates of cities and towns in the world of ancient Greece. However, in the literature of Gnosticism, archons take on a special meaning. They are inferior gods, and their legions who rule over the visible world are responsible for every human vice born of ignorance of the True God: greed, envy, vanity, self-centeredness, concupiscence, jealousy, and the rest. In psychological terms, archons represent the projections of our unconscious egocentrism upon external factors in the world.

THE WAY OF ASCENT

The myth concludes:

> When the soul had again adorned herself in her beauty, she enjoyed her
> beloved and he also loved her.
> And when she had intercourse with him,
> She got seed from him that is the life-giving spirit, so that by him she
> bears good children, and rears them.
> For this is the great perfect marvel of birth, and this marriage is made
> perfect by the will of the Father.
> Now it is fitting that the soul regenerate herself and become again as she
> formerly was.
> The soul then moves of her own accord.
> She receives the divine nature from the Father for her rejuvenation so that
> she might be restored.
> This is the resurrection from the dead, the ransom from captivity.
> This is the way of ascent to the Father. (*Exegesis on the Soul,* Robinson
> 1988, p. 196)

The consummation of the Sacred Marriage of the soul and the Self
is not an ending, but a beginning on another level of consciousness.
As the soul had once conveyed the breath of earthly life to carnal
man, Adam, so now does the Self bring eternal life through intercourse with the soul. The seeds of the Spirit are placed in her womb
so that she may bring forth beings in whom the spirit of the Father
lives.

To be whole means to be at one with the divine Self. Wholeness is
the original condition of life, before the first thought enters and
begins to discriminate "this" from "that." Although we are whole at
the moment of our birth, our lives become more and more fragmented as we live in the world. Each moment demands something
else from us, and we are pulled away from our center. We lose our
sense of the natural rhythms of life and of the Light that empowers
their harmonious actions. We become like automatons, going where
we are led by the information that is fed to us, by the fashions of the
times, and by the words of those whose wisdom we fail to question.
We become as the living dead. This used to be called "loss of soul,"
but in our time it is termed depression, ennui, or complacency.

When the soul emerges at last from this darkness and is able to see
with new eyes, we are free to move of our own accord. We can
discriminate between those who are deceiving us and those who are
worthy of our love. We need no longer remain captive in the web of
senses and emotions but can move as the Spirit moves in us, with

greater freedom. This, as I see it, is the meaning of "resurrection." When consciousness is enlightened, it happens in the here and now. The upward journey, the ascent into heaven, is a practice in which we can engage day by day—not an end that we must seek. Renewal is not "being born again." It is an ongoing process that, like a garden, requires continuous hard work to bring forth an abundance of excellent flowers and fruit.*

REFERENCES

Robinson, James M., ed. 1988. *The Nag Hammadi Library in English.* 3rd ed. San Francisco: Harper & Row.

Singer, June. 1990. *Seeing through the Visible World: Jung, Gnosis, and Chaos.* San Francisco: Harper & Row.

———. 1992. *A Gnostic Book of Hours: Keys to Inner Wisdom.* San Francisco: HarperCollins.

---

*This essay is a revision of pp. 96–111 of June Singer's *A Gnostic Book of Hours: Keys to Inner Wisdom* (San Francisco: HarperCollins, 1992), and is reprinted here with permission.

[5]

"BEGOTTEN, NOT CREATED": THE GNOSTIC USE OF LANGUAGE IN JUNGIAN PERSPECTIVE

Schuyler Brown

G NOSIS, broadly defined,[1] might be called *introverted religious knowledge*. If understood in this way, gnosis poses a continuing challenge to religious orthodoxy, whether Jewish, Christian, or Muslim.

Within the New Testament canon, Paul and the author of the Fourth Gospel, not to mention Jesus himself, exhibit a spiritual knowledge which commended them to later Gnostic writers. But Paul's letters and the Johannine corpus also show a concern for the threat that religious individualism can represent for any collective Church structure.

The creative tension which we find in these New Testament writings was abandoned in later letters attributed to Paul, where "what is falsely called knowledge" (1 Timothy 6.20), with its "myths and genealogies," was rejected in favor of "sound doctrine" (1 Timothy 1.4, 10; 4.7; 6.3; 2 Timothy 1.13; 4.3, 4; Titus 1.9, 14; 2.1; 3.9).

This exclusion of the Gnostics from the Church was more damaging to the Christian movement, from a psychological point of view, than any subsequent schism, whether between the Eastern and Western Churches or between Catholics and Protestants. For this first Christian schism involved not simply different interpretations of revelation but differences over the nature of revelation itself.

In my opinion, the Church and gnosis need each other. Without gnosis, Christianity ossifies into a dogmatic structure, and "faith" comes to mean paying lip service to that structure. But once gnosis had been excluded from the Church, it simply disappeared from history, except as an underground phenomenon. The reappearance in our own day of Gnostic churches suggests that the collective and individual expressions of religious experience need to remain on speaking terms.

In declining to respond to "the Gnostic question" with a simple pro or con, I am following the lead of C. G. Jung, who affirmed the importance of gnosis for Christian renewal[2] but who also acknowledged the psychological value of the Church as a protective container against the destructive inroads of the unconscious.[3]

My appreciation of the importance of gnosis did not come easily. Since I had been reared in the rationalism of mainline Christianity and schooled in the rationalism of the university, my initial reaction to Gnostic literature was one of bewilderment and disdain. I wondered how such material could ever have constituted a serious threat to the Church.

In 1978, when I entered Jungian analysis, my attitude began to change, as I noticed the correspondence between my own strange dream world and the strange world of the Nag Hammadi texts. I came to realize that whatever has not yet been incorporated into consciousness must seem alien to the rational ego. But such alien intrusions, over which the ego has no control, may point to a way out of a diminished existence which has become insupportable.

The relationship between the image and the text in gnosis is the subject of this essay. I have come to believe that the significance of the rediscovery of ancient gnosis lies not so much in the bizarre ideas attacked by the heresiologists as in the use of the written word to express and evoke a visual image. Gnosis and orthodoxy represent two different ways of thinking, two different ways of reading, and two different ways of using language.

GNOSIS AND ORTHODOXY: FANTASY THINKING VERSUS DIRECTED THINKING

C. G. Jung (1911–12/1952) has distinguished between "directed," or logical, thinking and "fantasy," or "dream," thinking (p. 18). Directed thinking is adapted to reality. It takes for granted the principle of contradiction, and it imitates the causal sequence of events taking place outside the mind. Fantasy thinking works spontaneously and is guided by unconscious motives. It sets free subjective tendencies. Rather than adapting itself to reality, fantasy thinking adapts external reality to its own inner world. Contradictions abound, as our own dreams testify every night. In Freudian terms, fantasy thinking is primary process thinking, directed thinking secondary process thinking.

Fantasy thinking, for Jung, is characteristic of antiquity: "to the classical mind everything was still saturated with mythology" (1911– 12/1952, p. 20). Jung's characterization of mythic thinking describes many of the texts which we now know from Nag Hammadi: "This creative urge explains the bewildering confusion, the kaleidoscopic changes and syncretistic regroupings, the continual renovation of myths in Greek culture" (1911–12/1952, pp. 20–21). The prevalence of this kind of thinking in Gnostic literature explains why the Church Fathers regarded gnosis as a relapse into paganism.

Directed thinking finds its ultimate achievement in modern science and technology. Mythic projections upon the universe are withdrawn in the interest of "devising formulas to harness the forces of nature" (Jung 1911–12/1952, p. 20).

Christian orthodoxy is linked to the thinking of antiquity insofar as its subject matter is religious fantasy, but this fantastic subject matter is treated dialectically, through directed thinking. In this sense, orthodox scholasticism "is the mother of our scientific method" (Jung 1911–12/1952, p. 20).

The Gnostic and the orthodox had the same Scripture, but they read it differently. The directed thinking which is characteristic of doctrinal orthodoxy leads to directed reading: the reader constructs a story "behind" the text. A directed reading of the opening chapters of Genesis leads to the orderly sequence of "salvation history" which is familiar to us from dogmatic theology: the creation of the world, the creation of Adam and Eve,[4] the Fall, and the promise of redemption contained in the *protoevangelium* (Genesis 3.15). In such an "objective" reading, a distinction must be made between the historical events (objective redemption) and the appropriation of this redemption by the individual (subjective redemption).

The Gnostic reading of Scripture is characterized by the infrequency of explicit Scriptural citations, which inhibits any distinction between text and interpretation, or between "then" and "now." "Salvation history" is indistinguishable from the psychic awakening of the reader: the creation story is paradigmatic for anyone who receives the revelatory gnosis.[5] In a Gnostic reading, the ceaseless crisscrossing and interweaving of themes and characters preclude referentiality: the feminine characters in particular—Barbelo, Sophia, the serpent, heavenly Eve, Epinoia—all seem to be expressions of the same force, rather like Olympia, Antonia, and Giulietta in Offenbach's opera "Tales of Hoffmann." The Gnostic creation stories do not show us a world distinct from ourselves: "objective" reality is renounced for the sake of an imaginal noesis which can exist only in a twilight which rational clarity dispels.

Gnostic interpretation of Scripture gives free rein to the inner promptings of the imagination. The text serves as a catalyst for the release of natural symbols arising out of the unconscious, and the text becomes, in turn, the screen upon which these unconscious contents are projected. The inner is expressed in terms of the outer. By pointing away from itself, in order to express an experience which is beyond rational discourse, the imagistic language of gnosis forestalls any idolatry of the word. Gnostic writing does not point to self-consistent and unchanging realities beyond the empirical world but rather uses religious images to interpret existence (LaFargue 1985, p. 207).

A Difference in Root Metaphors: Speech versus Sexuality

Gnostics and orthodox seem to be guided by two different root metaphors, both of them derived from a common Scripture. In the Genesis story, creation comes about through God's word: "God said, . . . and it was so." The Prologue to the Fourth Gospel personifies this divine word: "The Word was with God, . . . and without him not one thing came into being" (John 1.1,3). The masculine Logos replaces the feminine figure of Sophia, who, according to the Old Testament wisdom tradition, was beside God "like a master worker" (Proverbs 8.30).

Sophia (personified Wisdom) becomes the protagonist of the Gnostic creation story. She is given the epithet *prouneikos* (Pasquier 1988), which suggests impetuosity, wantonness, libido (in the inclusive sense used by Jung [1911–12/1952] of any form of psychic energy [pp. 132–70]). As the connecting principle between the deity and creation, on the one hand Sophia is God's "delight," while on the other hand she is "delighting in the human race" (Proverbs 8.30–31).

In the Johannine Prologue, where the feminine principle has been excluded, the sexual imagery is still present insofar as the incarnate Word is the "Father's only Son" (John 1.14). In the Gnostic reading of Scripture, sexuality, not speech, is the root metaphor. The beginning of the cosmic process is not the divine word but an act of autoeroticism. Sophia conceives a thought from herself, through the invisible spirit's foreknowledge, and reveals an image from herself, but without her consort's approval (*Apocryphon of John,* Robinson 1988, pp. 119–23).[6]

Sexuality is also operative in the Gnostic interpretation of the Adam and Eve story. Death comes into being through the separation of Eve from Adam, and it will only be overcome through the reintegration of the masculine with the feminine, as symbolized by the sexual act (*Gospel of Philip,* Robinson 1988, p. 150).

The Gnostic preference for fantasy thinking has consequences for the evaluation of the senses. In the orthodox conception, hearing is the most important sense, and it is through hearing that the word of faith is received (Romans 10.8, 14, 17). For gnosis, however, seeing, tasting, and smelling are more highly valued. The Gnostic is the fragrance of the Father, and what comes through the ears is less effective, less direct, and less intimate than what comes through *pneuma,* which has the double meaning of "spirit" and "breath" (*Gospel of Truth,* Robinson 1988, p. 47).

Psychological and Philosophical Critique of Religious Rationalism

Having grown up in a parsonage of the Swiss Reformed Church, Jung was keenly aware of the devastating psychological consequences of religious rationalism.[7] His concern was for those parts of the psyche which are not reached by rational discourse and which, in turn, rational discourse is unable to bring to expression.[8]

Jung was also thoroughly familiar with Kant's philosophical critique of metaphysics and metaphysically based theology. The language of directed thinking turns outwards and is used for the purpose of communication (Jung 1911–12/1952, p. 18). For communication to take place effectively, language must be used as univocally as possible, so that misunderstanding can be avoided. Language is a social artifact, and for it to function in the public arena it must be strictly governed by social convention.

The truth of such rational discourse is measured by its correspondence with external reality, which it is presumed to mirror. Such discourse is an essential tool for *homo faber,* as he strives to control the world in accordance with his intentions.

When, however, such discourse ventures into areas where no empirical verification is possible, its truth claims are suspect. In this conviction Jung was at one with the tradition of apophatic theology, also called the *via negativa,* which believes that we can know only what God is *not.*

This philosophical position has been confirmed by modern studies of language. No element can function as a sign without relating to another element which is not itself present. This means that every linguistic element is constituted by the trace of something absent. Nothing in language is ever simply there (Derrida 1981, p. 26).

In other words, there can be no one-to-one correspondence between language and external reality. The common-sense position of philosophical realism is an illusion. Language does not mirror the outer world but interprets it, and no interpretation is uninfluenced by the interpreter. "Objective" reality finds expression in language as a creation of human consciousness.

If this is true even of discourse concerning the familiar world we think we know, its consequences for religious rationalism are devastating. The *deus absconditus* is revealed not through the powers of human reason but only through "metaphors transparent to transcendence" (Campbell 1989, p. 28).

LANGUAGE AND THE POETIC IMAGINATION

Although for some religious traditions the ineffability of God excludes the use of Scripture, the Gnostics did not go this route. Yet instead of using language to try to construct a rationally consistent theological system, the Gnostics related the word to the image through which the divine is revealed. In *Thunder: Perfect Mind* Sophia proclaims, "I am . . . the word whose appearance is multiple" (Robinson 1988, p. 298). The *Gospel of Philip* declares, "Truth did not come into the world naked, but it came in types and images. The world will not receive truth in any other way" (Robinson 1988, p. 150). Using the paired opposites which are characteristic of mythic speech, Sophia declares, "I am the honored and the scorned one. I am the whore and the holy one. I am the wife and the virgin. I am the mother and the daughter" (*Thunder: Perfect Mind,* Robinson 1988, p. 297).

The primacy of the image in Gnostic writing and the lack of concern for rational consistency suggest that we are dealing here with poetic discourse. This realization has been missed by many students of the Nag Hammadi texts, for they, like the ancient heresiologists, interpret gnosis as a doctrinal system.

Paul Kugler (1982) has related the poetic language of the soul to a psychology of the imagination. The approach applies beautifully to the Gnostic writings. Ever since Ferdinand de Saussure, it has been customary to distinguish the manifestation of linguistic competence in speech and writing (*parole*) from the supra-individual stock of linguistic elements and the rules for combining them. This linguistic system (*langue*) is what makes human communication possible, but it is not consciously known or reflected upon in the act of speaking or writing (Culler 1976).

Through the unconscious assimilation of this linguistic system, which begins in earliest childhood, "man is separated from the material world (external objects of reference) and initiated into a shared archetypal system of meaning-relations—a system that collates meanings imaginally through a parity of phonetic values" (Kugler 1982, p. 117). The unconscious web of linguistic associations, both semantic and phonetic, interacts with emotionally charged patterns of meaning, which also lie outside consciousness and which are called complexes.[9] These inner connections between language and the psyche are particularly crucial for fantasy, where the ordinary reference of language is abolished and where phonetic associations seem to predominate.

Kugler is concerned with the relation between language and images in dreams, but the Nag Hammadi texts cannot be considered to be direct transcriptions of psychic material. The ancient Coptic manuscripts are translations, perhaps by Pachomian monks, of lost Greek originals. However, Kugler has shown that the invariant relationship among concepts, realized by an invariant phonetic pattern, transcends the differences among particular languages (1982, pp. 51–52). That is to say, the same phonetic pattern is found in languages which have no relationship with one another. It is therefore possible that the correspondence between phonetic patterns, unified by acoustic archetypal images, and psychologically charged patterns of meaning may have been preserved in the transmission of these texts from Greek to Coptic and from Coptic to modern vernacular translations.

In rational discourse the individual uses language; in poetic discourse language uses the individual, who is said to be "inspired" by the Muse. What is thereby brought to expression is an underlying deep structure which imaginally connects disparate concepts. Conceptual language is not abolished but transcended.

For analytical psychology, rational discourse is not the highest form of symbol making. Behind and beneath the word there is always something more ultimate: the image, which is the expression of archetypal energy that is simply there. As Jung has written, "The protean mythologem and the shimmering symbol express the processes of the psyche far more trenchantly and, in the end, far more clearly than the clearest concept; for the symbol not only conveys a visualization of the process but—and this is perhaps just as important—it also brings a re-experiencing of it" (1942, pp. 162–63).

In the *descensus ad inferos,* familiar to the mystics, human reasoning is of no avail, and the imaginative function of mythology replaces the use of rational discourse.

The doctrinal interpretation (and discreditation) of gnosis ignores not only the central importance given to the image in the passages already cited but also some clearly deconstructionist statements about language, found particularly in the *Gospel of Philip.*

In an extraordinary anticipation of Derrida, we find this statement about the differential nature of language: "Light and darkness, life and death, right and left, are brothers of one another. They are inseparable" (Robinson 1988, p. 142). From this point it follows that nothing can be understood in isolation: "Because of this neither are the good good, nor the evil evil, nor is life life, nor death death" (Robinson 1988, p. 142).

The text goes on to draw the consequences for "God-talk:" "Thus one who hears the word 'God' does not perceive what is correct, but perceives what is incorrect. So also with 'the father' and 'the son' and 'the holy spirit' and 'life' and 'light' and 'resurrection' and 'the church' and all the rest" (Robinson 1988, p. 142). The literalistic interpretation of religious language leads to deception, which only the inner knowledge of the Gnostic can escape (Robinson 1988, p. 142).

Of course, the Nag Hammadi texts include didactic as well as mythic material, and the Gnostic creation myth itself has been given a doctrinal interpretation. But these explicit statements from the *Gospel of Philip* give an indication of what kind of language game is being played.

To be sure, Nag Hammadi scholars can readily identify a welter of ideas and doctrines with parallels in other writings from late antiquity. But from a psychological point of view, the crucial thing is how such ideas and doctrines are being used.

A Gnostic Parable about Language?

There is an obscure passage in the *Gospel of Philip* which suggests the contrast between the rational and the archetypal dimensions of language that has been the central focus of this discussion. The text is stressing the difference between creating and begetting. A creator works openly, but begetting is done in private (Robinson 1988, pp. 157–58).

In the Gnostic creation myth it is the Demiurge and his archons who create Adam from the elements. But Adam has no real life in him. Only the highest being can confer upon him the divinity that will exalt him above the Demiurge and make him capable of receiving salvation (Rudolph 1987, pp. 94–95). The Demiurge who vainly boasts, "I am a jealous God [Exodus 20.5]; besides me there is no god [Isaiah 45.5]," corresponds psychologically to the rational ego, which proclaims its self-sufficiency, unaware of its own roots in the unconscious.

The primary expression of ego consciousness is rational discourse. It "works openly." It is exoteric and relies for its intelligibility upon social convention. Begetting is an esoteric action, done "in private," away from ego consciousness. It is also instinctual, thus paralleling the archetypes, which, like biological instincts, "direct all fantasy into its appointed paths" (Jung 1959, p. 66).

If understood with reference to language, "begetting" can refer to the unconscious associations which are grouped around an archetypal image. The author challenges the orthodox view that the same creator God is responsible for both the creation of the world and the begetting of the Son: "he who creates cannot beget." That is to say, rational discourse and fantasy language come from different parts of the psyche. Gnostic texts are esoteric because their meaning depends not on the public conventions of rational discourse but on correspondences hidden in the deep structure of language, to which ego consciousness has no direct access.

According to the instruction of Father Zosima in Dostoevsky's novel *The Brothers Karamazov*, "Much on earth is hidden from us, but to make up for that we have been given a precious mystic sense of our living bond with the other world, with the higher heavenly world, and the roots of our thoughts and feelings are not here but in other worlds" (1976, p. 299). For the Gnostic, the link between "things visible and invisible" is founded not on an act of creation but on a begetting from above (cf. John 3.3). The connection between the visible image and its invisible source is the result of inner process, like the resemblance between a woman's child and the man who loves her (*Gospel of Philip,* Robinson 1988, p. 156).

Consequently, the paradigm for the Gnostic use of language is to be sought not in the Word's creative power but in the eternal process of generation through which the Word came to be: "begotten, not created." The hidden correspondences between the two worlds are expressed not through rational discourse, the creation of ego consciousness, but through the power of fantasy language, which wells up from the deep structure which is eternally there.

JUNG AND THE GNOSTIC WORLD VIEW

Jung's attraction to gnosis raises a question which calls for comment. Jung tells us that, for him, the irreality to which Nietzsche succumbed "was the quintessence of horror, for I aimed, after all, at *this* world and *this* life" (1961, p. 214). How, then, could Jung have anything but a negative reaction to Gnostic writings, which have nothing good to say about the material world, the body, and human sexuality, and which understand the purpose of life to be escape from the world back to the divine *pleroma?*

I propose two responses to this question. First of all, our critique of the doctrinal interpretation of gnosis should make us cautious about taking such dark statements at face value. Of course, it is possible that the Gnostics shared the disparagement of the body and sexuality which was common in late antiquity. But far more important, the body, for the Gnostics, was a symbol of the ignorance of the spiritual world which gnosis strives to overcome. The cosmos, the body, and human sexuality all have powerful symbolic potential, and statements made about them in our texts may well represent the inner work of active imagination.

Second, the interest which Jung expressed in the Gnostics had to do not with their lifestyle but with the proximity of their writings to unconscious processes:

> Most of [the Gnostics] were in reality theologians who, unlike the more orthodox ones, allowed themselves to be influenced in large part by inner experience. They are therefore, like the alchemists, a veritable mine of information concerning all those natural symbols arising out of the repercussions of the Christian message. (1951, p. 269)

In *Symbols of Transformation* Jung wrote a commentary on the fantasies of a young woman who became psychotic because, in Jung's view, she had been unable to understand the significance of her own unconscious material and so was unable to draw the consequences for her personal life.[10] Unfortunately, the Nag Hammadi texts provide no biographical information about the authors, all of whom are anonymous.[11] We can therefore draw no inferences about how they interacted with the world in which they lived. Whether, from a modern psychological point of view, they were successfully individuated human beings we simply do not know.

CONCLUSION: READING THE NAG HAMMADI TEXTS TODAY

The characters in the Gnostic creation myth bear a striking resemblance to the Jungian model of the psyche: the *pleroma* = the unconscious; the Demiurge = the ego; Sophia = the anima. For a Jungian, such correspondences confirm the psychological origin of these texts. Nevertheless, this kind of interpretation runs the risk of becoming just one more variant of the doctrinal interpretation of gnosis criticized in this essay.

In keeping with the position which I have taken, I would suggest that we read the Nag Hammadi texts as poetry, whatever their formal literary genre. Speaking for an ironic age, W. H. Auden declared, "Poetry makes nothing happen."[12] Nevertheless, no one who actually reads poetry believes this to be true. Poetry *has* the power to make something happen, and reading the Nag Hammadi texts can be a highly activating experience, if only the reader is able to defer the critical question: what does this *mean?*

Jung has said, "Every interpretation is an hypothesis, an attempt to read an unknown text" (1954b, p. 150). From this it would seem to follow that, before beginning the interpretive task, the reader must encounter the unknown text, in all its strangeness, on the experiential level. For Jung, the encounter with Gnostic literature is bound to be disorienting:

> I read like mad, and worked with feverish interest through a mountain of mythological material, then through the Gnostic writers, and ended in total confusion. I found myself in a state of perplexity similar to the one I had experienced at the clinic when I tried to understand the meaning of psychotic states of mind." (1961, p. 186)

The proximity of these texts to the unconscious stirs up unconscious contents in the reader, breaking the grip of the fixed structures of objectivity and referentiality.

The world of gnosis, now available to us as never before through the Nag Hammadi texts, is a world from which mythological thinking has not yet been banished in the interest of doctrinal and ethical uniformity. Such mythological understanding returns the Christian symbols to the psychic matrix from which they once came and removes the barrier between religion and experience. It is that barrier which Jung considered to be the greatest weakness of Western religion.

NOTES

1. Since my interest in this essay is in the broad definition of the Gnostic phenomenon, I shall use the Greek word "gnosis" ("knowledge") rather than the English neologism "Gnosticism," which refers specifically to the developed Christian systems of the second and third centuries.

2. "Disparagement and vilification of Gnosticism are an anachronism. Its obviously psychological symbolism could serve many people today as a bridge to a more living appreciation of Christian tradition" (Jung 1954b, p. 292).

3. Jung refers to the Church as "a mighty, far-spread, and venerable institution," and he illustrates its containing function with the example of the Swiss mystic and hermit, Brother Nicholas of Flüe. Brother Klaus received a vision "so terrible that his own countenance was changed by it," but by means of an illustrated devotional booklet by a German mystic, Klaus was able to "elaborate" his visionary experience into the so-called "Trinity Vision," which he painted on the wall of his cell (1959, pp. 8–9). Referring specifically to gnosis, Jung remarks, "Recognizing the danger of Gnostic irrealism, the Church, more practical in these matters, has always insisted on the concretism of the historical events" (1954a, p. 287).

4. "These two sections of this 'primal history' [i.e., cosmogony and anthropogony] belong closely together and are only artificially separated by us" (Rudolph 1987, p. 95).

5. "Adam or the first earthly man is for Gnosis the prototype of men in general; his destiny anticipates that of the mankind which is to follow. For this reason all these narratives have not only an illustrative but above all an existential significance. They are expressions of knowledge about the whence and whither of mankind" (Rudolph 1987, p. 95).

6. The Gnostic texts cited in this essay are all to be found in Robinson 1988.

7. "[T]he distinguishing mark of the Christian epoch, its highest achievement, has become the congenital vice of our age: *the supremacy of the word,*

of the Logos, which stands for the central figure of our Christian faith" (Jung 1964, p. 286).

8. "The spirit does not dwell in concepts. . . . Words butter no parsnips" (Jung 1961, p. 167).

9. Kugler builds upon the word association experiments carried out by Jung (1973) at the Burghölzli Clinic.

10. "Had I treated Miss Miller I would have had to tell her some of the things of which I have written in this book, in order to build up her conscious mind to the point where it could have understood the contents of the collective unconscious" (Jung 1911–12/1952, p. 442).

11. What the heresiologists have to say about the lives of Gnostic teachers is naturally suspect.

12. Quoted in Culler 1981, p. 140.

REFERENCES

Campbell, Joseph. 1989. *This Business of the Gods: in conversation with Fraser Boa.* Caledon East, Ontario: Windrose Films.

Culler, Jonathan. 1976. *Saussure.* Glasgow: Fontana.

———. 1981. *The Pursuit of Signs.* Ithaca: Cornell University Press.

Derrida, Jacques. 1981. *Positions,* tr. Alan Bass. Chicago: University of Chicago Press.

Dostoevsky, Fyodor. 1976. *The Brothers Karamazov,* tr. Constance Garnett. New York: Norton.

Jung, C. G. 1911–12/1952. *Symbols of Transformation. Collected Works,* vol. 5. Princeton, NJ: Princeton University Press, 1967.

———. 1942. "Paracelsus as a Spiritual Phenomenon." In *Collected Works* 13:109–89. Princeton, NJ: Princeton University Press, 1968.

———. 1951. *Aion. Collected Works,* vol. 9, pt. 2. Princeton, NJ: Princeton University Press, 1968.

———. 1954a. "Transformation Symbolism in the Mass." In *Collected Works* 11:201–96. Princeton, NJ: Princeton University Press, 1969.

———. 1954b. *The Practice of Psychotherapy. Collected Works,* vol. 16. Princeton, NJ: Princeton University Press, 1977.

———. 1959. *The Archetypes and the Collective Unconscious. Collected Works,* vol. 9, pt. 1. Princeton, NJ: Princeton University Press, 1968.

———. 1961. *Memories, Dreams, Reflections,* ed. Aniela Jaffé, trs. Richard and Clara Winston. Glasgow: Fount.

———. 1964. *Civilization in Transition. Collected Works,* vol. 10. Princeton, NJ: Princeton University Press, 1970.

———. 1973. *Experimental Researches. Collected Works,* vol. 2. Princeton, NJ: Princeton University Press, 1973.

Kugler, Paul. 1982. *The Alchemy of Discourse: An Archetypal Approach to Language.* Toronto: Associated University Presses.

LaFargue, Michael. 1985. *Language and Gnosis: The Opening Scenes of the Acts of Thomas.* Philadelphia: Fortress.

Pasquier, Anne. 1988. "Prouneikos. A Colorful Expression to Designate Wisdom in Gnostic Texts." In *Images of the Feminine,* ed. Karen L. King (Philadelphia: Fortress), pp. 47–66.

Robinson, James M., ed. 1988. *The Nag Hammadi Library in English.* 3rd ed. San Francisco: Harper & Row.

Rudolph, Kurt. 1987. *Gnosis,* trs. Robert McLachlan Wilson and others. San Francisco: Harper & Row.

[6]

MARY MAGDALENE IN THE CANONICAL AND GNOSTIC GOSPELS

Bradley TePaske

THE CANONICAL MARY

All four New Testament Gospels describe the experiences of Mary Magdalene at the tomb of the resurrected Christ. According to Matthew, Mary first encounters an angel at the newly opened tomb and then meets Jesus before the other disciples do. Jesus even instructs her to go and tell the others to meet him in Galilee (28.1–10). Mark records, "Now after he rose early on the first day of the week, he appeared first to Mary Magdalene, from whom he had cast out seven demons" (16.9). It is ironic and revealing that this single verse combines both Magdalene's claim to prime credentials for heading the Roman Catholic Church with the fateful pathology from which she suffered![1] Luke recounts how Mary's words concerning the Resurrection were received by the Apostles as "an idle tale" and not believed (24.10–11). John describes a poignant conversation between the grieving Magdalene and a compassionate gardener whom she suddenly recognizes as her Master (20.1–16).

While Magdalene's place in the entourage of Jesus is familiar, the complexity of her nature and the magnitude of her importance are generally underestimated. For example, Mary is seldom acknowledged as a woman of means, with upper-class connections, rather than a person of marginal standing:

> Soon afterwards he went on through cities and villages, proclaiming and bringing the good news of the kingdom of God. The twelve were with him, as well as some women who had been cured of evil spirits and infirmities: Mary, called Magdalene, from whom seven demons had gone out, and

Joanna, the wife of Herod's steward Chuza, and Susanna, and many others, who provided for them out of their resources. (Luke 8.1–3)

We know that Mary possessed sufficient courage to witness the Crucifixion (John 19.25) and, more often than anyone else, beheld and conversed with angels at the tomb. She readily appears larger than life. Indeed, the propinquity of Magdalene to so many crucial aspects of Jesus's fate, particularly the tomb and the Resurrection, irresistibly calls to mind the revivifying ministrations of Isis upon Osiris.

Conspicuously absent from the canonical record is any mention of Magdalene as a prostitute. There simply are no Scriptural references to support this traditional Christian prejudice. Rather, a cluster of women and two discrete instances of an anointing of Jesus's feet have frequently been confounded. The Mary who anoints the feet of Jesus at Bethany with "costly perfume made of pure nard" (John 12.3) is another Mary, the sister of Martha and Lazarus. The "woman in the city, who was a sinner" (Luke 7.37) and who anoints the feet of Jesus with tears and ointment, is likewise someone else. And though attempts have been made, any identification of Magdalene with the "woman who had been caught in adultery" (John 8.3) is even more strained.

THE GNOSTIC MARY

What our selection of noncanonical Gnostic gospels adds to the image of Mary Magdalene are the erotic quality of her bond with Jesus, her difficult relationship with the other disciples, and her prominence as a visionary. The *Gospel of Philip* is explicit concerning her personal relationship with Jesus:

> And the companion of the [. . .] Mary Magdalene. [. . . loved] her more than [all] the disciples [and used to] kiss her [often] on her [. . .]. The rest of [the disciples . . .]. They said to him, "Why do you love her more than all of us?" The savior answered and said to them, "Why do I not love you like her?" (Robinson 1988, p. 148)

Translated here as "companion," the original Greek *koinonos* indicates a very intimate friend, who may possibly have been a lover.

In the Gnostic accounts the closeness between Jesus and Mary makes the Apostles, all of them male, extremely jealous and bitter. For example, at the end of the *Gospel of Thomas,*

> His disciples said to him, "When will the kingdom come?" [Jesus said,]

"It will not come by waiting for it. It will not be a matter of saying 'here it is' or 'there it is'. Rather, the kingdom of the father is spread out upon the earth, and men do not see it." Simon Peter said to them, "Let Mary leave us, for women are not worthy of life." Jesus said, "I myself shall lead her in order to make her male, so that she too may become a living spirit resembling you males. For every woman who will make herself male will enter the kingdom of heaven. (sayings 113–14, Robinson 1988, p. 138)

The equation of "living spirit" with "male" would strike the modern ear as misogynous even without the specific directive that Mary be excluded. This becoming "male" refers to a specific ascetic notion of receiving gnosis. The essential role of women and the feminine in other groups demonstrates that this attitude was not characteristic of Gnosticism as a whole. For example, the teachings of Valentinus affirm the equality of the sexes and include an elaborate mythology of Sophia, the feminine personification of wisdom.

In the *Gospel of Mary* the Apostles are gathered together after the Crucifixion in a tense and disconcerted mood. The jealous Peter places Mary in center stage, saying, "Sister, we know that the Savior loved you more than the rest of women. Tell us the words of the Savior which you remember—which you know (but) we do not, nor have we heard them" (Robinson 1988, p. 525). The text continues directly with Magdalene's forthright disclosure of a powerful vision of Christ, who commends her for her unflinching reception of mystic sight:

Mary answered and said, "What is hidden from you I will proclaim to you." And she began to speak to them these words: "I," she said, "I saw the Lord in a vision and I said to him, 'Lord, I saw you today in a vision.' He answered and said to me, 'Blessed are you, that you did not waver at the sight of me. For where the mind is, there is the treasure.' I said to him, 'Lord, now does he who sees the vision see it [through] the soul [or] through the spirit?' The Savior answered and said, 'He does not see through the soul nor through the spirit, but the mind which [is] between the two—that is [what] sees the vision and it is [. . .].' (pp. 11–14 missing)

"[. . .] it. And desire [states] that, 'I did not see you [i.e., soul] descending, but now I see you ascending. Why do you lie, since you belong to me?' The soul answered and said, 'I saw you. You did not see me nor recognize me. I served you as a garment, and you did not know me.' When it had said this, it went away rejoicing greatly.

"Again it came to the third power, which is called ignorance. [It (the power)] questioned the soul saying, 'Where are you going? In wickedness are you bound. But you are bound; do not judge!' And the soul said, 'why do you judge me although I have not judged? I was bound though I have not bound. I was not recognized. But I have recognized that the All is being dissolved, both the earthly (things) and the heavenly.'

"When the soul had overcome the third power, it went upwards and saw the fourth power, (which) took seven forms. The first form is darkness, the second desire, the third ignorance, the fourth is the excitement of death, the fifth is the kingdom of the flesh, the sixth is the foolish wisdom of the flesh, the seventh is the wrathful wisdom. These are the seven [powers] of wrath. They ask the soul, 'Whence do you come, slayer of men, or where are you going, conqueror of space?' The soul answered and said, 'What binds me has been slain, and what surrounds me has been overcome, and my desire has been ended, and ignorance has died. In a [world] I was released from a world, [and] in a type from a heavenly type, and (from) the fetter of oblivion which is transient. From this time on will I attain to the rest of time, of the season, of the aeon, in silence.'" (Robinson 1988, pp. 525–26)

Mary accordingly falls silent before the Apostles, who are dumbfounded and seek to repudiate these "strange ideas." Andrew takes exception to Mary even as Peter grumbles concerning the Master: "Did he really speak with a woman without our knowledge (and) not openly? Are we to turn about and all listen to her? Did he prefer her to us?" (Robinson 1988, p. 526). Mary begins to weep at not being believed. At last, the group comes to some reconciliation and goes forth to preach.

In this vision, from which four pages of the original text are missing, the ascending soul reaches a rarefied and virtually unconditioned state, but not without a spirited colloquy with a succession of contentious symbolic figures. In an ancient Gnostic frame of reference, the four would refer to the material elements, even as the seven forms of the four would refer to the planetary archons which hinder the return of the soul to its origin. The focus of this essay is, rather, with Mary's vision as the authentic psychological experience of an individual human being.

A PSYCHOLOGICAL UNDERSTANDING OF THE VISION

What we witness with Mary is a dynamic struggle of "partial personalities." The tension is not merely between Mary's ego consciousness and her inner world but also among a number of autonomous psychic figures which interact with one another. Mary, Christ, and soul as well as the four or seven powers are all decisive participants. These figures at once reflect the arrangement of complexes in Mary's individual personality and display an archetypal structure and dynamic. Mary has a soul even as she witnesses "soul" as an autonomous and objective phenomenon. This ambiguity of the personal and archetypal is an essential mystery of personality. In any case, each figure in the vision possesses its own affective, imagistic, and ideational quality as well as its own quantum of dispersed consciousness. The vision is a classic example of C. G. Jung's broad description of the psyche as a "field of multiple luminosities."[2]

In the *Gospel of Mary* Christ distinguishes the mind from both the soul and the spirit. Located between the two, the mind alone receives the "treasure." This emphasis on mind as that which centrally mediates the experience of gnosis is typical of the tripartite variety of Gnosticism. In discussing Gnostic designations of psychological types, Jung states:

> Gnostic philosophy established three types, corresponding perhaps to three of the basic psychological functions: thinking, feeling, and sensation. The *pneumatikoi* could be correlated with thinking, the *psychikoi* with feeling, and the *hylikoi* with sensation. The inferior rating of the *psychikoi* was in accord with the spirit of Gnosticism, which, unlike Christianity, insisted on the value of knowledge. (1921, p. 14)[3]

In ordinary tripartite Gnosticism, to which Jung's categorization refers, the discrete parts of the human being are body, soul, and spirit, which is highest. In Mary's vision soul is apparently the most important aspect, even though mind is the recipient of the treasure. Certainly the text concentrates on soul. Desire, one of the four powers, arrogantly confronts soul only to learn that soul cloaks it like a garment of which the wearer is unaware. Consider the blind immediacy of a physical prompting which is intent on concrete gratification. Soul's words suggest that those same energies may be held reflectively within and contemplated as image or awareness. This activity of the imagination would reveal the fabric of soul's garment. Next ignorance, another power, boldly confronts soul, only to learn that though it sought to bind soul, soul cannot be bound. Soul's ascending freedom is triumphant.

Psychologically, soul, as the reflective consciousness *par excellence,* sees beyond the ego and displaces its limited conceptions of reality. Soul says, "I was not recognized. But I have recognized that the All is being dissolved both the earthly (things) and the heavenly" (Robinson 1988, p. 526). In the ensuing succession of personifications comes the fourth power, which takes seven forms:

darkness, desire, ignorance, excitement of death, the kingdom of the flesh, the foolish wisdom of the flesh, and wrathful wisdom. As if threatened and confused, the powers collectively ask soul, "Whence do you come, slayer of men, or where are you going, conqueror of space?" (Robinson 1988, p. 526). Clearly, the sudden ascendancy of a perspective based on soul spells death for the old ego and heralds an expansion of consciousness which is far beyond the ken of the seven powers of wrath.

The influence of the seven powers is fundamental to the concretism and literalism of an ego which has rejected the unconscious and has remained uninitiated by soul. But it would be simplistic to say that the ego is synonymous with the powers, at least without recalling a fundamental psychoanalytic observation that the ego is, to begin with, a "body-ego." However pneumatic and ascending Mary's vision, most of the seven powers have a distinct somatic reference. Intuition suggests that they are related to the seven demons which originally afflicted Magdalene.

A parallel Gnostic document, the *Apocryphon of John,* not only amplifies the theme of bodily spirits but grants those spirits a somewhat more positive estimation:

> And the powers began. The first, Goodness, created a soul of bone; the second, Pronoia, created a soul of sinew; the third, Deity, created a soul of flesh; the fourth, Lordship, created a soul of marrow; the fifth, Kingdom, created a soul of blood; the sixth, Zeal, created a soul of skin; the seventh, Understanding, created a soul of hair. And the multitude of angels stood up before it. They received from the powers the seven hypostases in order to make the joining of the limbs and the joining of the pieces and the synthesis of the adornment of each of the members. [. . .] And all the angels and demons worked until they had adorned the psychic body, but their entire work was inert and motionless for a long time. (Pearson 1990, p. 32)

The multitude of angels and demons recognize seven divine principles as the essential organizing factors in their creation of the body. (How similar this is to the seven *chakras* of Hindu physiology!) Psychologically, this "psychic body" is the intuitive visualization of a deep psychosomatic mystery. Most immediately, the angelic host pertains to the perpetual experiential fluctuations of our organismic awareness and mood. Magdalene's seven demons and the seven powers of her vision may likewise be understood as essential structures which manifest themselves in a variety of ways. They represent a subtle dimension of reality in which psychic or somatic symptoms are fatefully generated or transformed and which any inquiry into spiritual healing must comprehend.

In ancient Gnosticism these bodily things are never created by the ineffable, transcendent God. They are finely fashioned by the "angels and demons" who serve the baleful Demiurge. Ancient Gnosticism considered the body, as part of the created world, to be altogether evil. Accordingly, in Magdalene's vision the soul seeks to ascend from precisely this transient "fetter of oblivion" to the immaterial godhead. At its extreme, such a radical dualism represents a profound challenge to the Jungian psychologist, who would welcome the rediscovery of the soul but would seek to reunite the soul with the body and the world. The question is whether Mary's earthly powers are destined to appear only as wrathful, foolish, dark, and deadly. Mircea Eliade, the historian of religions, makes a more optimistic observation of pantheons worldwide that is more in accord with the Jungian outlook:

> We must not forget that many of the divinities and powers of the earth and the underworld are not necessarily "evil" or "demonic." They generally represent autochthonous and even local hierophanies that have fallen in rank as a result of changes within the pantheon. Sometimes the bipartition of gods into celestial and chthonic-infernal is only a convenient classification without any pejorative implication for the latter. (Eliade 1951, p. 186)

MARY'S HEALING EXPERIENCE

Even without the traditional prostitute fantasy, Mary Magdalene introduces the factors of body, sex, psychopathology, soul, and a uniquely feminine wisdom into a predominantly masculine sphere. She is an intimate companion of Jesus, who repeatedly defends her. Mary may well have first sought Jesus out as a healer. One wonders what moved so daemonically in Mary's psyche before and after she knew Jesus and what discerning capacity for relationship he brought to their healing encounter. In Luke 8.2 "seven demons" are said to have "gone out" of Mary. Were these demons driven out by Jesus through confession, exorcism, or some external agency? As teacher and companion, he surely encouraged Mary to face her inner world and offered seminal ideas with which to understand it. But one must not suppose that the healing sprang merely from a discursive process. Our larger psychosomatic understanding is appropriate. Palsy was an ailment frequently healed by Jesus. Luke speaks of "evil spirits and infirmities" in connection with Magdalene.

A basic principle of Jungian psychology holds that the energy needed to heal an illness is concealed within the symptoms themselves. When the ego is stressed by emotional turmoil or severe physical sufferings, the unconscious tends to manifest itself directly to consciousness in symbolic forms. One must consider the casting out of Magdalene's demons in terms of an inner transformation, a coming to consciousness of what had been present all along but until now had existed in a pathological state of unconsciousness and somatization. The initiatory illness characteristic of the shamanic vocation includes many examples of such psychosomatic suffering as the prelude to a visionary and healing gift.[4] Frequently even frightening or horrific symbols from the unconscious have a stabilizing effect on consciousness. The fundamental healing factor seems to lie in a recognition of the soul's deep reality through a fearless acceptance of both suffering and the psychic experiences which unfold in the process. The spiritual healing attributed to Jesus is holistic. It must have touched Mary's totality at the most subtle and essential level. From her early encounter with Jesus through the development of their intimate relationship, what Mary found in Jesus contributed immeasurably to an ongoing cure.

A feature distinguishing the Gnostic outlook from that of the orthodox Christian was the experience of a nonphysical Jesus at the Resurrection. While Matthew 28.9 states that Mary and her female companions "came to him, took hold of his feet, and worshipped him," Elaine Pagels explains that "Gnostic Christians interpret resurrection in various ways. Some say that the person who experiences the resurrection does not meet Jesus raised physically back to life; rather, he encounters Christ on a spiritual level. This may occur in dreams, in ecstatic trance, in visions, or in moments of numinous illumination" (Pagels 1979, p. 5). The appearance of Christ in the vision of Magdalene is a vivid example of just such a spiritual experience. This reunion is a thrilling affirmation of a deep bond which continues even beyond this life. Addressed as "Lord" and "Savior," Christ appears with an impact which might have made Mary waver at the sight. Viewed psychologically, the Christ-figure within Mary's psyche definitely possesses the qualities of a positive animus: that contrasexual figure within a woman which supports her creative endeavors and affirms her mission in the world.

It must not be forgotten that Mary is a woman in mourning. She has recently witnessed the public execution of the most important person in her life. Her own longing for recognition and her need of human companionship are apparently only enhanced by so grave a loss and by her vision of the spiritual world. This bodes well for her. The possibility of reestablishing her equilibrium is indicated by soul's statement that "the All is being dissolved, both the earthly (things) and the heavenly," and more particularly by the statement that "In a [world] I was released from a world, [and] in a type from a heavenly type" (Robinson 1988, p. 526). Psychologically, soul mediates a world of opposing emotions and images. In Mary's vision, soul is clever, authoritative, resilient, and capable of rejoicing even in affliction. The liberation of soul's reflective consciousness may well have enabled Mary to achieve some critical distance from an inner world swarming with horrific images and to enhance her emotional independence from the inevitable fate of the body and the traumatic memory of the Crucifixion.

NOTES

1.   This issue of priority is discussed by Pagels: "But orthodox churches that trace their origin to Peter developed the tradition—sustained to this day among Catholic and some Protestant churches—that Peter had been the 'first witness of the resurrection,' and hence the rightful leader of the church" (1979, p. 8).

2.   Complimentary to both the theory of complexes and archetypes, this notion is perhaps most clearly articulated in Jung's "On the Nature of the Psyche" (1947, pp. 388–96).

3.   The broader significance of the ancient typology is discussed by Rudolph, who states that "Only the pneumatics are Gnostics and capable of redemption" (1977, p. 92).

4.   See "Initiatory Sicknesses and Dreams" (Eliade 1964, pp. 33–66).

REFERENCES

Eliade, Mircea. 1964. *Shamanism,* tr. Willard R. Trask. Princeton, NJ: Princeton University Press.

Jung, C. G. 1921. *Psychological Types. Collected Works,* vol. 6. Princeton, NJ: Princeton University Press, 1971.

———. 1947. "On the Nature of the Psyche." In *Collected Works* 8:343–442. Princeton, NJ: Princeton University Press, 1969.

Pagels, Elaine. 1979. *The Gnostic Gospels.* New York: Random House.

Pearson, Birger. 1990. "Biblical Exegesis in Gnostic Literature." In his *Gnosticism, Judaism and Egyptian Christianity* (Minneapolis: Fortress), pp. 29–38.

Robinson, James M., ed. 1988. *The Nag Hammadi Library in English.* 3rd ed. San Francisco: Harper & Row.

Rudolph, Kurt. 1977. *Gnosis,* trs. Robert McLachlan and others. San Francisco: Harper & Row.

[7]

SEX, SUFFERING, AND INCARNATION: FEMALE SYMBOLISM IN GNOSTICISM

Jorunn Jacobsen Buckley

FEMALE imagery in Gnosticism takes two predominant forms: female divine figures, and elements within human beings designated female, regardless of the gender of the humans. Gnostic speculations on the female seem to derive particularly from the Adam and Eve story in Genesis 2–3 and from Greek, partly Platonic traditions about the soul—the soul here being female. Orthodox Jewish and Christian views tend to present Eve in a negative light, and the classical Greek heritage stresses the fallenness of the soul. How, then, should modern readers deal with this strongly negative outlook toward the feminine?

My answer is: by considering the alternatives. Heretical Jewish and Christian views form part of the Western heritage, too, and heretical views function to objectify and publicize unformulated experiences, challenging the orthodox claims of self-evidence and indisputability (Bourdieu 1977, pp. 169–70).

I wish to show how Gnostic texts portray the female along a spectrum from the most negative evaluation through androgyny (which can be taken either negatively or positively) to a most positive assessment: a heavenly "Lightworld" female, an autonomous, supreme principle, even a savior. Such a positive female is depicted as acting alone, as an androgyne, or as a member of a pair. One may even find all three models mixed together. Mixtures may involve paradox, puns, and other features of lived experience. It is the tendency of orthodox, canonical views to limit such richness and multiplicities. For canonicity entails a closed system, to which only texts passing scrutinizing, standardized tests gain access.

THE *EXEGESIS ON THE SOUL*

I begin with the *Exegesis on the Soul,* one of the Nag Hammadi texts (Robinson 1988, pp. 190–98). This text belongs to no particularly recognizable Jewish or Christian group, but it makes use of biblical traditions and of Homer's *Odyssey.* The soul—female, androgynous, virgin—lives with her Father in the upper, heavenly Lightworld. Everything is blissful and static until she falls into a body. This fall means loss of virginity, estrangement from the Father, and subjection to a series of men who rape her and turn her into a prostitute.

Fallen from virgin status to whore, the soul becomes a "desolate widow," even though she was never married! Because of her prostitution, she bears imperfect offspring: they are dumb, blind, and sick. Repenting, the soul appeals to the Father to be restored to him. He saves her by turning her womb from outside her body to inside, for "the womb of the soul is around the outside like the male genitalia, which are external" (*Exegesis on the Soul,* Robinson 1988, p. 194).

The text's statement can be understood on the basis of ancient Greek medical theories, according to which the uterus, ovaries, and vagina are internal, precise correlates to the male's outward scrotum, testicles, and penis (Smith 1988). Female sexual organs are created like the male ones, but simply on the inside (Smith 1988; Fredriksen 1979). However, when the soul acts as a prostitute, her sexual organs, especially the womb, are turned out, and her salvation depends on the Father's pushing the womb back inside.

Next, the text states that the soul begins to rage like a woman in labor, although she is not even pregnant. To prevent a phantom, monstrous birth (a theme I will return to) and to avoid any hint of paternal incest, the Father sends her a bridegroom: her own brother. When he arrives, they engage in spiritual intercourse devoid of bodily desire, and she bears spiritual children. Thus rejuvenated, the soul is rescued and finally ascends home to the Father.

THE *APOCRYPHON OF JOHN*

The pregnant soul is a central mythical theme in many Gnostic texts, though only alluded to in the *Exegesis on the Soul.* The *Apocryphon of John* (Robinson 1988, pp. 104–23) elaborates on the theme, telling the prototypical story of the daughter figure in the Lightworld, Sophia, who, as the last of the Father's offspring, decides to undertake a creation of her own. Predominantly female androgynes should not need a mate to procreate but, in contrast to male androgynes, nevertheless do so (Buckley 1986, pp. 132–33). In the *Apocryphon of John* Sophia on her own brings forth an imperfect, snake-like monster with a lion's head: Yaltabaoth.

Because Yaltabaoth has no father, his character is overly "female." Born from Sophia in a fit of ignorance, he grows up to become the Hebrew god Yahweh, who creates a world of imperfection, a world he cannot understand or control. Disgusted by her son, Sophia throws him into a realm of his own—where he will create the world as we know it—and goes searching for her Father. Like the soul in the *Exegesis on the Soul,* Sophia is eventually paired with a husband and rescued by the Father.

This pattern of obligatory marriage as a first step toward return to the Father demonstrates a highly ambivalent, though predominantly negative, attitude toward the female. Females simply cannot be left to act on their own. Putting the womb back in place—putting women in their place—is the Father's action in the *Exegesis on the Soul.* In the *Apocryphon of John* Sophia's autonomous creation constitutes a threat to the male. The price paid is the deformed, expelled child. Both the soul and Sophia are restored to the Father once they obtain union with a male of the same generation. Male "ownership" of the female must thus be established in two generations.

THUNDER: PERFECT MIND

I now move from these two texts with negatively evaluated females (although the *Apocryphon of John* also has positive ones) to one featuring a more complexly drawn female. One of the most mystifying Nag Hammadi texts is *Thunder: Perfect Mind* (Robinson 1988, pp. 297–303; Buckley 1980b), a monologue by a female revealer, Thunder, who speaks of herself largely in terms of antitheses. She is the first and the last, the honored and the scorned, whore and holy, wife and virgin, mother and daughter (Robinson 1988, p. 297; Buckley 1980b). Paradoxically, she is also barren, but with many sons; she is knowledge and ignorance, shame and boldness, strength and fear, war and peace.

Thunder collapses various gender and family categories: she is bride and bridegroom; her husband is her begetter; she is her father's mother and her husband's sister; and her husband is her child. Plays on paradoxes, violations of Aristotelian logic, and divine complaints about the lack of intelligent adherents characterize Thunder's utterances. A believer in this goddess would serve a divinity truly beyond recognition in rational terms.

Thunder's entire list of oppositions—her "I am" statements in particular—expresses the problem that medieval European philosophers set up as their favorite debate: realism versus nominalism. Does an entity exist apart from its name (realism), or is the name alone real (nominalism)? Are Thunder's designations real, or is the experience of her as revealed Truth real? She says, "I am the one whom they call Life, and you have called Death" (Robinson 1988, p. 299). The polemical "you," opposed to "they," perhaps refers to religious factions quibbling over the reality of names. Thunder seems to say that designations do nothing but hide realities. Both parties are therefore wrong: both those who call her "Life" and those who call her "Death."

The text is an excellent example of a religious polemical stance against the power of names, labels, designations. Yet both those who call her "Death" and those who call her "Life" are also correct. For if anything on earth is to be understandable and communicable at all, names are necessary. Still, names and other concepts try in vain to catch experiences and realities. Residing beyond distinctions such as Life/Death and light/darkness, Thunder says that she is the original source that makes it possible to use names, labels, and designations. She provides the humans with the capacity to perceive and think in terms of oppositions. At the end of the text, she exhorts her believers to give up sins, passions, and pleasures so that they may rise up to the place of rest, "and they will find me there, and they will live and they will not die again" (Robinson 1988, p. 303).

One may see a link between Sophia in the *Apocryphon of John,* who acts ignorantly, and Thunder, who reveals herself through dichotomies. "To be made body" demands of every divinity who embarks on this path the risk of being understood in merely human terms. Hence there ensue battles of dogma, which Thunder would dismiss as demonstrating allegiance to nominalism. The task for believers is simultaneously to affirm and to deny divine oppositional traits and designations.

Thunder seems particularly vulnerable to being despised in her incarnated aspects. Any worthy believer would have to overcome resistance to paradox and to the distasteful facets of incarnation, and would also need to understand the dynamics of Thunder's symbolism. No symbol is identical with the meanings it signifies, but a symbol supplies the possibility for inexhaustible meanings. A divine being is not limited to the incarnation in which it reveals itself at any given time. Playing on the paradox of its ineffable identity and of that identity's earthly manifestations, a symbol at the same time hides and discloses itself. This observation is as old as the pre-Socratic philosopher Heraclitus (Wheelwright 1966, sects. 17–18, p. 70), who might have made a good Thunder-devotee!

RUHA IN MANDAEISM

Another double-natured female is Ruha, or "Spirit," in Mandaean Gnosticism (Buckley 1982). The still surviving Mandaeans, anti-Jewish and anti-Christian, probably were originally heretical Jews, and they make an ironic statement by calling the personified evil spirit "ruha d-qudsha," or "Holy Spirit." Ruha is mainly evil insofar as she is the mother of the planets and zodiac-spirits and is a devious collaborator with the helpless Mandaean creator god.

Ruha's correlate in the human being is *ruha* (with a "small" *r*), which designates the middle element of every person. The Mandaean anthropological model posits the soul as the highest, the spirit as the middle, and the body as the lowest element. The spirit is a wobbly entity, torn between the higher soul and the lower body, between good and evil inclinations. In her good moments, the spirit knows who she is, where she hails from, and how to gain salvation. At other times, she works aggressively against gnosis and the Lightworld. Scholars have traditionally seen Ruha, the mythological figure, as an indisputably evil female entity, a devilish she-monster.

But Ruha's more mixed status is clearly shown by her middle position in the human body. Her status is also evinced in a number of stories in which the personified Ruha exhibits mood swings, sudden shifts in allegiances between good and evil forces, and outright divine attributes. Some of the most perplexing sections of the vast Mandaean literature—and the places in which Ruha most resembles Thunder—equate Ruha with female entities in the Lightworld and with opposites like light and darkness and life and death.

In *Right Ginza* 6 (Lidzbarski 1925, pp. 206–7) Dinanukht, who is half man, half book, sits and reads in himself, pondering the mysteries of the universe. He is approached by another hybrid, Disai, who proclaims that there is both life and death, both light and darkness, both truth and error, and other dichotomies. After having tried in vain to burn and to drown Disai, Dinanukht falls into a trance, and Ruha reveals herself to him, saying that she is all of these dichotomies. The story reveals an isolated female figure, one similar to Thunder, who nevertheless includes in herself the totality of life and its dichotomous concepts.

Mandaeism was not (and is not now) an ascetic religion: its people marry and procreate, and priests must do so. The religion espouses a complex gender balance, despite some of the expected Gnostic ambivalences regarding females and sexuality. Therefore the religion has room for Ruha as a positive figure. The Lightworld is populated by both male and female Light beings. The positive Mandaean view of marriage and procreation is an earthly parallel to the divine order. Because females exist on high, the balance of gender there functions as a blueprint for how things ought to be on earth.

The disadvantages of a monotheistic system spring immediately into sight, for where a single, male god reigns and no female partner is assigned to him in heaven, there arises an obsessive interest in female culpability. The Mandaeans know of Eve but take no interest in her as a sinner; they are unacquainted with (or do not care about) Eve's birth out of Adam or the fall in Eden. In Judaism and orthodox forms of Christianity the emphasis on the sinful Eve becomes a major justification for viewing women as the sources of temptation and fall.

The pattern of gender balance in heaven and on earth may not always hold in Gnosticism, for there is no necessary correlation between women's positive status on earth and the presence of goddesses above. But at least Mandaeism furnishes gender balance, which perhaps derives from inner-"heretical" Jewish conflicts.[1]

THE *GOSPEL OF PHILIP*

An example of gender balance generally suppressed in orthodox Christianity is that of the Trinity. Some types of early Semitic Christianity accepted a female divine entity, who obviously could not be the Father or the Son and so who had to be the Holy Spirit. She is both God's wife or lover and Jesus's mother. "Spirit" in Semitic languages (*ruach, ruh*), is feminine, and ancient Near Eastern goddesses reverberate in the female Holy Spirit.

The Gnostic *Gospel of Philip* (Robinson 1988, pp. 139–60) deals with the Spirit as female. The document states that it is a sign of inferior understanding to believe that the Holy Spirit impregnated Mary. For when has one ever heard of a female making another female pregnant? The diatribe is intelligible only if one knows the Semitic basis for the joke. This gospel, one of the most philosophically sophisticated among the Nag Hammadi texts, is extremely interested in the female figure, and the document conflates the female Truth with Holy Spirit, Mary Magdalene, and Sophia (Buckley 1986, pp. 105–25). All four have earthly as well as heavenly aspects, and their earthly manifestations necessarily imply some kind of imperfection or destructive characteristic.

In identifying these females with one another and giving them a double nature, the *Gospel of Philip* exemplifies the kind of gnosis that takes the nominalist-realist dispute seriously. The text states outright that when names come into the world, they distort the divine entity to which they are attached. The reality is out of reach—hidden by names, labels, and symbols. Truth, which comes into the world "in types and images" (Robinson 1988, p. 150), is also distorted and spurned because it is forced to reveal itself in material terms.

Both Holy Spirit and Sophia are deadly as well as life-giving figures, and Mary has a threefold character: she is Jesus's mother; his aunt; and his lover, Mary Magdalene. He kisses her often, and the male disciples become envious and ask Jesus why he loves her more than he loves them. As is common in this category of Gnostic texts, Jesus offers no straight answer but mockingly echoes the question—as if to say: if you have to ask, you show how ignorant you are. He kisses his favorite disciple, Mary Magdalene, because she is the only one who understands who he is—and who she herself is: a female counterpart to the divine teacher (Buckley 1986, pp. 109–10). Their kisses produce spiritual children, who are the *real,* not the nominal, Christians.

Christians in this gospel similarly engage in kissing in order to receive grace from one another. When this grace takes root in the receiver, that person becomes a spiritual, reborn entity. We may assume that proponents of this kind of Christianity claimed to be such reborn spirituals. The engendering of spiritual entities takes place in the ritual setting of the bridal chamber, though we do not know what went on there (Buckley 1986, pp. 120–24; 1980a). The bridal chamber is the primary locus for salvation. The activity there heals the split suffered by the conflated Lightworld entity: Truth/Sophia/Holy Spirit/Mary Magdalene. When human beings identify themselves with her in her suffering, they, too, are healed.

Philip and other Gnostic texts testify to two models of healing operating simultaneously. One is the same-sex merging of one's lower aspect with its Lightworld prototype. For example, the lower, sinful Sophia becomes united with her upper, positive, real self. The other model shows a merging of opposite genders. Here the human beings in the ritual of the bridal chamber—in a kind of spiritualized sex-act—make the two genders one, which is to say, *none*. This is the hint that Jesus provides when he kisses Mary, for it is an activity that the male disciples, still on a lower level of gnosis, cannot comprehend.

THE IMPLICATIONS OF INCARNATION

Where merging takes place between a lower, earthly self and an upper, same-sex counterpart, Gnostics accord an inherent dynamic to the upper image. This entity's lower counterpart may become manifest in the earthly realms below, thanks solely to the existence of the upper image. As Gnostic figures tend to possess this doubleness (and human beings, too), it is improper to form categorical, static judgments of "good" or "evil" for these personages. When a heavenly self co-exists with—and gives form to—an earthly one, we have a case of incarnation.

Here one might consider that the example *par excellence* of "made flesh," Jesus, is dependent on the myths of the Jewish female Wisdom. These traditions are clearly visible in the Hebrew Bible—for example, Proverbs 8.22–31. Wisdom is an "avatar," a manifestation, of God. She constitutes his female aspect: his playmate, lover, and fellow world creator. Incarnate in human women and, more abstractly, in philosophical insight, Wisdom suffers misunderstanding and rejection in the world. Unable to find a home there, she returns home to heaven.

This pattern is played out in Christianity, which substitutes Jesus for Wisdom. Gnostic texts such as the *Apocryphon of John* evince outright competition between Wisdom and Jesus. Both are incarnations of the divine, both are God's children, both have messages to give humankind, and both suffer before returning home (Buckley 1986, pp. 42, 55, 58). Gnostic texts show the gender competition more clearly than does orthodoxy. The budding Christian orthodoxy thus usurps the Jewish territory of female Wisdom, a figure that often produces problems in Judaism because her relationship to Yahweh is too close.

Medieval Christians saw Jesus's incarnation as an essentially *female* condition (Bynum 1987). Jesus acquired his spirit from his father but his body from his mother. Even early Christian views of Mary's supernatural impregnation show the need for a female body to house the presumably male spirit. When the emphasis rests on Jesus's life on earth, his female nature may be stressed. But his spirit itself needs embodiment. This is a frequently neglected element in scholarship on Christianity: to make spiritual salvation possible, a "female body" is needed. It is in the bodily, material realm that the work of salvation begins and persists. Disembodied spirits cannot live on earth for long.

Take the case of exorcism in the New Testament. Demons need a home and prefer a human body. In many of the New Testament accounts, the demons, *not* the patients in whose bodies they reside, immediately recognize who Jesus is: they know a fellow spirit when they meet one. When Jesus casts them out of bodies, they know they are in danger of dying. After a successful exorcism, the patient must at once fill the vacated space with faith in Jesus. If not, the demon will return, and will be accompanied by seven even more powerful demons, who will set up their household in the patient who thought he had been permanently healed (Luke 11.24–26).

The bodily home may be regarded as female if we maintain the possibility that Jesus had his body from his mother. According to a "gender-integrative" view, spirit is male and body female, regardless of a person's gender (Bynum 1987). The relationship between spirit and body is expressed in the familiar relationship between Jesus and the Church. If Christ, the spiritual, "male" aspect of Jesus, is married to his bride, then the believers, irrespective of gender, are cast into a female role. Male Christians take on a female role in relationship to their bridegroom, Christ.

Women devotees may assume the female role more naturally. But Jesus's own, lower, female embodied self will at his resurrection be subsumed into his upper, male aspect. This is why resurrection is crucial: Jesus needs to go safely back home, to achieve yet again his spiritual status unencumbered by earthly, bodily form.[2] Now we see why he asks Mary Magdalene, who tries to hold him back (John 20.16–17), to let him go. In the Coptic *Manichaean Psalmbook,* he explicitly asks her not to touch him, "for I have not yet seen the face of my Father" (Hennecke and Schneemelcher 1963, p. 353).

In reentering heaven, Jesus may, like the female Gnostic double-natured figures, regain his upper self. At the same time, this self and his earthly one can be seen as merging in a "same-sex" union, like Holy Spirit and Sophia in the *Gospel of Philip.* But because he is also married to the heavenly Church, the mythology furnishes a male-female merging as well. Christianity, however, only rarely admits a female entity to heaven. Like the female Gnostic figures, Jesus may have regained his full, heavenly, spiritual status, but his female, earthly body cannot find another female Lightworld model for itself.

A spiritual transformation that retains the female identity conceptually implicit in incarnation seems impossible for mainstream Christianity.

One of the early Christian Church Fathers, the "half-Gnostic" Clement of Alexandria, goes as far as to declare, "And God Himself is love, and out of love to us became feminine. In His ineffable essence He is Father; in His compassion to us He became Mother. The Father by loving became feminine: and the great proof of this is He whom he begot of Himself; and the fruit brought forth by love is love" (Roberts and Donaldson 1925, sect. 37, p. 601b). A Valentinian Gnostic text, transmitted by Clement, states that the visible part of Jesus is Wisdom while the special seeds of the Church are "borne-apart." Jesus puts on these female entities, Wisdom and Church, when he is incarnated; thus he becomes fleshly and psychic, "soul-ly" (*Excerpta ex Theodoto,* sect. 26, Casey 1934, pp. 60–61; Buckley 1986, pp. 66–67).

Another Gnostic example of Jesus's becoming female when he becomes incarnate comes from the Manichaean text *Kephalaia.* At the beginning of time, according to this vast and complex Manichaean creation myth, Jesus descended to settle matters after a great earthquake had occurred in the three prototypical earth realms. In descending, Jesus appeared as Eve (*Kephalaia,* sect. 38, Schmidt 1940, p. 94). One might have expected him to take on the guise of Adam, but instead he, one of whose central aspects in Manichaeism is suffering, donned the more despised half of the first human couple.

Thus there are several early Christian testimonies to the view that incarnation is a female condition. It is possible that the Manichaeans were influenced by Jewish Wisdom speculations. Jesus and Eve both play the scapegoat role, suffer, and are bearers of embodiment. Recall the curses that God put on Eve after the fall in Genesis: subjection to her husband and pain in childbearing. These are female burdens and important ways for women to imitate Jesus's sufferings.

Even as Jesus becomes the despised Eve, he retains his higher self, his supreme spiritual identity. Doubleness is a characteristic he shares with the Gnostic female figures treated in this study. Eve is not so lucky. Orthodox Christianity allows Eve no upper, positive, same-sex image. She remains on the earthly, embodied, sinful level. By contrast, *Philip* balances upper and lower images for its four females. Orthodox Christianity cannot afford to make a bold connection between sinful Eve and her own, heavenly counterpart, let alone to see her as a negative aspect of the elevated Holy Spirit.

But what dogma excludes sneaks in by the back door, and

Catholicism elevates Mary to a nearly divine status as the mother, albeit a not very sexy mother, of Jesus. Meanwhile Protestants— perhaps secretly envying Catholics—submit to a stern prohibition against any positive female figure on equal footing with the male god.

The mainstream Western Christian tradition views the female either all negatively (Eve) or all positively (Mary). Either way, the female often proves irrelevant for modern Christian contexts. Oddly, Christian feminism has neglected to seize on the third person in the Trinity, the Holy Spirit, as at once a positive and a negative powerful female image, as in *Philip* and *Thunder.* Perhaps the issue is merely one of access to heretical texts. In any case it seems necessary to take into account heresy as well as orthodoxy in order to make feminism workable in the modern world. The mental health of Western Christianity might have been better if the religion had incorporated more nuanced, Gnostic ideas of the female.

In a recent review in the *New York Review of Books* of a painting by Max Ernst, the art historian Leo Steinberg judged that its foregrounded theme is "theologically absurd" (Steinberg 1993, p. 93). The huge (196 × 130 cm) painting, *The Blessed Virgin Chastizing the Child Jesus before Three Witnesses,* shows Mary spanking her four- or five-year-old son, whose halo has rolled to the ground while hers remains in place. Puzzled, Steinberg said that "Jesus cannot have misbehaved, and Mary cannot chastize unjustly" (Steinberg 1993, p. 93). Had Steinberg been more familiar with Gnostic theologies and therefore with alternative standards for "Mother of God" behavior, he might have appreciated a relentlessly punitive *divine* mother and a deserving *human* child. The surrealist Max Ernst may be a "crypto-Gnostic" well suited to make a heterodox theological statement. Far from the commonly seen, sweetly "demure mother and divine child" depictions, here the mother beats the demons of disobedience out of her child. Had she not, how could he later have graduated to his role as healer?

NOTES

1. For the possibility of Mandaean women priests, see Buckley 1992, p. 34, note 9, and p. 44. Manichaeism, which was influenced by early Mandaeism and formed a dangerous opponent to the budding orthodox Christianity of the third century, had predominantly negative female figures in its mythologies. Still, the upper-class Manichaean Elect included ascetic women as missionaries and preachers, while the lower-class Auditors married, procreated, and belonged on a lower level of salvation. A compara-

tive study of Mandaean and Manichaean social and gender strata remains to be written.

2. Exactly *what* kind of body is capable of resurrection is a thorny issue in early Christian debate. For the *Gospel of Philip,* see Buckley 1988. For the necessity of creating new limbs in order to have a resurrection body, see my treatment of pertinent logia in the *Gospel of Thomas* (especially 11 and 22) in Buckley 1986, ch. 5.

REFERENCES

Bourdieu, Pierre. 1977. *Outline of a Theory of Practice,* tr. Richard Nice. Cambridge Studies in Social Anthropology. New York and London: Cambridge University Press.

Buckley, Jorunn J. 1980a. "A Cult-Mystery in the *Gospel of Philip.*" *Journal of Biblical Literature* 99: 569–81.

———. 1980b. "Two Female Gnostic Revealers." *History of Religions* 19: 159–69.

———. 1982. "A Rehabilitation of Spirit Ruha in Mandaean Religion." *History of Religions* 22: 60–84.

———. 1986. *Female Fault and Fulfilment in Gnosticism.* Chapel Hill: University of North Carolina Press.

———. 1988. "Conceptual Models and Polemical Issues in the *Gospel of Philip.*" *Aufstieg und Niedergang der römischen Welt,* I, 25, 5, eds. Hildegard Temporini and Wolfgang Haase (Berlin: Walter de Gruyter), pp. 4167–94.

———. 1992. "The Colophons in *The Canonical Prayerbook of the Mandaeans.*" *Journal of Near Eastern Studies* 51: 33–50.

Bynum, Caroline W. 1987. *Holy Feast and Holy Fast: The Religious Significance of Food to Medieval Women.* Berkeley and Los Angeles: University of California Press.

Casey, Robert P., ed. and tr. 1934. *Excerpta ex Theodoto of Clement of Alexandria.* Studies and Documents. Vol. I. London: Christopher's.

Fredriksen, Paula. 1979. "Hysteria and the Gnostic Myths of Creation." *Vigiliae Christianae* 33: 287–90.

Hennecke, Edgar, and Wilhelm Schneemelcher, eds. 1963. *The New Testament Apocrypha,* trs. Robert McL. Wilson and others. Vol. I. Philadelphia: Westminster.

Lidzbarski, Mark. 1925. *Der Ginza oder das grosse Buch der Mandäer.* Göttingen: Vandenhoeck and Ruprecht.

Roberts, Alexander, and James Donaldson, eds. 1925. *The Ante-Nicene Fathers.* Vol. II. New York: Scribner.

Robinson, James M., ed. 1988. *The Nag Hammadi Library.* 3rd ed. San Francisco: Harper & Row.

Schmidt, Carl, ed. 1940. *Kephalaia.* Vol. I, Pt. 1. Manichäische Handschriften der staatlichen Museen Berlin. Stuttgart: Kohlhammer.

Smith, Richard. 1988. "Sex Education in Gnostic Schools." In *Images of the Feminine in Gnosticism,* ed. Karen L. King (Philadelphia: Fortress), pp. 345–60.

Steinberg, Leo. 1993. "This is a Test." *The New York Review of Books* 40: 24.

Wheelwright, Philip, ed. and tr. 1966. *The Pre-Socratics.* Indianapolis: Bobbs-Merrill.

[8]

THE "MYSTERY OF MARRIAGE" IN THE
GOSPEL OF PHILIP

Elaine Pagels

T HE *Gospel of Philip* is not one of the more immediately accessible Gnostic texts. It does not, like the *Gospel of Thomas,* present a list of sayings of Jesus as startling as Zen koans; nor does it contain lyrical poetry like *Thunder: Perfect Mind.* Instead, this remarkable gospel consists of meditations on Christ and his message, meditations that are mysterious and provocative. After considerable struggle spent reading it in Coptic, I find this gospel to be extremely profound, and profound in a way that people who are familiar with the work of C. G. Jung will especially appreciate.

The *Gospel of Philip* is not a "gospel" in the sense of the New Testament Gospels. Unlike Matthew, Mark, and Luke, it does not follow the narrative pattern of historical biography. The *Gospel of Philip* does contain a few sayings attributed to Jesus and a few stories about him, but these either are taken from the New Testament or are startlingly different from it. Essentially, this "gospel" consists of cryptic reflections intended to hint at, or to reveal, the central mystery which its author sees at the heart of the Christian message—a mystery often referred to as the "mystery of marriage."

We do not know who actually wrote this gospel, any more than we know who actually wrote Matthew and Mark, but its author chose the *persona* of the apostle Philip. For this reason, without presuming that we actually know his or her gender, I have decided to follow this author's chosen *persona* and so to use the masculine pronoun.

In describing the "mystery of marriage," the author of *Philip* apparently takes his clue from the apostle Paul's letter to the Ephesians, where Paul speaks of the primordial union of Adam and

Eve. There Paul quotes the Genesis passage traditionally taken as describing the origin of marriage: "Therefore a man leaves his father and his mother and clings to his wife, and they become one flesh" (2.24). Commenting on this passage in his letter to the Ephesians, Paul adds, "This is a great mystery, and I am applying it to Christ and the church" (5.32).

I will explore several interrelated themes in the *Gospel of Philip:* the "mystery of marriage," the relationship between opposites, and the practical question of what such insights have to do with human relationships.

THE MYSTERY OF MARRIAGE

The author of *Philip* envisions an original androgynous union of the sexes which he reads into Genesis 1.27, a passage which says, "So God created humankind in his image, in the image of God he created *him;* male and female he created *them.*" That ambiguity between the singular and the plural led some Rabbis to speculate that Adam was originally an androgyne. The subsequent story in Genesis 2 tells how God, having put Adam to sleep, drew out of his body a part that he fashioned into Eve. The author of *Philip* thus reasons that before humanity was separated into two distinct sexes, the two were originally joined in one, in the perfect harmony of primordial union: "When Eve was still in Adam, death did not exist. When she was separated from him, death came into being. If he enters again and attains his former self, death will be no more" (Robinson 1988, p. 150 [all translations revised by Elaine Pagels]). Only when Adam reenters that primordial state and reunites with Eve can he "attain to his former self" and transcend his present isolated existence, along with its inevitable result. According to *Philip,* it was the woman who first separated herself from the man: "If the woman had not separated from the man, she should not die with the man. His separation became the beginning of death. Because of this Christ came to repair the separation which was from the beginning and again unite the two, and to give life to those who died . . ." (Robinson 1988, p. 151).

One remarkable feature of the *Gospel of Philip* is that it often mentions a secret Gnostic sacrament called the "bridechamber" (*nymphion*), a sacrament that is the culmination of all the other sacraments and that transforms the recipient.

This gospel's author sees the first sacrament, baptism, as a mystery, too. He seems to assume that the initiate already has received all the preceding sacraments: baptism, anointing (*chrism*), the Eucharist (which Latin Catholics call the "mass"), and redemption. The final initiation occurs in the bridechamber: "The Lord [did] everything in a mystery, a baptism and a chrism and a eucharist and a redemption and a bridal chamber [bridechamber]. . . . Those who have united in the bridechamber will no longer be separated" (Robinson 1988, pp. 150–51).

The divine prototype of the bridal sacrament ritual that the Gnostic initiate receives is the union of the "the Father of the all" with the "virgin who descends"—that is, the union of God the Father with God the mother, the Holy Spirit. When they were joined together, "a fire shone for them on that day" (Robinson 1988, p. 152). The author of *Philip* explains that the union of these masculine and feminine divine energies brought forth Jesus and the "body of Christ, his bride." As the author says, "He [Jesus] appeared in the great bridal chamber" (Robinson 1988, p. 152).

Now this sacrament probably was acted out in various ways. One account says that certain Gnostics, followers of the teacher Valentinus, used for this purpose an actual bridal chamber surrounded with mirrors. Others say this ritual involved a bridal bed.

According to the *Gospel of Philip,* the myth of the separation of Adam from Eve, symbolically interpreted, describes how we, as human beings, became separated—alienated—from our spiritual selves, how we become literally "dis-integrated." Thus the myth shows how we have lost consciousness of our spiritual potential and consequently of our innate need for spiritual growth. Adam represents *psyche,* the ordinary self—or, we could say, the *psychological* self. Eve represents the *pneuma,* the spirit. According to *Philip,* "Adam came into being from a breath (*psyche*) and Eve came into being from a spirit (*pneuma*)" (Robinson 1988, p. 152). What this means is that originally a human being consisted of ordinary self joined with spirit in bodily form. But once our ordinary sense of self was wrenched apart from the spirit, each separate element deteriorated. In the language of this myth, Eve committed adultery with the serpent. The spirit, severed from her grounding with the ordinary self, became immersed in material things alone; and the ordinary self, equally distorted in its separation from the spirit, became obsessed with everyday life, preoccupied with mere survival and reproduction.

Once Eve, the spiritual self, had separated from Adam, both

elements remained estranged until Christ came. The very purpose of his coming was "to repair the separation which was from the beginning and again unite the two, and to give life to those who died as a result of the separation and unite them" (Robinson 1988, p. 151). Only then does the initiate "become himself again," reintegrated and whole. The secret ritual of "bridechamber" thus places the initiated of either gender into the role of a bride, who now comes with joyful anticipation to be joined with her spiritual self, her divine bridegroom. What certain Gnostic Christians were actually enacting in a secret ritual was, then, the discovery of the spiritual self and the reunion with it.

Once initiated, such Christians actually perceived the whole significance of Christianity with different eyes. The ritual of the Eucharist in mainstream Christianity provides a similar transformation. Catholic Christians (like Protestants after them) are taught to see the bread and wine of the Eucharist as embodying an atonement sacrifice for sins. The bread is broken, symbolizing the broken body of Christ, broken upon the cross. According to the New Testament Gospels, Jesus himself offered this interpretation: "This is my body, which is given for you" (Luke 22.19). The wine sacramentally becomes his blood, "poured out for many for the forgiveness of sins" (Matthew 26.28). So the traditional celebrant, whether Roman Catholic, Orthodox, Episcopal, Lutheran, or whatever, pronounces these words from the Gospel of John while holding up the Eucharistic bread: "[Behold] the Lamb of God who takes away the sin of the world" (John 1.29).

Yet through the ritual of the bridechamber, the Gnostic Christian comes to perceive the Eucharist in very different terms. *Philip* paraphrases John 6.53 in saying that "unless you eat my flesh and drink my blood, you have no life in you" (Robinson 1988, p. 145). But *Philip* reinterprets these terms. For *Philip deprecates* the sacrificial view of Christ's death. John, he suggests, turns a divine mystery into a kind of cannibalism! Instead, *Philip* explains, the saying is a symbolic one: "His flesh is the *logos,* and his blood is the *holy spirit"* (Robinson 1988, p. 144). Since *logos* and *spirit* are in Hebrew masculine and feminine divine emanations, the mingling of the two in the bread and wine effects a union of opposites—that is, a marriage. As the celebrant says in prayer, "You who have joined the perfect light with the images, unite the angels with us also" (*Philip,* Robinson 1988, p. 145). According to *Philip,* then, not everyone sees Jesus in the same way: "[Jesus] did not appear as he was, but in the way in which [they would] be able to see him. To the small he appeared as small; to the great he appeared as great" (Robinson 1988, pp. 144–45).

SEXUALITY

In the forty years since Professor Hans-Martin Schenke first edited and published the *Gospel of Philip*, many scholars have asked the following question: what does this pervasive use of sexual symbolism in this gospel have to do with Gnostic attitudes toward actual sexuality? The question of sexual attitudes is not only contemporary; during the first and second centuries of our era Christians hotly debated the same question. The issue became, in fact, the storm center of the divisions among various groups of Christians. This same issue was also that which divided Jews and Christians from the majority of their pagan contemporaries. The majority of pagans tolerated a wide diversity of sexual practices, ranging from legalized prostitution (involving men, women, and children) to the everyday sexual use and abuse of slaves by owners. Christians inherited from Jews a strict code of sexual morality and proceeded to make it stricter still. Indeed, the question was not *whether* a Christian must be self-disciplined in sexual matters but *how* strict one must be. Many in the early movement, observing that Jesus was celibate (as was Paul) and that Jesus had praised celibacy as a way of living "like angels" (Luke 20.36), insisted that the true Christian, like Jesus and Paul, must observe total celibacy. Those who were already married at the time of conversion were to curtail or terminate their sexual relations.

To these views, however, more liberally minded Christians objected. Invoking Jewish precedent, they argued that marriage is, on the contrary, divinely ordained and blessed. These Christians insisted that marriage is good, not evil, and some went so far as to say that celibacy is suspect and unnatural.

So central was the controversy about sexual practice, especially about celibacy versus marriage, that virtually every Christian writing during the first two centuries took a stand on one side or the other. The distinctiveness of the *Gospel of Philip* is that, despite the centrality of sexual symbolism, it is very hard to tell *where* the Gospel stands on the issue. It is so hard that scholars are completely divided in their readings of this gospel!

Schenke contended that the bridechamber ritual was a symbolic sacrament, enacted "through a holy kiss that the *mystes* received from the *mystagogue*" (Schenke 1959, p. 5). Schenke assumed that such ritual practices had nothing to do with actual marriage and certainly had nothing to do with ordinary sexual practice. While Schenke himself refrained from speculating about actual Valentinian attitudes toward marriage, many scholars since have gone on to argue that *Philip* sides with those who advocated strict celibacy: the total renunciation of married life.

By contrast, Professor Gilles Quispel insists on the opposite interpretation. He maintains that Valentinian Christianity, here represented by *Philip,* is unique among Christian doctrines of the past two thousand years in that it offers a positive theology of sexuality. According to Quispel, such Gnostic Christians not only encouraged their members to marry but regarded marriage as a virtual prerequisite for Gnostic initiation. One of Quispel's students, the Danish scholar Jorunn Buckley, insists that the bridechamber sacrament, too, was enacted sexually. As she sees it, this ritual enabled the participants to embody spiritual union (Buckley 1980).

As I was reading the text, I was astonished that two groups of scholars could come up with such totally contradictory readings of *Philip.* On studying the text more carefully, I began to see that each group of scholars was selecting and emphasizing certain passages from the texts that fit their argument and was ignoring passages that did not. Furthermore, each group was translating its selected passages in ways that made one or the other argument more plausible. At first, I tried to figure out which of these interpretations was right. But as I puzzled over the Coptic text, I became convinced that both groups of scholars are equally wrong—or, to be generous, equally right. What I see in the *Gospel of Philip* is an author fully aware of the controversy ranging among his Christian contemporaries—with some insisting that marriage is good and celibacy is bad and the rest insisting on the opposite. What makes this text striking, as I read it, is the author's deliberate *refusal* to take sides.

MORALITY

The author simply will not stand on one side of the argument or the other because, as *Philip* explains, taking a stand on either side against the other does not really answer the essential underlying question: which actions are moral. That question is difficult to answer. For one thing, he says, as people's needs differ, so their level of spiritual development differs. Any spiritual advisor must therefore prescribe a different "diet," both literally and figuratively, for each person according to the needs and capacity of that person.

On a more theoretical level, the author of *Philip* argues that taking a stand on either side of these opposites misses the point that all the things which we ordinarily regard as opposites actually involve one another, as Jung so well understood. Calling one thing *light* and another *dark* thus fails to characterize reality: "Light and darkness, life and death, right and left, are brothers of one another. They are inseparable. Because of this neither are the good good, nor the evil evil, nor is life life, nor is death death. . . . Names given to things in the world are very deceptive for they divert our thoughts from what is real to what is not real" (Robinson 1988, p. 142).

Philip goes so far as to say that this deceptive habit of thinking in oppositional terms is the delusion that the serpent introduced to Adam and Eve in the Garden of Eden! For when the serpent offered Adam and Eve the fruit of the tree of the "knowledge of good and evil," he seduced the man and woman into believing that good and evil are opposites:

> In the place where I will eat all things is the tree of knowledge. That one killed Adam, but here the tree of knowledge made people alive. The law was the tree. . . . [I]t created death for those who ate of it. For when he said, "Eat this, do not eat that," it became the beginning of death. (Robinson 1988, p. 153)

As *Philip* sees it, the "tree of the knowledge of good and evil" caused Adam's spiritual death. For "the law was the tree," and when the creator said, "'Eat this, do not eat that,'" it became the beginning of death" (Robinson 1988, p. 153).

This statement is nothing less than an indictment of all traditional Christian morality. For the great majority of Christian teachers, from the first century to the present, essentially have composed *lists* distinguishing between acts they regard as *moral* and acts they regard as *immoral:* "These things are *good* to do (or to believe); these people are *good.* Conversely, these acts are *bad;* these people are *bad."* By contrast, the author of *Philip* is trying to show that *both* those who say "marriage is bad and celibacy good" and those who say "celibacy is bad and marriage good" are deluded. For, this author insists, neither marriage nor celibacy is good or bad in itself. Its moral quality depends upon the person involved and upon what "diet" (way of life) is beneficial to that person.

In the true Paradise, *Philip* declares, no one, least of all God, will say, "Eat this, do not eat that." On the contrary, *Philip* says, "God [has] a garden. . . . This garden [is the place where] they will say to me, 'Eat this, or do not eat that, just as you wish'" (Robinson 1988, p. 153). Such an astonishingly open view of morality is unprecedented in the Christian literature of its own time and of virtually any time since.

EVIL

Let us consider a serious objection. Does this mean that there is *nothing* we can say is really evil? Would not such a view lead to total moral relativism and allow Gnostic Christians to turn a blind eye to such undeniably evil acts as rape, murder, and even genocide?

Apparently aware of this question, *Philip* shifts the whole discussion, transforming it into a new key. Where Christian moral teaching typically consists of a person in authority dictating to others what is good or evil, *Philip* declares, on the contrary, that each person (or at least each Gnostic) must decide for himself or herself. No one can decide for someone else. The way for a Christian to live involves choosing the action that balances *gnosis*—spiritual consciousness— with *love*.

Now this may sound like a facile formula, but what makes it profound is the way *Philip* draws on the Jewish teaching of the *yetzer hara:* the "evil impulse" which the author takes seriously as potential energy in every person. *Philip* calls "the root of evil" the impulse toward anger, lust, or hatred that can grow and fester within any one of us. The root of evil is hidden within everyone. The author goes on to explain to his fellow Gnostics what we would today call the power of the unconscious. As long as we remain unaware of this potential for evil within us, it remains hidden from our consciousness, and it thereby holds great power:

> What is hidden within a person has great power, until it comes to light and is exposed. . . . Thus, so long as the root of evil is hidden, it is powerful. But when it comes to consciousness (*gnosis*), its power is dissolved. When it is revealed, it dies. This root is like the root of a tree; so long as the root is hidden the tree grows. But if the root is exposed, the tree withers and dies. (Robinson 1988, p. 158)

For this reason, *Philip* says, Jesus declared, "Already the ax is laid to the root of the trees" (Robinson 1988, p. 158). The ax does not merely cut the root, for what is cut may grow again, but the ax penetrates until it uproots the whole plant.

The text continues:

> As for ourselves, let each of us dig down after the root of evil within us, and pull out the root from the heart. It will be plucked out if we recognize it. But if we do not recognize it, it takes root in us and produces its fruits in our heart. It masters us and makes us its slaves. It takes us captive so

that we do what we do not want, and what we do not want to do, we do. It grows powerful because we have not recognized it. (Robinson 1988, p. 158)

One essential element of *gnosis* is, then, to know one's own potential for evil. Remaining unaware of the potential for evil within one is ignorance, which leads to sin and death: "Ignorance is the mother of all evil. Ignorance will result in death" (Robinson 1988, p. 158). Yet recognizing evil within is necessarily an individual process: each one must strive to recognize his or her own truth and to identify impulses and acts that come from the "root of evil."

Recently, I was at a gathering where Terry Anderson, former bureau chief for Associated Press in Lebanon, described his seven years as a hostage, during which he was chained to a wall, beaten, spat upon, and subject to constant abuse and several mock executions. During those years, he said, he came to know his kidnappers intimately. One day one of them said to him rather apologetically, "No man thinks that he is doing evil."

This terrible statement suggests that harming others often requires a person to repress his or her awareness of such motives as rage, envy, lust, and hatred. Those who do harm to others often insist instead that they are acting out of necessity, or, worse, in the name of some higher principle. When the same guard finally admitted to Anderson, "I hate doing this," his prisoner answered, "Then why don't you stop?" The man quit the next day and never returned. For to acknowledge the impulses here called the "root of evil" apparently decreases the power of conviction needed to sustain them.

Present experience as well as past history demonstrates that the "root of evil" thrives especially in people who are certain that they are right, and all of us have seen that such people can commit nearly unimaginable atrocities. On an everyday level, any of us may find ourselves launching into an angry tirade against another and then suddenly recognizing that the root of the action involves primarily our envy, pride, or rage. That insight often dissipates the energy fueling the tirade. What the *Gospel of Philip* offers, then, are practical insights into the nature of opposites, moral action, and its relation to consciousness.*

*This essay is a revised version of "The 'Mystery of Marriage' in the *Gospel of Philip* Revisited," which originally appeared in *The Future of Early Christianity: Essays in Honor of Helmut Koester,* ed. Birger A. Pearson (Minneapolis: Fortress, 1991), pp. 442–54, and which is reprinted here by permission. The author wishes to thank Anne Merideth for her help with the revision.

REFERENCES

Buckley, Jorunn J. 1980. "A Cult-Mystery in the *Gospel of Philip.*" *Journal of Biblical Literature* 99: 569–81.

Robinson, James M., ed. 1988. *The Nag Hammadi Library in English.* 3rd ed. San Francisco: Harper & Row.

Schenke, Hans-Martin. 1959. "Das Evangelium nach Philippus." *Theologische Literaturzeitung* 84: 1–26.

[9]

GNOSTICISM AND MODERN NIHILISM

Hans Jonas

I

NIETZSCHE, in his time, said that nihilism, "the most uncanny of all guests," "stands before the door."[1] Meanwhile the guest has entered and is no longer a guest, and, as far as philosophy is concerned, existentialism is trying to live with him. Living in such company is living in a crisis. The beginnings of the crisis reach back into the seventeenth century, where the spiritual situation of modern man takes shape.

Among the features determining this situation, the one that Pascal faced in all its awful implications and expounded with the full force of his eloquence is man's loneliness in the physical universe of modern science. "Cast into the infinite immensity of spaces of which I am ignorant, and which know me not, I am frightened." "Which know me not": more than the overawing infinity of the silent spaces and of limitless cosmic time, more than the quantitative disproportion, the insignificance of man as a magnitude in this vastness, more than these it is the utter indifference of the Copernican universe to human aspirations—the not-knowing of things human on the part of that within which all things human have preposterously to be enacted—which constitutes the utter loneliness of man in the sum of things.

As a part of this sum, man is only a reed, liable to be crushed at any moment by the forces of an immense and blind universe in which it is but a particular blind accident. As a thinking reed he is no part of the sum, not belonging to it, but radically different, incommensurable, for the *res extensa* does not think, and nature is nothing but *res extensa*—body, matter, external magnitude. If she crushes him, she does so unthinkingly, while he, being crushed, is aware of being crushed. He alone thinks, not because of but in spite of his being part of nature. If he has no share in nature's grandeur, which has become a foreign spectacle, nature has none in his inner concerns. Thus that which makes man superior to all nature, his unique distinction, mind, no longer results in a higher integration of his being into the totality of being, but on the contrary marks the unbridgeable gulf between himself and the rest of existence. Estranged from the community of being in one whole, his consciousness only makes him a foreigner in the world, and in every act of true reflection tells of this stark foreignness.

This is the human condition. There is no longer the *cosmos* with whose immanent *logos* my own can feel kinship, no longer the order of the whole which gives meaning to man's part in it, and therefore to his place in it. That place appears now as a sheer and brute accident. "I am frightened and shocked," continues Pascal, "at being here rather than there; for there is no reason why here rather than there, why now rather than then." There had always been a reason before, so long as the world had been regarded as life's cosmic home. But Pascal speaks of "this remote corner of nature" in which man has to "regard himself as lost," of "the little cell in which he finds himself lodged, I mean the universe." The utter contingency of man's existence in the scheme deprives that scheme of any human sense as a possible frame of reference for man's understanding of himself.

But there is more to this situation than the mere mood of homelessness, forlornness, and dread. The indifference of nature also means that nature has no reference to ends. With the ejection of teleology from the system of natural causes, nature, herself purposeless, ceased to provide any sanction to possible human purposes. A universe without an intrinsic hierarchy of being, as the Copernican universe is, leaves values ontologically unsupported, and the self is thrown back entirely upon itself in its quest for meaning and value. Meaning is no longer found, but is "given." Values are no longer beheld in the vision of objective reality, but are posited as feats of valuation. As functions of the will they are solely my own responsibility. Will replaces vision; temporality of the act ousts the eternity of the "good in itself." This is the Nietzschean phase of the situation in which European nihilism breaks the surface. Now man is alone with himself.

The world's a gate
To deserts stretching mute and chill.
Who once has lost
What thou hast lost stands nowhere still.

Thus spoke Nietzsche (in *Vereinsamt*)—closing the poem with the line, "Woe unto him who has no home!"

Pascal's universe, it is true, was still one created by God, and solitary man, bereft of all mundane props, could still stretch his heart out toward the transmundane God. But this God is essentially an unknown God, an *agnostos theos,* and is not discernible in the pattern of his creation. The universe does not reveal his purpose by its order of created things, or his goodness by their abundance, or his wisdom by their fitness, or his perfection by the beauty of the whole—but reveals solely his power, by its magnitude, its spatial and temporal immensity. And though the contingency of man, of his existing here and now, is still a contingency upon God's will, that will, which has cast me into just "this remote corner of nature," is inscrutable, and the "why?" of my existence is here just as unanswerable as atheistic existentialism makes it out to be. The *deus absconditus,* of whom nothing but will and power can be predicated, leaves behind as his legacy, upon leaving the scene, the *homo absconditus,* a concept of man characterized solely by will and power—the will for power, the will to will.[2]

The point that particularly matters for the purposes of the present discussion is that a change in the vision of nature, that is, of the cosmic environment of man, is at the bottom of that metaphysical situation which has given rise to modern existentialism and to its nihilistic implications. But if this is so, if the essence of existentialism is a certain dualism, an estrangement between man and the world, with the loss of the idea of a kindred *cosmos*—in short, an anthropological acosmism—then it is not necessarily modern physical science alone which can create such a condition. A cosmic nihilism as such, by whatever historical circumstances it may have been begotten, would be the condition in which some of the characteristic traits of existentialism might evolve. And the extent to which this is found to be actually the case would be a test for the relevance which we attribute to the described element in the existentialist position.

There is one situation, and one only that I know of in the history of Western man, where—on a level untouched by anything resembling modern scientific thought—that condition has been realized and lived out with all the vehemence of a cataclysmic event. That is the Gnostic movement, or the more radical ones among the various Gnostic movements and teachings, which the deeply agitated first three centuries of the Christian era proliferated in the Hellenistic parts of the Roman empire and beyond its eastern boundaries. From them, therefore, we may hope to learn something for an understanding of that disturbing subject, nihilism, and I wish to put the evidence before the reader as far as this can be done in the space of a brief essay.

II

The existence of an affinity or analogy across the ages, such as is here alleged, is not so surprising if we remember that in more than one respect the cultural situation in the Greco-Roman world of the first Christian centuries shows broad parallels with the modern situation. Spengler went so far as to declare the two ages "contemporaneous," in the sense of being identical phases in the life cycle of their respective cultures. In this analogical sense we would now be living in the period of the early Caesars. However that may be, there is certainly more than mere coincidence in the fact that we recognize ourselves in so many facets of later post-classical antiquity. Gnosticism is one of those facets, and here recognition, difficult as it is rendered by the strangeness of the symbols, comes with the shock of the unexpected, because it fits neither the picture of an age which a superficial historical consciousness characterizes mostly by Stoicism and Epicureanism, nor the picture of modern nihilism as—in line with the Nietzschean definition—essentially a post-Christian phenomenon.

In the following discussion I refer to existentialism as more or less a known quantity. Unfortunately I cannot do the same with Gnosticism. It lies off the main road of historical knowledge, and philosophers do not usually come across it. I am therefore compelled to dwell much more on the Gnostic side of my subject than a just balance in the comparison would warrant. In the circumstances, however, I do not see how this lopsidedness in my presentation can be avoided.

The term Gnostic refers to a group of religious doctrines at the beginning of our era which either explicitly identified themselves by the word *gnosis* or implied it as a central point of their message.[3] *Gnosis* means knowledge, and the historical connotations of the term have caused many observers, ancient and modern, to see in Gnosticism the inroad of Greek philosophy into Oriental religious thought. In content, manner, and aim, however, the "knowledge" of the Gnostics has little to do with rational thought, and the Hellenic associations of the name are more misleading than enlightening.

Also easily misleading is the fact that the majority of the recorded Gnostic sects appear within the still fluid boundaries of the early church, thus investing the very name, in the minds of observers, with the meaning of a Christian heresy, a mere epiphenomenon to Christianity. Modern research, however, has shown the existence of non-Christian Gnostic religions as well, coincident with the rise of Christianity in the declining ancient world, and there is evidence even of pre-Christian Gnosticism. As a matter of fact, the Gnostic movement—such we must call it—was a comprehensive phenomenon in those critical centuries, feeding like Christianity on the impulses of a widely prevalent human situation, and therefore erupting in many places, many forms, and many languages.

The salient feature to be emphasized here is the radically dualistic mood which underlies the whole Gnostic attitude and unifies the widely diversified, more or less systematic expressions which that attitude gave itself in Gnostic ritual and literature. It is on this primary human foundation of a dualistic mood, a passionately felt experience of man, that the formulated dualistic doctrines rest. The dualism is between man and the world, and concurrently between the world and God. It is a duality not of supplementary but of contrary terms, a polarity of incompatibles, and this fact dominates Gnostic eschatology. Basic to it is the feeling of an absolute rift between man and that in which he finds himself lodged: the world. The feeling is explicated in terms of doctrine. In its theological aspect it states that the Divine has no part and no concern in the physical universe; that the true God, strictly transmundane, is not revealed or even indicated by the world, and is therefore the Unknown, the totally Other, unknowable in terms of any worldly analogies. Correspondingly, in its cosmological aspect it states that the world is the creation not of God but of some inferior principle; and, in its anthropological aspect, that man's inner self—called the *pneuma*—is not part of the world, of nature's creation and domain, but, within that world, is as totally transcendent and as unknown by all worldly categories as is its transmundane counterpart, the unknown God without.

That the world is created by someone is generally not doubted in the mythological systems (though in some of the subtler systems a sort of dark autogenesis from orts of divinity is contemplated). But whoever has created the world, man, according to Gnosticism, does not owe him allegiance; and neither his creation, though incomprehensibly encompassing man, nor his proclaimed will offers the standards by which man can set his course. Since the true God cannot be the creator of that to which selfhood feels so utterly a stranger, nature must have been created by a lowly Demiurge, a power far removed from the supreme source of Being, a perversion of the Divine, retaining of it only the power to act, but to act blindly, without knowledge; he created the world out of ignorance and passion.

Thus the world is the product, and even essentially the embodiment, of the negative of knowledge. What it reveals is unenlightened and therefore malignant force, proceeding from the spirit of self-assertive power, from the will to rule and coerce—which, as spiritual, is foolish and bears no relation to understanding and love. The laws of the universe are the laws of this rule, and not of divine wisdom. Thus the essence of the *cosmos* is ignorance (*agnosia*). In this negativity the idea of knowledge (*gnosis*) finds its first application, an application in the privative mood. The positive complement is in the fact that the essence of man is knowledge: this determines the situation of man as that of the knowing in the midst of the unknowing, of light in the midst of darkness, and this relation is at the bottom of his being alien, without companionship in the dark vastness of the universe.

That universe has none of the venerability of the Greek *cosmos.* Contemptuous epithets are applied to it: "these miserable elements" (*paupertina haec elementa*), "this puny cell of the creator" (*haec cellula creatoris*)—both quotations from Marcion, the second offering literally the same expression that we found in Pascal. Yet it is still *cosmos,* an order—but order with a vengeance. Not only is the name *cosmos* retained for the world; it is called that now with a new and fearful emphasis, an emphasis at once awed and disrespectful, troubled and rebellious, for that order is alien to man's aspirations. The blemish of nature lies not in any deficiency of order, but in the all too pervading completeness of it. Far from being chaos, the creation of the Demiurge, that antitype of knowing, is a comprehensive system, governed by law. But cosmic law, once regarded as the expression of a reason with which man's reason can communicate in the act of cognition, is now seen only in its aspect of compulsion which thwarts man's freedom. The cosmic *logos* of the Stoics is replaced by *heimarmene,* oppressive cosmic fate.

This *heimarmene* is dispensed by the planets, or the stars in general, the mythical exponents of the inexorable and hostile law of the universe. The change in the emotional content of the term *cosmos* is nowhere better symbolized than in this depreciation of the formerly most divine part of the visible world, the celestial spheres. The starry sky—which from Plato to the Stoics was the purest embodiment of reason in the cosmic hierarchy, the paradigm of intelligibility and therefore of the divine nature of reality as such— now stared man in the face with the fixed glare of alien power and necessity. Its rule is tyranny, and not providence. Deprived of the venerability with which all sideric piety up to then had invested it, but still in possession of the prominent and representative position it had acquired, this stellar firmament becomes now the symbol of all that is terrifying to man in the towering factness of the universe. Under this pitiless sky, which no longer inspires worshipful confidence, man becomes conscious of his utter forlornness, of his being not so much a part of, but unaccountably placed in and exposed to, the enveloping system.

And, like Pascal, he is frightened. His solitary otherness, discovering itself in this forlornness, erupts in the feeling of elementary dread. Dread as a fundamental mood of being-in-the-world first became articulate not in existentialism but in the Gnostic writings. It is the self's reaction to the discovery of its situation, actually itself an element in that discovery: it marks the awakening of selfhood from the slumber or intoxication of the world; it is the way in which the inmost spirit becomes originally aware of itself and of the fact that it is not really its own, but is rather the involuntary executor of cosmic designs. Knowledge, *gnosis,* might liberate man from this servitude; but since the *cosmos* is contrary to life, the saving knowledge cannot aim at the knower's integration into the cosmic whole, cannot aim at compliance with the laws of the universe, as did Stoic wisdom, which sought freedom in the knowing affirmation of universal necessity. For the Gnostics, contrary to the Stoics, man's alienation is not to be overcome, but is to be deepened and pushed to the extreme for the sake of the self's redemption.

III

Before going any further, let us stop to ask what has here happened to the old idea of the *cosmos* as a divinely ordered whole. Certainly nothing comparable to modern physical science was involved in this catastrophic devaluation or spiritual denudation of the universe. We need only observe that this universe became thoroughly demonized in the Gnostic period. Yet this, taken with the transcendence of the acosmic self, resulted in curious analogies to the phenomena of existentialism in the vastly different modern setting. If not science and technology, what caused, for the human groups involved, the collapse of the cosmos piety of classical civilization, on which so much of its ethics was built?

The answer is certainly complex, but at least one angle of it may be briefly indicated. The classical ontological doctrine of whole and parts—according to which the whole is prior to the parts, is better than the parts, and is that for the sake of which the parts are and wherein they find the meaning of their existence—had lost the social basis of its validity. The living example of such a whole had been the classical *polis,* whose citizens had a stake in the whole, and could affirm its superior status in the knowledge that they, the parts, however passing and exchangeable, maintained it with their own being, and that their actions made a difference to the being and perfection of the whole. This whole, the condition for the existence and wellbeing of the individual, was thus in addition the framework for the fulfillment of man's aspirations.

The ontological principle survived the conditions of its conception. With the absorption of the city states into the monarchies of the Diadochs and finally into the Roman empire, which deprived the *polis* intelligentsia of its constructive function, the relation no longer held politically. But Stoic pantheism, the physico-theology of post-Aristotelian monism, substituted for it the relation between the individual and the *cosmos,* the larger living whole. By this substitution the classical doctrine of whole and parts was kept in force even though it no longer reflected the actual situation of man. Now the *cosmos* was declared to be the great "city of gods and men," and to be a citizen of the universe, a *cosmopolites,* was now considered to be the goal by which otherwise isolated man could set his bearings. He was asked, as it were, to adopt the cause of the universe as his own, that is, to identify himself with that cause directly, across all intermediaries, and to relate his inner self, to relate his *logos,* to the *logos* of the whole.

The practical side of this identification consisted in his affirming and faithfully performing the role allotted to him by the whole, in just that place in which cosmic destiny had set him. "To play one's part"—that figure of speech on which Stoic morals dwelt so much—unwittingly reveals the fictitious element in the structure. A role played is substituted for a real function performed. The actors on the stage behave "as if" they acted their choice, and "as if" their actions mattered. What actually matters is only to play well rather than badly, with no genuine relevance to the outcome. The actors, bravely playing, are their own audience.

In the phrase of playing one's part there is a bravado that hides a deeper despair, and only a shift in attitude is needed to view the great spectacle quite differently. Does the whole really care, does it concern itself in the part that is I? The Stoics averred that it does by equating *heimarmene* with *pronoia,* cosmic fate with providence. And does my part, however I play it, really contribute, does it make a difference to the whole? The Stoics averred that it does by their analogy between the *cosmos* and the city. But the very comparison brings out the artificiality of the construction, for—in contrast to what is true in the *polis*—no case can be made out for my relevance in the cosmic scheme, which is entirely outside my control and in which my part is thus reduced to a passivity which in the *polis* it had not.

To be sure, the strained fervor by which man's integration in the whole was maintained, through his alleged affinity to it, was the means of preserving the dignity of man and thereby of saving a sanction for a positive morality. This fervor, succeeding that which had formerly been inspired by the ideal of civic virtue, represented a heroic attempt on the part of the intellectuals to carry over the life-sustaining force of that ideal into fundamentally changed conditions. But the new atomized masses of the empire, who had never shared in that noble tradition of *areté,* reacted very differently to a situation in which they found themselves passively involved: a situation in which the part was insignificant to the whole, and the whole alien to the parts. The Gnostic aspiration was not to "act a part" in this whole, but—in existentialist parlance—to "exist authentically." The law of empire, under which they found themselves, was an external dispensation of dominating, unapproachable force; and, for them, the same character was assumed by the law of the universe, cosmic destiny, of which the world state was the terrestrial executor. The very concept of law was modified in all its aspects— natural law, political law, moral law.

I leave it to the reader to draw whatever analogies there are between this alienation of man from his world and the situation of atomized industrial society. Such analogies, I am sure, would supplement from the social angle the effects I have attributed to the cosmology of modern science, on the testimony of Pascal. As in late antiquity, so today, the term "world" contains two meanings at once: nature in general, and social reality. And it may well be the latter which preeminently determines man's relation to "the world," the sum of things.

IV

The subversion of the idea of law, of *nomos,* leads to a moral consequence in which the nihilistic implications of the Gnostic acosmism, and at the same time the analogy to the Nietzsche-Heidegger-Sartre strain of existentialism, become even more obvious than in the cosmological aspect: the antinomism of Gnosticism. To begin with, it is to be conceded that antinomism—the rejection of any objective norm of conduct—is argued on vastly different theoretical levels in the two cases, and that antinomistic Gnosticism appears crude, and perhaps less profound, in comparison with the subtlety and pitiless historical self-elucidation of antinomistic existentialism. What is being liquidated, in the one case, is the moral heritage of a thousand years of ancient civilization; added to this, in the other, are two thousand years of Occidental Christian metaphysics as background to the idea of a moral law.

Nietzsche expressed the root of the nihilistic situation in the phrase "God is dead," meaning primarily the Christian God. The Gnostics, if asked to summarize similarly the metaphysical basis of their own nihilism, could have said only "the God of the cosmos is dead"—is dead, that is, as a god, has ceased to be divine for us and therefore to afford the lodestar for our lives. Admittedly the catastrophe in this case is less comprehensive and thus less irremediable, but the vacuum that was left, even if not so bottomless, was felt no less keenly.

To Nietzsche the meaning of nihilism is that "the highest values become devaluated" (or "invalidated"), and the cause of this devaluation is "the insight that we have not the slightest justification for positing a transcendence, or an 'in itself' of things, which is 'divine,' which is morality incarnate."[4] This utterance, taken with that about the death of God, bears out Heidegger's statement that "the names God and Christian God are in Nietzsche's thought used to denote the transcendental (supra-sensible) world in general. God is the name for the realm of ideas and ideals" (*Holzwege,* p. 199). Since it is from this realm alone that any sanction for values can derive, its fading, that is, the "death of God," means not only the actual devaluation of highest values, but the loss of the very possibility of obligatory values as such. To quote once more Heidegger's interpretation of Nietzsche, "The phrase 'God is dead' means that the transcendental world is without effective force."

In a modified, rather paradoxical way this statement applies also to the Gnostic position. It is true, of course, that its extreme dualism is of itself the very opposite of an abandonment of transcendence. The transmundane God represents transcendence in the most radical form. In him the absolute beyond beckons across the enclosing cosmic shells. But this transcendence, unlike the "intelligible world" of Platonism or the world lord of Judaism, does not stand in any positive relation to the sensible world. It is not the essence of that world, but its negation and cancelation. The Gnostic God, as distinct from the Demiurge, is the totally different, the other, the unknown. Like his inner-human counterpart, the acosmic self or *pneuma,* which, otherwise hidden, also reveals itself only in the negative experience of otherness, of non-identification and of protested indefinable freedom, this God has more of the *nihil* than the *ens* in his concept. A transcendence withdrawn from any normative relation to the world is equal to a transcendence which has lost its effective force. In other words, for all purposes of man's relation to existing reality, this hidden God is a nihilistic conception: no *nomos* emanates from him, no law for nature and thus also no law for human conduct as a part of the natural order.

On this basis the antinomistic argument of the Gnostics is as simple as for instance that of Sartre. Since the transcendent is silent, Sartre argues, since "there is no sign in the world," man, the "abandoned," reclaims his freedom, or rather, cannot help taking it upon himself: he "is" that freedom, man being "nothing but his own project," and "all is permitted to him."[5] That this freedom is of a desperate nature, and, as a compassless task, inspires dread rather than exultation, is a different matter.

In Gnostic reasoning we sometimes meet the merely subjectivist form of the antinomistic argument: nothing is naturally bad or good, things in themselves are indifferent, and only by human opinion are actions good or bad. Spiritual man, in the freedom of his knowledge, has the indifferent use of them all. While this reminds one of nothing more than of classical Sophism, the real metaphysical background to this superficially skeptical subjectivism comes to light in the deeper Gnostic reflection on the source of such human opinions.

The ultimate source turns out to be not human but demiurgical, and common with that of the order of nature. Its product, the "law," is thus not really indifferent, but is part of the great design upon our freedom. Being *nomos,* the moral code is but the psychical complement to the physical *nomos* and, as such, the internal aspect of the all-pervading cosmic rule. Both emanate from the lord of the world as agencies of his power, unified in the double aspect of the Jewish God as creator and legislator. Just as the law of the physical world, the *heimarmene,* integrates the individual bodies into the general system, so the moral law integrates the souls, and thus makes them subservient to the demiurgic scheme.

For what is the law—either as revealed through Moses and the prophets or as operating in the actual habits and opinions of men—but the means of regularizing and thus stabilizing the implication of man in the business of the world and worldly concerns; of setting by its rules the seal of seriousness, of praise and blame, reward and punishment, on his utter involvement; of making his very will a compliant party to the compulsory system, which thereby will function all the more smoothly and inextricably? In so far as the principle of this moral law is justice, it has the same character of constraint on the psychical side that cosmic fate has on the physical side. "The angels that created the world established 'just actions,' to lead men by such precepts into servitude" (Simon Magus). In the normative law man's will is taken care of by the same powers that dispose of his body. He who obeys it has abdicated the authority of his self.

It is not possible here to go into the anarchical and sometimes libertinistic consequences of this attitude. Incidentally, the consequences can be either libertinistic or ascetic, and actually, except for a brief period of revolutionary extremism, they have probably more often been the latter than the former. But the two seemingly opposite attitudes are really of the same root, and are capable of strange combinations. The same basic argument supports them both. The one repudiates loyalty to nature through excess, the other through abstention. The one sometimes makes of the permission to do everything a positive obligation to perform every kind of action, with the idea of rendering to nature its own and thereby exhausting its powers; the other flouts those powers by denying them opportunity and reducing commerce with them to the minimum. Both are lives outside the law. Freedom by abuse and freedom by non-use, equal in their indiscriminateness, are thus only alternative expressions of the same acosmism.

The reference to this root makes it clear that, far beyond what the merely skeptical argument of "subjectivism" suggests, there was a positive metaphysical interest in repudiating allegiance to any objective norm. It was the assertion of the authentic freedom of the self. But it is to be noted that this freedom is not a matter of the "soul," which is as adequately determined by the moral law as the body is by the physical law; it is wholly a matter of the *pneuma,* the indefinable spiritual core of existence, the foreign spark. The soul, *psyche,* is part of the natural order, created by the demiurge to envelop the foreign *pneuma,* and in the normative law the creator exercises control over what is legitimately his own. Psychical man, definable in his natural essence, for instance as rational animal, is still natural man, and is no more admitted to be the authentically existing self of the *pneuma* than in modern existentialism any determinative essence is admitted to prejudice authentic existence.

It is pertinent here to compare an argument of Heidegger's. Against the classical definition of man as the rational animal, Heidegger, in his Letter on Humanism, argues that this definition places man within animality specified only by a differentia which falls within the genus "animal" as a particular quality. This, Heidegger contends, is placing man too low. I suspect there is a verbal sophism involved in thus arguing from the term "animal" as used in the classical definition. But apart from that, in his rejection of the concept of any definable "nature" of man which would subject his sovereign existence to a predetermined essence and thus make him part of an objective order of essences in the whole of nature—in this whole conception of trans-essential, freely "projecting" existence— there is a significant analogy to the Gnostic concept of the trans-psychical negativity of the *pneuma.* This *pneuma* is the bearer of a knowledge peculiar to itself which is radically different from the rational knowledge of the *psyche.* Psychical man, through his reason, owes allegiance, indeed, to the moral law laid down by his creator, the Demiurge, and in obediently fulfilling it he has the only chance of being just, that is, properly "adjusted" to the externally established order, and thus of playing his allotted part in the cosmic scheme. But the *pneumaticos,* "spiritual" man, is above the law, beyond good and evil, and a law unto himself in the power of his "knowledge."

Only in passing I wish to remark that Paul's antinomism, though sharing in the general climate of the Gnostic one, is a vastly different matter. It certainly does not grant freedom from the law to any superior "knowledge."

V

But what is this knowledge about, this cognition which is not of the soul but of the spirit, and in which the spiritual self finds its salvation from cosmic servitude? A famous formula of the Valentinian school thus epitomizes the content of *gnosis:* "What makes us free is the knowledge who we were, what we have become; where we were, wherein we have been thrown; whereto we speed, wherefrom we are redeemed; what is birth and what rebirth."[6] A real exegesis of this programmatic formula would have to unfold the complete Gnostic myth. Here I wish to make only a few formal observations.

First we note the dualistic grouping of the terms in antithetical pairs, and the eschatological tension between them, with its irreversible directedness from past to future. We further observe that all the terms used are concepts not of being but of happening, of movement. The knowledge is of a history, in which it is itself a critical event.

Among these terms of motion, the one of having "been thrown" into something strikes our attention, because we have been made familiar with it in existentialist literature. We are reminded of Pascal's "Cast into the infinite immensity of spaces," of Heidegger's *Geworfenheit,* "having been thrown," which with him is a fundamental character of the *Dasein,* of the self-experience of existence. The term, as far as I can see, is originally Gnostic. In the Mandaean literature it is a standing phrase: life has been thrown into the world, light into darkness, the soul into the body. It expresses the original violence done to me in making me be where I am and what I am, the passivity of my choiceless emergence into an existing world whose law is not mine. But the image of the throw also imparts a dynamic character to the whole of the existence thus initiated. In our formula this is taken up by the image of speeding toward some end. Ejected into the world, life is a kind of trajectory projecting itself forward into the future.

This brings us to the last observation I wish to make apropos the Valentinian formula: that in its temporal terms it makes no provision for a *present* on whose content knowledge may dwell and, in beholding, stay the forward thrust. There is past and future, where we come from and where we speed to, and the present is only the moment of *gnosis* itself, the peripety from the one to the other in a supreme crisis of the eschatological *now*. There is this to remark, however, in distinction to all modern parallels: the context makes it clear that, though thrown into temporality, we had an origin in eternity, and so also have an aim in eternity. This constitutes a metaphysical background to innercosmic nihilism which is entirely absent from its modern counterpart.

To turn once more to the modern counterpart, let me put before you an observation which must strike the close student of Heidegger's *Sein und Zeit,* that most profound and still most important manifesto of existentialist philosophy. In this book Heidegger develops an ontology of the self according to the modes in which it exists, that is to say, in which it constitutes its being by its existing, and these modes are explicated in a number of fundamental categories which Heidegger prefers to call "existentials." Unlike the objective categories of Kant, they define structures not of reality but of realization—of the active movement of inwardness by which a world of objects is entertained and the self originated as a continuous event. They have, therefore, each and all, a profoundly temporal meaning. The "existentials" are categories of internal or mental time, the true dimension of existence, and they articulate that dimension in its tenses. This being so, they must exhibit, and distribute between themselves, the three horizons of time—past, present, and future.

Now if we try to arrange these "existentials," Heidegger's categories of existence, under these three heads, as it is possible to do, we make a striking discovery—at any rate one that struck me very much when I made it many years ago (at the time even going so far as to draw up a diagram, in the classical manner of a "table of categories"). This is the discovery that the column under the head of "present" remains practically empty. I must hasten to add that this statement, and what follows, is an extreme abridgment. Actually a great deal is said about the existential "present." But it is nothing original in its own right. As far as the term is meant to denote an aspect of *genuine* "existence," it is the present of the "situation," which is wholly defined in terms of the self's relation to its "future" and "past." It flashes up, as it were, in the light of decision when the projected "future" reacts upon the given "past," and in this meeting constitutes what Heidegger calls the "moment" (*Augenblick*): moment, not duration, is the temporal mode of *this* present—a creature of the other two horizons of time, a function of their ceaseless dynamics, and no independent dimension to dwell in. Detached, however, from this context of inner movement, by itself, "present" denotes precisely the renouncement of genuine future-past relation in the "abandonment" or "surrender" to talk, curiosity, and the like (*Verfallenheit*): a failure of the tension of true existence, a kind of laziness of being. Indeed, *Verfallenheit,* a negative term which also includes the meaning of degeneration and decline, is *the* "existential" proper to "present" as such, showing it to be a derivative and "deficient" mode of existence.

To return, then, to our original statement, we find that all the relevant categories of existence, those having to do with the possible genuineness of existence, fall in correlate pairs under the heads of either past or future: "facticity," necessity, having become, having been thrown, are existential modes of the past; being ahead of oneself, anticipation of death, care and resolve, are existential modes of the future. No present remains for genuine existence to repose in. Leaping off, as it were, from its past, existence projects itself into its future; faces its ultimate limit, death; returns from this eschatological glimpse of nothingness to its sheer factness, the unalterable datum of its already having become this, there and then; and carries this forward with its death-begotten resolve, into which the past has now been gathered up. I repeat, there is no present to dwell in, only the crisis between past and future, the pointed moment between, balanced on the razor's edge of decision which thrusts ahead.

This breathless dynamism holds a tremendous appeal for the contemporary mind, and my generation in the German twenties and early thirties succumbed to it wholesale. But there is a puzzle in this evanescence of the present as the holder of genuine content, in its reduction to the inhospitable zero point of mere formal resolution. What metaphysical situation stands behind it?

Here an additional observation is relevant. There is, after all, besides the existential "present" of the moment, the presence of things. Does not the co-presence with them afford a "present" of a different kind? But we learn from Heidegger that things are primarily *zuhanden,* that is, usable (of which even "useless" is a mode), and therefore related to the "project" of existence, therefore included in the future-past dynamics. Yet they can also become merely *vorhanden* (standing before me), that is, indifferent objects, and the mode of *Vorhandenheit* is an objective counterpart to what on the existential side is *Verfallenheit,* false present. *Vorhanden* is what is merely and indifferently "extant," the "there" of bare nature, there to be looked at outside the relevance of the existential situation and of practical concern. It is being, as it were, stripped and alienated to the mode of neutral object. This is the status left to "nature"—a deficient mode of reality—and the relation in which it is so objectified is a deficient mode of existence, its defection from the futurity of care into the spurious present of mere onlooking curiosity.

This existentialist depreciation of the concept of nature (the absence of "nature" as a relevant topic from Heidegger's philosophy is in itself a revealing fact) obviously reflects its spiritual denudation at the hands of physical science, and it has something in common with the Gnostic contempt for nature. No philosophy has ever been less concerned about nature, which, for it, has no dignity left to it: this unconcern is not to be confounded with Socrates' refraining from physical inquiry as being above man's understanding.

To look at what is there, at nature as it is in itself, at Being, the ancients called by the name of contemplation, *theoria*. But the point here is that, if contemplation is left with only the irrelevantly extant, then it loses the noble status it once had—as does the repose in the present to which it holds by the presence of its objects. *Theoria* had that dignity because of its Platonic implications—because it beheld eternal objects in the forms of things, a transcendence of immutable being shining through the transparency of becoming. Immutable being is everlasting present, in which contemplation can share in the brief durations of the temporal present.

Thus it is eternity, not time, that grants a present and gives it a status of its own in the flux of time; and it is the loss of eternity which accounts for the loss of a genuine present. Such a loss of eternity is the disappearance of the world of ideas and ideals in which Heidegger sees the true meaning of Nietzsche's "God is dead": in other words, the absolute victory of nominalism over realism. Therefore the same cause which is at the root of nihilism is also at the root of the radical temporality of Heidegger's scheme of existence, in which the present is nothing but the moment of transcience from past to future. If values are not beheld in vision as being (like the Good and the Beautiful of Plato), but are posited by the will as projects, then indeed existence is committed to constant futurity, with death as the goal; and a merely formal resolution to be, without a *nomos* for that resolution, becomes a project from nothingness into nothingness. In the words of Nietzsche quoted before, "Who once has lost what thou hast lost stands nowhere still."

VI

Once more our investigation leads back to the dualism between man and *physis* as the metaphysical background of the nihilistic situation. There is no overlooking one cardinal difference between the Gnostic and the existentialist dualism: Gnostic man is thrown into an antagonistic, anti-divine, and therefore anti-human nature, modern man into an indifferent one. And only the latter case represents the

absolute vacuum, the really bottomless pit. In the Gnostic conception the hostile, the demonic, is still anthropomorphic, familiar even
in its foreignness, and the contrast itself gives direction to
existence—a negative direction, to be sure, but one that has behind it
the sanction of the negative transcendence to which the positivity of
the world is the qualitative counterpart. Not even this antagonistic
quality is granted to the indifferent nature of modern science, and
from that nature no direction at all can be elicited.

This makes modern nihilism infinitely more radical and more
desperate than Gnostic nihilism ever could be, for all its panic terror
of the world and its defiant contempt of its laws. That nature does not
care, one way or the other, is the true abyss. That only man cares, in
his finitude facing nothing but death, alone with his contingency and
the objective meaninglessness of his projecting meanings, is a truly
unprecedented situation.

But this difference, which reveals the greater depth of modern
nihilism, also challenges its self-consistency. Gnostic dualism, fantastic as it was, was at least self-consistent. The idea of a demonic
nature against which the self is pitted, makes sense. But what about
an indifferent nature which nevertheless contains in its midst something to which its own being does make a difference? The phrase of
having been flung into indifferent nature is a remnant from a
dualistic metaphysics, a phrase to whose use the existentialists' own
monistic beliefs give them no right. What is the throw without the
thrower, and without a beyond whence it started? Rather should the
existentialist say that life—conscious, caring, knowing self—has
been "thrown up" *by* nature. If blindly, then the seeing is a product
of the blind, the caring a product of the uncaring, a teleological
nature begotten unteleologically.

Does not this paradox cast doubt on the very concept of an
indifferent nature, that abstraction of physical science? So radically
has anthropomorphism been banned from the concept of nature that
even man must cease to be conceived anthropomorphically if he is
just an accident of that nature. As the product of the indifferent, his
being, too, must be indifferent. Then the facing of his mortality
would simply warrant the reaction "Let us eat and drink for
tomorrow we die." There is no point in caring for what has no
sanction behind it in any creative intention. But if the deeper insight
of Heidegger is right—that, facing our finitude, we find that we care,
not only whether we exist but how we exist—then the mere fact of
there being such a supreme care, anywhere within the world, must
also qualify the totality which harbors that fact, and, having given

rise to it physically, cannot be only the indifferent externality of a-teleological science.

The disruption between man and total reality is at the bottom of nihilism. The illogicality of the rupture makes its fact no less real, or its seeming alternative more acceptable: the stare at isolated selfness, to which it commits man, may seek release—and has found it—in a monistic naturalism which, along with the rupture, would abolish also the idea of man as man. Between that Scylla and this her twin Charybdis, the modern mind hovers. Whether a third road is open to it—one by which the fatal dualism can be overcome and yet enough of the dualistic insight saved to uphold the humanity of man—philosophy will have to find out.*

NOTES

1. *Der Wille zur Macht,* § 34.

2. The role of Pascal as the first modern existentialist, which I have here very roughly sketched as a starting point, has been more fully expounded by Karl Löwith in his article on "Man Between Infinites," in *Measure, A Critical Journal* (Chicago), vol. 1 (1950), from which also the quotations from Pascal have been borrowed.

3. What follows is a brief summary of certain basic features of Gnosticism. The full argument for the view presented here, which differs from the conventional one, may be found in my *Gnosis und spätantiker Geist,* vol. 1 (Göttingen 1934). Note also two articles of mine on this subject in *Theologische Zeitschrift* (Basel): vol. 4, no. 2 (1948), and vol. 5, no. 1 (1949).

4. *Wille zur Macht,* §§ 23, 24; cf. *ibid,* § 4, "to live alone, 'without God and morals.' "

5. *L'existentialisme est un humanisme,* pp. 33 ff.

6. Clemens Alex., *Exc. ex Theod.,* 78, 2.

*This essay was originally published in *Social Research* 19 (1952): 430–52, and is reprinted here with permission. The essay was subsequently published in revised form as "Gnosticism, Existentialism, and Nihilism" in the second edition of Jonas's *The Gnostic Religion* (Boston: Beacon, 1963), pp. 320–40. That revised version was in turn republished in Jonas's first collection of essays, *The Phenomenon of Life* (New York: Harper & Row, 1966), pp. 211–34.

[10]

ERIC VOEGELIN AND THE CHANGING PERSPECTIVE ON THE GNOSTIC FEATURES OF MODERNITY

Stephen A. McKnight

THE 1940s and 1950s saw major developments in Gnostic studies, especially in the analysis of parallels between ancient Gnosticism and modern thought and experience. Three scholars played major roles in this development. Carl Jung, the renowned psychologist, recognized the archetypal significance of the Gnostic experience of the world and found striking parallels in his patients and in modern culture. Hans Jonas, Heidegger's famous student, said that his reading of Gnostic texts provided the skeleton key that opened the door to understanding the experiential foundations of modern existentialism. Eric Voegelin, the internationally known political scientist and philosopher of history, analyzed the parallels between ancient Gnosticism and modern revolutionary political movements and philosophies.

In this essay, I want to focus on Voegelin's analysis of the Gnostic features of modern epistemology and utopianism. I will begin by explaining Voegelin's original thesis as it developed in the forties and fifties and then indicate how his theory began to change in the 1970s and 1980s. Discussion of the nature of his change in perspective will lead to an examination of Renaissance hermeticism, an esoteric tradition similar to Gnosticism.[1] My intent is to demonstrate that Hermeticism is gnostic in the generic sense of having a doctrine of saving knowledge but is fundamentally different from the radically pessimistic, dualistic world view associated with ancient Gnosticism. The significance of the differentiation between Gnostic pessimism and Hermetic optimism will become apparent in relation to the discussion of Voegelin's analysis of the traditions shaping modernity.

VOEGELIN: GNOSTICISM AND MODERNITY

Voegelin's analysis of modernity is concerned with the origin and development of three characteristic features. The first and foremost is the claim of an epochal break with the methods of the past. The second is the claim that the source of this epochal break is an extraordinary epistemological advance which provides humanity with both the knowledge and the ability to perfect society. The third element of this modern configuration is the conviction that this epistemological breakthrough allows humanity to alter the conditions of existence and for the first time to be able to shape its own destiny. Modernists from the seventeenth century to the present have linked this epistemological leap and this confidence in humanity's capacity for self-determination with science and secularization. Voegelin makes these claims the focus of his critical analysis and develops the counterposition that the epistemological foundations of modernity are Gnostic in nature (see Voegelin 1952, 1968, 1975).

Voegelin's principal interest and his major contribution are in his analysis of the parallels between ancient Gnostic and modern concepts of knowledge. The Gnostic believes that he has a direct grasp of the ultimate issues concerning human nature, human purpose, human meaning, and human destiny. With the possession of this knowledge, he is convinced that he is able to recognize accurately the sources of alienation and to escape from the prison of the world. Voegelin found this characteristic Gnostic element in the epistemological operations of modern political revolutionaries like Comte and Marx, who sought to use knowledge to overcome the alienated state of existence. The knowledge that modern revolutionaries put their faith in is, of course, modeled after science, but Voegelin demonstrates that these "social science" projects took science far beyond the boundaries proper to it. Whereas Galileo and Newton readily acknowledged the limits of the field to which the new methodologies could be applied, the philosophes and nineteenth-century "social scientists" like Comte and Marx disregarded those limitations and used the method in the way that the ancient Gnostics had used esoteric knowledge: as a means to escaping alienation and transforming existence.

Voegelin's analysis of the transformation of science into the equivalent of an esoteric religion by radical social and political reformers not only undermines the powerful link that social science attempts to establish with natural science but also undercuts another basic tenet of modernity: that it is secular. Secularization is another fundamental modernist theme that develops in the eighteenth century and expands in our own time to the point that Hans Blumenberg (1983) can claim that the terms *modernity* and *secularization* are virtually identical. Voegelin's analysis shows, however, that modernity is not overwhelmingly secular. The root concept of knowledge and the basic views of society and history are religious in origin and function.

The juxtaposition of science with *gnosis* was a central feature of Voegelin's analysis of modernity in the 1940s, 1950s, and 1960s. Beginning in the 1970s, however, Voegelin acknowledged that other esoteric traditions had also played a major role in shaping the character of the modern age. This realization came from the study of new historical data and from new theoretical insights which convinced him that the configuration of ideas that he was analyzing was far more complex than he had originally realized. He indicated, for example, that the influence of Renaissance Neoplatonism would now have to be re-evaluated in light of the work being done on its relation to magic and alchemy, and he published essays (1971, 1981) on magic and sorcery in the writings of Hegel and others. Voegelin's death in 1984 prevented him from making a thorough study of these other esoteric traditions. We know, however, from his lectures and from his research notes that he had a strong interest in the work on the Renaissance recovery of Hermeticism and related esoteric traditions.

The work in Renaissance studies and in the history of science that was most directly relevant to Voegelin's analysis of modernity focused on what is called the *prisca theologia,* or ancient wisdom, tradition. This *prisca theologia* tradition is a compendium of a wide array of esoteric religious and pseudoscientific traditions, including Orphism, Zoroastrianism, Hermetism, Kabbalah, alchemy, and magic. The term *prisca theologia,* which was used by Ficino (1433–99) and other theologians and philosophers of the Renaissance, reflects their opinion that these materials contained the pristine theological and philosophical revelations to the great wise men, the magi, of the ancient Near East and the Mediterranean.[2]

One of these Ancient Wisdom traditions, the Hermetic, was of particular interest. A clear indication of the high regard for Hermes Trismegistus is the fact that Ficino, the head of the Platonic Academy, set aside his work on newly acquired Platonic dialogues to analyze newly found Hermetic materials. The reason for giving primacy to Hermes Trismegistus was that he was believed to be the first in a series of ancient wise men who received revelations regarding the true nature of the world and of humanity's place in it (see Walker 1958, 1972).[3]

Scholarship on the *Corpus Hermeticum* has long recognized that it is a compendium of a wide range of materials—some radically dualistic, others intensely immanentistic. It has only fairly recently been recognized, however, that Ficino and other influential early modern thinkers concentrated on the highly optimistic, immanentist elements of the Hermetic tradition that portrayed man as a terrestrial god able to master nature and perfect society. I want to examine the optimistic, immanentist strands that profoundly affected Renaissance thought and show their similarities and differences with ancient Gnosticism. I want to make two points through this comparison: (1) the Hermetic materials are gnostic in the generic sense of having a doctrine of saving knowledge, but (2) the optimistic world view of the Hermetic materials is profoundly different from the pessimistic Gnostic view. To demonstrate that this is the case, I will briefly compare the features of ancient Gnosticism found in the "Hymn of the Pearl" with themes in the Hermetic creation story. The reason for choosing the "Hymn of the Pearl" is that there is general agreement that it is a representative Gnostic text. Equally important for our purposes, Hans Jonas uses it as the text to compare Gnosticism with modern existentialism and nihilism.

THE GNOSTIC "HYMN OF THE PEARL"

This text opens as follows:

> When I was a little child and dwelt in the kingdom of my Father's house and delighted in the wealth and splendor of those who raised me, my parents sent me forth from the East, our homeland, with provisions for the journey. From the riches of our treasure-house they tied me a burden: great it was, yet light, so that I might carry it alone. . . . They took off from me the robe of glory which in their love they had made for me, and my purple mantle that was woven to conform exactly to my figure, and made a covenant with me, and wrote it in my heart that I might not forget it: "When thou goest down into Egypt and bringest the One Pearl which lies in the middle of the sea which is encircled by the snorting serpent, thou shalt put on again thy robe of glory and thy mantle over it and with thy brother our next in rank be heir in our kingdom." (Jonas 1963, pp. 113–14)

The narrator then gives an account of his journey into Egypt. While in Egypt, he meets "one of my race" who warns against the Egyptians and "contact with the unclean ones." Despite his precaution, the Egyptians "ingratiated themselves with me, and mixed me [drink] with their cunning, and gave me to taste of their meat; and I forgot that I was a king's son and served their king. I forgot the Pearl for which my parents had sent me. Through the heaviness of their nourishment I sank into deep slumber" (Jonas 1963, p. 114).

This "ingratiation" is a trap deliberately sprung on the royal visitor by the Egyptians. The son's predicament causes great anxiety in his father's kingdom, and it is decided that all of the royal governors and officers of the land will prepare a letter and send it to the son, reminding him of his true nature and his real home.

Upon receipt of the message, the son remembers his royal origin and awakens from the slumber into which he had fallen. Immediately he sets out to recover the pearl and return home to his father's kingdom: "Their filthy and impure garment I put off, and left it behind in their land, and directed my way that I might come to the light of our homeland, the East" (Jonas 1963, p. 114). Upon his return, there is much joy that the pearl has been returned and that the son is safely home.

Even without being familiar with the specific Gnostic meaning of certain symbols, the thrust of this myth is clear. The king of kings is, of course, the supreme God. In attempting to recover the pearl, the son of God becomes trapped in matter and forgets his divine origin and mission. The pessimistic, dualistic view of the physical world is expressed in references to food and drink as the source of trickery, to the garments put on to be like the Egyptians as filthy, and to the consequences of the treachery as slumber and sleep walking. Myths of a great treasure lost in the dross of the world are a frequent component of dualistic religions and most often refer to the soul that becomes imprisoned in matter and that has to be rescued by divine action. This is the meaning here. Without explaining how the divine soul becomes entrapped, the myth nevertheless expresses entrapment as the fundamental condition. The effects of the material world are so strong that even God's son forgets his true nature and his real home.

HERMETIC VIEWS OF HUMAN NATURE: MAN AS A TERRESTRIAL GOD

The Hermetic text that Ficino was responsible for translating and introducing into the mainstream of modern thought was the

Pimander, which contains a creation myth often referred to as the "Egyptian Genesis." This compact but comprehensive myth is revealed after a spiritually restless Hermes has struggled to advance beyond normal sensory knowledge in order to gain a fuller and more complete understanding of reality. His efforts are rewarded by his being called into the presence of Pimander, "the mind of absolute sovereignty," who asks Hermes: "What do you want to hear and see; what do you want to learn and know?" Hermes replies: "I wish to learn about the things that are, to understand their nature, and to know god" (Copenhaver 1992, p. 1).

Pimander tells him that God created the Demiurge, who created the seven celestial Governors who encompass the world and whose rule is known as Fate. He is then told of Man's creation, which is by the Supreme God and not by the Demiurge: "But the Mind, the father of all, who is life and light, gave birth to a man like himself whom he loved as his own child. The man was most fair: he had the father's image. The father, who was really in love with his own form, bestowed on him all his handicrafts" (Copenhaver 1992, p. 3). When Man sees the creation of the Demiurge, he wants to participate in creation, and God the Father orders the celestial powers to teach Man how the cosmos was governed. After receiving knowledge and creative power from the cosmic sources, Man enters into the world of Nature and Matter:

> Having all authority over the cosmos of mortals and unreasoning animals, the man broke through the vault and stopped to look through the cosmic framework, thus displaying to the lower nature the fair form of god. Nature smiled for love when she saw him whose fairness brings no surfeit [and] who holds in himself all the energy of the governors and the form of god. . . . When the man saw the form like himself as it was in nature, he loved it and wished to inhabit it; wish and action came in the same moment, and he inhabited the unreasoning form. Nature took hold of her beloved, hugged him all about, and embraced him for they were lovers. (Copenhaver 1992, p. 3)

The narrator then explains the implications of this union for human nature: "Because of this, unlike any other living thing on earth, mankind is twofold—in the body mortal but immortal in the essential man. Even though he is immortal and has authority over all things, mankind is affected by mortality because he is subject to fate" (Copenhaver 1992, p. 3).

Later on, Pimander asks whether Hermes understands how death (loss of immortality) can be avoided, and Hermes replies that man must turn toward the light (knowledge/*nous*) because it is the essence of

God and the essence of man. But Hermes is still somewhat troubled. Don't all men possess god-given minds; are not all men capable of salvation? Pimander answers that "I myself, the mind, am present to the blessed and good and pure and merciful—to the reverent and my presence becomes a help. . . . But to these I remain distant—the thoughtless, and evil and wicked and envious and greedy and violent and irreverent—giving way to an avenging demon." Hermes then asks about the stages of the ascent to God and is told of the seven stages and of the final union with God: "This is the final good for those who have received knowledge: to be made god" (Copenhaver 1992, pp. 5–6). Pimander then commands Hermes to use what he has learned to save others from damnation.

Several important features emerge from this compact myth. First of all, the cosmogony makes the creation a work of beauty and harmony that is divinely inspired and maintained by celestial influences. The material world is not intrinsically evil or an inherent threat to man. On the contrary, Primal Man and Nature love each other. Admittedly, there are aspects of the world that are turned away from the divine influence and that retain the properties of the *prima materia*—viz., the tendency to dissolve or to revert to their original state as part of moist/humid Nature. Still, the world is a work of beauty and a suitable home for man, especially when he becomes actively involved in it. The explanation of man's loss of immortality makes it clear that the world is not inherently evil. For the man whose life is oriented toward the light (knowledge and God) the world is not a temptation or an obstruction. Only if man has turned from the light is he susceptible to the attraction of the flesh and inclined toward darkness (material existence). This pursuit of material pleasure is a willful choice; it is not the result of original sin or of the inherent evil in the world. The myth therefore stands in dramatic contrast to dualistic views of the tension between the flesh and the spirit, the secular and the sacred.

Another feature to note is the emphasis which the myth places on man's capacity for godlike knowledge and on knowledge as the means of salvation. At his creation God provides Man with the knowledge needed to exercise his role as a divine co-creator, and the myth contains repeated references to parallels between the divine *Nous* and man's *nous* and to the role of the *Logos* as the link among man, the creation, and the Supreme God.[4] Man becomes damned to a material existence only if he willfully ignores or denies the noetic dimension of his soul.

The *Aesclepius,* which Ficino regarded as the second divine book of Hermes Trismegistus, contains a section worthy of brief note because of its explanation of the problem of evil in the world. In the texts we have already examined, evil is not inherent in the world, and man is not flawed with original sin. Yet the *Aesclepius* warns that it is possible for humanity to become so disoriented that chaos and despair will consume the world. Egypt, the holy land where Hermes has served as priest-king, will be overrun by barbarians who will destroy the true religion; and the gods will leave the earth and go back to heaven, leaving only evil angels, who will goad men to commit every conceivable crime: "Then neither will the earth stand nor the sea be sailable; stars will not cross the heaven nor will the course of the stars stand firm in heaven. . . . The fruits of the earth will rot; the soil will no more be fertile; and the very air will droop with gloomy lethargy" (Copenhaver 1992, p. 83). The lament does not explain the origin of this time of troubles, except to say that it will occur when barbarians, who do not understand the true religion, overrun Egypt. Instead, the purpose of this passage is to provide reassurance that the condition is only temporary and that God will intervene to renew the world and man:

> Such will be the old age of the world, irreverence, disorder, disregard for everything good. When all this comes to pass, Asclepius, then the master and father, the god whose power is primary, governor of the first god, will look on this conduct and these willful crimes, and in an act of will— which is god's benevolence—he will take his stand against the vices and the perversion in everything, righting wrongs, washing away malice in a flood or consuming it in fire or ending it by spreading a pestilential disease everywhere. Then will he restore the world to its beauty of old so that the world itself will again seem deserving of worship and wonder, and with constant benedictions and proclamations of praise the people of that time will honor the god who makes and restores so great a work. And this will be the geniture of the world: a reformation of all good things and a restitution, most holy and most reverent, of nature itself, reordered in the course of time [but through an act of will] which is and was everlasting and without beginning. (Copenhaver 1992, pp. 39–40)

Here again, evil and disorder are not the permanent state of the world. They are temporary conditions that will be alleviated by divine redemption, which will turn the world again into paradise and restore man to his proper state. It is apparent that Ficino and other early modern thinkers believed themselves to be living at the beginning of the new age of light that would end the reign of darkness.

GNOSTIC PESSIMISM AND HERMETIC OPTIMISM

While the emphasis on saving knowledge parallels Gnosticism, Hermeticism's highly optimistic view stands in stark contrast. In the Gnostic myth, salvation—regaining one's divine station—depends on escaping from the world. In the Hermetic myth the world is necessary for mankind to exercise its divine creativity, and it is in the world that man creates the social microcosm that completes creation. The threat posed by the material world results not from its inherent evil but from human ignorance of the proper relation of the material and the divine. The two esoteric traditions also have very different understandings of the benefits of knowledge. In the Gnostic myth, knowledge frees humanity from an ignorant effort to find meaning and purpose in the world. In the Hermetic writings, knowledge enables humanity to master nature and perfect society—that is, to create a utopian existence.

Despite these fundamental differences, a sharp contrast between Gnosticism and Hermeticism has not usually been made. A.-J. Festugière, one of the most important early scholars of the *Corpus Hermeticum,* referred to it as Gnostic. His reason for doing so was that, as we have seen, the Hermetic texts regard right knowledge as the only means of salvation. But as we have also seen, the Hermetic materials contain a very different understanding of what is meant by salvation from the disorder of the world. Therefore to classify Hermeticism as Gnostic would mean that many esoteric traditions —e.g., Orphism, Pythagorianism, Zoroastrianism, and Kabbalah— would have to be placed under this broad rubric. To do so, however, obscures the characteristic differences that distinguish them.

Festugière attempted to deal with the differences between the Gnostic dread of the world and the Hermetic immanentism by distinguishing between optimistic and pessimistic forms of Hermeticism. But this attempt, which was subsequently introduced into Renaissance Hermetic studies by D. P. Walker and Frances Yates, only perpetuates the confusion, especially with regard to the parallels with modernity. We have seen, for example, that Hans Jonas identified the pessimistic, nihilistic elements of modernity with Gnosticism while Voegelin drew parallels between Gnosticism and the optimistic, utopian dreams of scientism and political revolution.

To avoid perpetuating this confusion, it is important to recognize that the themes that enter modern thought through Renaissance Neoplatonism/Hermeticism have a thrust profoundly different from those associated with ancient and modern Gnostic nihilism. Of course, in pleading for recognition of the Hermetic pattern in modern thought, I do not mean to discount the influence of Gnosticism as examined, for example, by Hans Jonas. Rather, my purpose is to argue that another mode of esoteric saving knowledge gains attention in the Renaissance and becomes part of a different pattern in modernity—one that emphasizes human dominance over nature and the transformation of the natural and social order into paradise. This pattern is crucial for analysts to explore because these elements of modernity are usually claimed to be derived from science and secularization and not from ancient esoteric religions and pseudoscience. Eric Voegelin opened the way into this productive field of inquiry, and work by Renaissance specialists makes it clear that the revival of Hermeticism in the Renaissance plays a key role in the development of modern utopian political ideologies and contributes to the modern belief that an epistemological breakthrough separates the new age from the past and equips modern humanity with the power to master nature and perfect society.

NOTES

1. Festugière (1949–54) and other scholars have, in fact, classified Hermeticism as a variety of Gnosticism. In the course of my analysis, I will explain why a differentiation is needed, especially with regard to the influence on modern patterns of thought.

2. For a discussion of the terms *prisca theologia* and *prisci theologi,* see Walker 1958 and 1972.

3. For a useful examination of this and other genealogies of the Ancient Wisdom developed by Ficino, see Walker 1954. In every instance Hermes is either first or second (following Zoroaster)—for example, in the *Theologia Platonica*—or contemporaneous with Zoroaster—for example, in the *Plotinus commentaries.*

4. The myth, like classical philosophy's concept of the cosmos, emphasizes the link between *Logos* as the source of order and *logos* as man's understanding of the ordering principles of creation.

REFERENCES

Blumenberg, Hans. 1983. *Legitimacy of the Modern Age,* tr. Robert Wallace. Cambridge, MA: MIT Press. A translation of the second revised edition of *Die Legitimität der Neuzeit* (1976).

Copenhaver, Brian. 1992. *Hermetica.* Cambridge: Cambridge University Press.

Festugière, A.-J. 1949–54. *La Révélation d'Hermès Trismégiste.* 4 vols. Paris: Librairie Lecoffe.

Jonas, Hans. 1963. *The Gnostic Religion* 2nd ed. Boston: Beacon.

Voegelin, Eric. 1952. *The New Science of Politics.* Chicago: University of Chicago Press.

———.1968. *Science, Politics and Gnosticism.* Chicago: Regnery.

———.1971. "On Hegel: A Study in Sorcery." *Studium Generale* 24:335–68.

———.1975. *From Enlightenment to Revolution.* Durham, NC: Duke University Press.

———.1981. "Wisdom and the Magic of the Extreme: A Meditation." *Southern Review,* N.S., 17:235–87.

Walker, D. P. 1954. "The Prisca Theologia in France." *Journal of the Warburg and Courtauld Institutes* 17:204–59.

———.1958. *Spiritual and Demonic Magic.* London: Routledge & Kegan Paul.

———.1972. *The Ancient Theology.* Ithaca, NY: Cornell University Press.

[11]

BETWEEN GNOSTICISM AND JEHOVAH: THE DILEMMA IN KAFKA'S RELIGIOUS ATTITUDE

Walter H. Sokel

K AFKA was certainly not religious in a conventional dogmatic sense. One of his few statements about God, for instance, suggests that belief in a personal God may be the cover under which man's faith in something indestructible in himself is concealed—a view which resembles Feuerbach's humanism rather than theistic religion.[1] Kafka views his lack of religion as symptomatic of his historical situation: "I have not been led into life like Kierkegaard by the already heavily drooping hand of Christianity and I have not, like the Zionists, still caught the last corner of the Jewish prayer shawl that is flying away. I am end or beginning" (H 121).

The great religions of the Western world themselves appear from this perspective as historical phenomena, not as absolute truths. Kafka mocks religion where, as in the case of his father's remnants of Judaism, it has been reduced to social convention and meaningless ritual. He found the obligatory visits to the synagogue of his childhood an occasion for boredom relieved by the comedy of the spectacle (H 197–98). Hugo Bergmann, Kafka's friend from his school days, attests to Kafka's inclination toward atheism and recalls that his own faith was threatened by Kafka's arguments against the existence of God (Bergmann 742)—arguments which Kafka himself also remembers in his diary. His strong and growing interest in Judaism, ever since the profound encounter with the Warsaw Yiddish Theater group in Prague in 1911, seems often more ethnically, morally, and existentially motivated rather than religious, a concern with rootedness in a communal way of life rather than with God.[2]

Nevertheless, if we take the term "religion" in a broader and deeper sense, then Kafka's very criticism of the conventionalized remnants of religion is in itself a sign of deep religious involvement. He took religion too seriously to have been satisfied with its involuntary self-mockery which the so-called "Yom Kippur Jews" of his social milieu represented. Similar to Kierkegaard, in this respect, Kafka would rather have no religion than its caricature.

The *religious* nature of Kafka's thinking and sensibility becomes clear if we look at one dominant explanation of the etymology of the word "religion." According to this etymology, the Latin word *religio* originally signified a holding or a tying back, a restraint, or a bond and denoted a sense of absolute obligation and dependence. In Kafka's case, such *religio* manifests itself as his sense of living under absolute laws which obligated him in his deepest being but remained incomprehensible to his rational understanding. The following aphorism articulates this sense of personal duty to an unknown superpersonal power:

> He does not live because of his personal life; he does not think because of his personal thoughts. It seems to him as though he were living and thinking under the compulsion of a family which in its own right, to be sure, had superabundance of life and thought, but for which he, according to a law unknown to him, represents a formal necessity. Because of that unknown family and those unknown laws, he cannot be released. (B 283)

Kafka's basic *religio* is a sense of responsibility to an unknown collectivity.

What complicates this case enormously is the duality of Kafka's laws. Kafka confronts not one law, but two, each absolute in its demand. These two absolutes stand in radical opposition to each other. Compliance with one violates the other, so that guilt is inescapable. If *religio* means "bond" or "bind," then one can speak in Kafka's case of a "double bind" in the most literal sense (Bateson et al. 251–64). This double bind works on all levels—psychological, ethical, metaphysical, salvational. Kafka describes someone who is bound around the neck by two chains which are fastened at opposite points, one on earth, the other in heaven:

> . . . Now, when he desires to move down toward earth, the necklace of heaven strangles him, and when he desires [to raise himself toward] heaven, the earthly chain strangles him. And yet he possesses all possibilities and feels them; indeed, he refuses to attribute the whole dilemma to a mistake at the original chaining. (H 46–47)

It would be misleading to see this double-bind in terms of a conflict merely between the religious and the worldly dimensions of the self. For the earthly chain has itself the force of *religio.* It constitutes an absolute law for Kafka which contradicts the other absolute that Kafka locates in heaven. In documents from Kafka's life this double-bind manifests itself as a conflict between two ways of life which are also absolute moral responsibilities for him. To bring it down to its essential character, the contradiction which rends him asunder inheres in the Judeo-Christian tradition from its beginnings. It derives from God's contradictory position to the world and the moral double-bind that follows from it. Let us then begin from the beginning, the book of Genesis, which had a particular significance for Kafka.

This paradox within the God of Genesis lies in His double nature. He is a god of immanence, creator and ruler of the universe. But He is also a god of transcendence, who stands outside His world, unrecognized by it, an unknown God to all except a select few of His creatures. He is a stranger to a world that He Himself has made. He re-enters this world only by making the Covenant with a special individual, Abraham, and his descendants.

I propose to call the moment of God's utmost estrangement from His world, prior to the Covenant with Abraham, the proto-Gnostic phase or aspect of God. For, at this moment in Genesis, between the Tower of Babel and Abraham, a possibility of religious thought emerges which will eventually lead to Christianity and culminate in Gnosticism. In Gnosticism, the transcendent strain of Judaism was to unite with Greek and Iranian dualisms at the beginning of our era. The Gnostic hypostatized one side of the Jewish paradox and eliminated the other. God for the Gnostic is pure transcendence. He dwells forever beyond this world, an eternal stranger to it, and is neither its creator nor its ruler. The cosmos is the handiwork of inferior beings, of a jealous Demiurge called Jehovah, of petty gods or demons, or else it is a delusion, the result of a fall, the self-estrangement of God from Himself. To those who are smitten by the inkling of true divinity, this physical universe is a huge prison. They turn away from this world, while condemned to live in it, and strain toward another life, a life unlike anything known here. Followers of an Alien God, they are sharers of a hidden knowledge, and therefore called Gnostics or "the knowing ones."

Judaism itself was preserved from developing its Gnostic potential by the idea of the Covenant. With Jehovah's pact with Abraham and Abraham's descendants a counter-movement to pure transcendence sets in, from which Judaism proper results. Judaism is a synthesis between the Edenic or immanent aspect of God and His transcendent or proto-Gnostic aspect. Even after the Covenant, God remains outside His creation. He is not domiciled in nature; He is not immanent in His cosmos. Yet, in another sense, He does dwell in it potentially, by virtue of His covenant with His chosen people. In and through the stream of generations of the Hebrew people, God lives toward a future in which the world will be entirely His again. This confluence of immanent and transcendent phase constitutes the properly Judaic concept of God.

This paradox that resides in the Judaic God entails a moral *aporia,* an ethical double-bind, for the individual Jew. God's demand and expectation confront the Jew with the same paradox which, as Kierkegaard saw, characterizes the existence of Abraham. To heed the call of God, the natural man, Abram, had to become the new man, Abraham. Abraham had to abandon his native home, his family, his natural world, and move toward a strange land to live as a stranger. He was to move in the Gnostic direction, out of and away from the familiar world. By the same token, however, he had to move back into this world, reconnect with nature, found a family, establish a home, fill the world with his seed. Following in Abraham's footsteps, the Jew, partner of a transcendent God, is to stand apart from the natural world of the gentiles. At the same time, he is to do God's bidding by means of nature. Procreating by the flesh, he is to serve and fulfill a promise of spirit.

The paradox within Judaism was fought out to an extraordinary degree of intensity in Kafka's life and work. Salvation lay for Kafka in two opposite directions—continuity of and apartness from earthly life. The continuity of past and future was for him, as an early dialogue in his diary makes clear, a circle of time in which the self is sheltered as long as it can stay within it (T 17–24). This feeling of the saving power of continuity received concrete content in the overwhelming impact which the Yiddish Theater exerted on him. Yiddish culture revealed to him the warmth and inner wealth on which a collective life, drawing sustenance from roots in the remote past, could thrive. In this continuous, ethnic-spiritual identity, Judaic religion revealed itself to Kafka in its most basic and archetypal form. What Kafka longed for, but found lacking in his own family, was revealed to him in the encounter with the extended family of Jewish people who seemed to live in still-unbroken connection with their distant origin. His diary of 1911 and 1912 shows Kafka elated and fascinated by the discovery of this "circle of blood"—his term for the continuity between father and son (T 296). But as a thoroughly estranged Western Jew, he found it impossible to enter the circle himself.

The only way in which, at least at this time, he could conform to the Judaic law was to marry and to found a family of his own. "A man without a wife is not human," he quoted the Talmud in his diary (T 174). The Talmudic inveighing against bachelorhood and child-lessness merely confirmed Kafka's own original guilt toward life which he felt he had incurred because of his natural tendency toward solitude and separateness which the demands of his writing rein-forced. The relationship to Felice, which lasted for five years, led to two engagements, and played an enormous role for his work, followed almost immediately upon the experience of the Yiddish Theater. Felice represented a test case for Kafka. His "judgment" that here was *his* challenge, was made the first time he met her (T 285). It was a "judgment" on the fundamental question: "Can I connect with Judaism on its deepest level and take my place, as a Jew must, in the chain of generations which bind the Jew in partnership to his God, who is a God of life and its promise on earth?" But the overwhelming power of Kafka's Gnostic sensibility proved to be the decisive obstacle to fulfilling Jehovah's commandment, at least at this point in his life.

Kafka seemed to have been familiar with Gnostic thought both directly and indirectly. According to Klaus Wagenbach's list of the volumes of Kafka's personal library, he owned Walter Köhler's book on Gnosticism, and he also seemed to be very interested in Jewish religion at the time of Jesus (Wagenbach 262–63), in which the origins of important strains of Gnosticism have to be looked for. Gnosticism was, as the recent discoveries of Nag Hammadi have shown, in essential respects an outgrowth of Judaic origin (Rudolph 36–38). The Gnostics formed an important part of the reception which the Old Testament found in late Hellenistic and Roman times. The Holy Book of Judaism served as a point of reference, a background against which the Gnostics were able to highlight their deviations (Rudolph 79, 81, 102, 111–112, 140, 148). Even their antagonism reveals their indebtedness. Gnosticism, in turn, left a lasting imprint on the Judaism from which it had sprung. As Gershom Scholem has shown, strong echoes of Gnosticism are found in the Kabbalah and other sources of Jewish mysticism (35, 49–50, 260–77). "Gnostic myth, and not history, provided the extra strength that Jewish memory needed for Jewry to survive its latest catastrophe" (Bloom 23–24). These words of Harold Bloom do not refer to the Holocaust, but to the expulsion of the Jews from Spain at the beginning of the modern era, and to the consequences of this event for the development of the Kabbalah in Palestine.

This close connection between Gnosticism and important trends within Judaism is of the greatest importance for understanding the Gnostic strain in Kafka.[3] Kafka's strong interest in the sources of the Jewish past, his growing preoccupation with the Kabbalah and Jewish mysticism, reinforced the Gnostic sensibility and predisposition that had been deeply implanted in his outlook and character long before he became acquainted with direct and indirect sources of Gnostic thought.[4] Much more decisive than external "influences," however, are the kinship and parallelism in patterns of interpreting life and the world that link Kafka to Gnosticism from the beginning of his writing, and long before we can detect any evidence of his acquaintance with the historic phenomenon of Gnosticism. We are faced here with a case analogous to the astounding parallelism prevailing between the narrative structure of Kafka's fiction and Freud's theory of human life (Sokel, "Freud," 145–58).

To be sure, Kafka's close relationship to Gnostic thinking is not a unique case in our century. We can speak of a powerful revival of Gnostic sensibility in the twentieth century, after Gnosticism had become a subject of historical scholarship which made its doctrines available to the broader public. For in Gnosticism of the Hellenistic and Roman world, the modern phenomenon of alienation first appeared in human history. This explains the intense appeal of Gnostic ideas to our time. Hans Jonas in his book, *The Gnostic Religion,* has pointed out striking analogies between Gnostic and existential thought. Any study of the revival of Gnostic ideas would have to include August Strindberg, Otto Weininger, C. G. Jung, Hermann Hesse (Quispel, "Hesse, Jung," 241–58), Oskar Kokoschka, Hans Henny Jahnn, Antonin Artaud, Robert Musil, and above all, Franz Kafka. Harold Bloom has found Gnosticism even in Norman Mailer's *Ancient Evenings.*

Kafka's exceptionally developed Gnostic sensibility resided in two factors: in his writing, and in his ingrained abhorrence not only of sexuality—"coitus" was, he said, "the punishment of the happiness of being together"—but all reminders of the material and sensory nature of human beings. Very much in the Gnostic vein, Kafka perceived life as imprisonment, and death as liberation. The wish to die was for him the dawn of a "knowledge" which corresponded exactly to the meaning which the Gnostics gave to the term (Rudolph 126, 130–31). It is the kind of knowledge that sees through the illusion which earthly, corporeal, individuated life represents:

> A first sign of beginning knowledge is the wish to die. This life seems unbearable, another life unattainable. One is no longer ashamed of wanting to die; one asks to be taken out of the old prison cell which one hates and to be brought to a new one which one will learn to hate. But in this wish there also glimmers a remnant of faith that during the transport the Lord will perchance pass by, look at the prisoner and say: "This one you shall not lock up again." (H 40)

This aphorism of Kafka's reproduces the exact structure of a particular sect of Gnostic religion. Marcion preached that an Alien God has gratuitously taken pity on the poor prisoners in Jehovah's cosmic jail and sent Christ into this world to liberate those who would heed His call of pure compassion (von Harnack; Jonas 137–45). To be sure, in Kafka, liberation is not knowledge, Gnosis, but only belief in a perhaps remote possibility. Knowledge in Kafka's case is purely negative. Knowledge sees the worthlessness of this life and the unattainability of any other.

Yet in contrast to Schopenhauerian pessimism,[5] there is in Kafka frequently the supposition or conjecture of another world, another life, or at least another standpoint from which the thoroughly distressing picture which earthly life presents might appear quite different:

> Viewed by earthly clouded eyes, we are in the situation of railroad passengers who have suffered an accident in a tunnel at a spot where one can no longer see the light from the entrance, while the light from the exit is so faint that the eyes of the passengers must make a constant effort and yet constantly lose sight of it; and, to top it all, neither entrance nor exit are certain. (H 73)[6]

Implied is the possibility that an unclouded, unearthly, and therefore truer vision would see the light, and know that a world exists outside the tunnel. From such a well-nigh Platonic perspective it would appear that

> Only down here is suffering suffering. This is not to be understood as an assertion that those who suffer here shall be raised elsewhere on account of their sufferings, but only in the sense that what is called suffering in this world is bliss in another world, without undergoing any change and merely freed from its opposite. (H 51)

Kafka's dualism is one of two diametrically opposed ways of being and experiencing, which frequently seems to hide behind the more traditional dualistic image of two worlds.[7]

The origin of this dualism and the positing of a higher and truer world or state of being than the one known to the earthly eye seems to lie in Kafka's perception and experience of writing. In an interview with the theosophist Rudolf Steiner in 1911, which Kafka recorded in his diary, Kafka asserts to have experienced in literature "states (not many) which in my opinion are very close to the clairvoyant states described by you [Dr. Steiner] . . . in which I felt not only at my own limits, but at the frontiers of the human altogether" (T 57). Kafka describes his writing, or rather his experiences of writing, frequently in terms customarily reserved for religion. It would exceed the limits of this paper to show the religious nature of the language with which Kafka depicted everything pertaining to his writing. Part of Kafka's poetics provides a fine example of what Hegel calls "the Religion of Art" (490–520). To be sure, Hegel had the Greeks in mind when he coined the term, while Kafka's concern with writing represents what I should like to call, in the terms of the dichotomy of styles that Erich Auerbach develops in *Mimesis,* the Hebrew variant of *Kunstreligion.* Auerbach's distinction between the mimetic, visual relationship of the Homeric style to physical reality and the auditory hearkening posture with which the biblical style refers to man's relationship to an invisible, inward reality is extremely relevant to Kafka. The Hebrew God manifests Himself not by images, but by the voice, and by the call. The call from beyond the world is also a fundamental theme of Gnosticism; it is the call that awakens us (Rudolph 137). Kafka, in whose work the call is a fundamental structural principle as well as a primary theme, obviously conforms to Auerbach's biblical type (Sokel, "Kafka's Poetics," 37–38). The exclusiveness with which literature fills Kafka and requires him to live in its service provides striking analogies to the demands God made on Abraham. Kafka, too, feels commanded to estrange himself from his family and indeed from all worldly concerns—his job, women, friends, and so on—in order to devote himself to an absolute task which fills him as completely as God wants His chosen ones to be filled by Him.

But, while alienating him completely from the world that he knows, writing opens another world to him. This strange unknown world dwells in his depths. It is inchoate, immaterial, indescribable. Only writing provides an approach to it, which, however, must remain mere allusion and the barest of hints.[8] Kafka is able to say of it only *that* it is, that it dwells inside him, urging to be revealed. For this task of revelation he must sacrifice his life. It is a task which, in its absoluteness, can only be described as holy. He feels that for the "uncertain liberation" of this inner world, a hammer might be needed that would smash *him* to pieces (T 321). His destruction would then be the birth of the "enormous world . . . in [his] head" (T 306). In a sense, Kafka stands in relation to his writing as Abraham and Isaac combined stand in relation to God. The sacrifice which *his* divinity (literature) demands of *its* "Abraham," Kafka, is his own life: "The enormous world which I have in my head. But how to release myself and how to release it without being torn to pieces. But rather be torn to pieces a thousand times than to hold it back in me or to bury it. For this task I exist; that is completely clear to me" (T 306).

What distinguished Kafka's *Kunstreligion* from the aestheticism fashionable in his youth was this religious dimension. Kafka's religion of literature was service in the cause of a world, strange and yet more real, deeper, truer, purer, more alive than anything experienced in empirical existence.

In the meditations and the aphorisms of his *Oktavhefte* of 1917/18, Kafka transformed the deep and inner world of his writing experience into a realm more akin to the higher world of traditional dualistic religion and metaphysics. A religion of art became an art of religious and metaphysical thinking which, far from constituting a system, must, in keeping with the tradition of the aphorism from Lichtenberg to Nietzsche and Karl Kraus, be seen as a series of stabs into, or momentary flashing points of contact with, a truth that can never be grasped, let alone formulated, in its totality.[9] "Truth is indivisible. It therefore cannot know itself. He who claims to know it must be a lie" (H 48).

In such an approach to truth, contradictions are essential. Thought that harbors contradictions comes closer to the infinite truth than the attempt to systematize neatly, and resolve or eliminate contradiction. Given the infinite discrepancy between the individual mind and the totality that is truth, any appearance of consistency is a symptom of what Kafka calls the cardinal sin of man, impatience—"a premature discontinuation of the methodical, an apparent fencing in of an apparent subject matter" (H 39). The meditations and aphorisms of the *Oktavhefte* in which Kafka's religious thought is most overtly expressed still belong to art, not to discursive reasoning. They are a different genre in the same body of writing to which his narrative fiction belongs.

The step from the religion of writing to the Gnostic dualism of the meditations and aphorisms can be followed in the way in which the absolute demand made by literature tends to strengthen Kafka's natural disposition to experience the world as a prison, a place of intolerable confinement, frustration, disruption, and estrangement.[10] The constant interruptions with which family, profession, and human relationships in general frustrate his writing, stealing precious moments from what should have been a perennial task, the noises of the world that interfered with concentration, and above all the conflict between the need to write and the long hours of office duty force a duality upon his life, dividing it between the true life away from the world and the false one within it. This divided self is the background for the emergence of a dualistic world view.

In the "Meditations," Kafka projects dualism into the heart of the Judeo-Christian tradition. His retelling of the story of Eden and the Fall is a reinterpretation of the Edenic myth from a dualistic, Gnostic perspective. For Kafka changes the expulsion from Paradise from a temporal event to a spatial separation. He posits the possibility of the continued existence of Paradise, and of our own continued residence in it, even while we live banished from it in the world:

> The expulsion from paradise is in its main portion eternal: That is, the expulsion from paradise is final; life in the world is unavoidable; but the eternity of the event (or expressed in temporal terms, the eternal repetition of the event) makes it possible nonetheless, not only that we might be living permanently in paradise, but that we actually are continuing to live there, regardless of whether we are aware of it here or not. (H 46)

Thus two worlds, or rather two forms of being, exist side by side. One is paradisiacal, the other is earthly. This duality is not merely one of two worlds or two distinct states of being. It resides in each of us as a split between our earthly and our heavenly nature, as beautifully expressed in this aphorism about the duality of love: "Sensuous love deludes us about heavenly love; it would be incapable of doing this by itself; but since it contains the element of heavenly love unconsciously within itself, it is able to do it" (H 48). Every one of us is a citizen of two universes. We live in Paradise and in the fallen world simultaneously. But, exactly as in Gnosticism, this knowledge may be, and usually is, hidden from man so that he lives unaware of his true nature and residence. The recognition that our sensuous existence is a state of self-alienation is precisely what gnosis means.

Such a dualistic anthropology is the means by which Kafka is able to universalize his double-bind. The double-bind appears in the "Meditations" as every human being's dual citizenship in a heavenly and an earthly world. Man's fall is the fall into the split existence. If man had stayed in Paradise, he would have remained unified and one with himself. This unity is what Kafka calls life.

The world view expressed in Kafka's "Octave Notebooks" of the Zürau period becomes most precisely analogous to the thinking of Gnosticism through the fact that, in both, the apparent dualism reveals itself as ultimate monism (Rudolph 65). In his Zürau writings, Kafka attempted an "experiment." Here, for once, he attempted to overcome the dualism in his own existence. During his whole life he had suffered the emotional and spiritual strangulation which two equally powerful, but contradictory demands performed on him. He tried to free himself from the double-bind of the two chains by resolutely giving sole allegiance to the one anchored in heaven. He did not succeed. The earthly absolute pulled him back; the strangulation persisted. However, the attempt of breaking loose toward the heavenly pole left us the unique genre in his *oeuvre,* the Gnostic meditations of the Zürau period.

In them, Kafka, like the Gnostics, assigned absolute primacy to the spiritual world over the sensory one: "There is nothing but a spiritual world; what we call the sensory world is the evil in the spiritual one . . ." (H 44). In the light of this aphorism, no reading of Kafka which seeks to view him as a Manichaean can be convincing (Heller 223). For while Manichaeism sees two autonomous principles—light and darkness, spirit and matter, good and evil—engaged in mortal combat, Kafka, in this aphorism, views the one as lodged in the other. Of all forms of Gnosticism, the Valentinian or Syro-Egyptian variety possesses the greatest relevance for Kafka. For in it, evil emerges within the good and the material world is the delusion of spirit. For the Valentinian Gnosis, the material universe is the result of the fall of divinity into self-estrangement. The main difference between this type of Gnosis and Judeo-Christian religion lies in the radically different view of the relationship between Creation and the Fall. According to Valentinian Gnosis, our world owes its being not to the free, beneficent act of God, but to His seduction which embroiled Him in matter. It is not the Fall of man, but the Fall of God that forms the point of origin of the historical world. In the words of Hans Jonas, it is

The distinguishing principle of the [Syro-Egyptian] type [of Gnosis] . . . to place the origin of darkness, and thereby of the dualistic rift of being, *within* the godhead itself, and thus to develop the divine tragedy, the necessity of salvation arising from it, and the dynamics of this salvation itself, as wholly a sequence of inner-divine events. Radically understood, this principle involves the task of deriving not only such spiritual facts as passion, ignorance, and evil but the very nature of *matter* in its contrariety to the spirit from the prime spiritual source: its very existence is to be accounted for in terms of the divine history itself. (Jonas 174)

The history of the cosmos is understood as a "defection" of God from Himself, as His self-fragmentation and exile into the world of corporeal individuation, and as a gradual remembering and return to Himself through the process of seeing through and recognizing the material world for what it is: the self-estrangement of divine reality, the "error and failure" of the godhead, the evil lodged within it (Jonas 175; Rudolph 93, 132–133).

Kafka's special interest, as that of the Gnostics, was devoted to the book of Genesis, and in it, to Paradise and the Fall. Many of his aphorisms concern themselves with these parts of the Judaic narrative. However, the above-quoted aphorism about the sensory world being the evil in the spiritual one points to a fall totally different from the sin of Adam and Eve as described in Genesis. Kafka's aphorism identifies the creation of our sensory world with evil. That which has made our world is the evil that inheres in spirit. The Fall thus appears conditioned by the divine itself. Finding evil in the bosom of the spiritual itself, Kafka stands infinitely closer to Gnosticism than to the Bible. His aphorism hints at a fall much more radical than the mere act of disobedience of the ancestral pair of mankind. What Kafka shares with Gnosticism, and what separates both from Genesis, is the view of evil as self-estrangement rather than rebellion. Evil, and with it the cosmos, is the self-defection of the divine.

It is this view of divine self-betrayal that moves Kafka so uncannily close to Gnosticism. For what predisposes him toward this particular Gnostic perspective is not only the split in the self between two contradictory demands, each of absolute validity, but also the radical division in the source of the law, the split in the father figures, power figures, and God figures of his life and work.

This split appears in its clearest form where the father figure first emerges in Kafka's work—in the early fragment, "Urban World," of February 1911. There a father heaps violent abuse upon his son, Oskar. The son rejects his father's accusations indignantly. His protest culminates in this exclamation in which we can see an important seed of Kafka's Gnostic attitude: "This is not my father who speaks to me in this way. Since noon something has changed you or you are an alien whom I meet in my father's room for the first time. My real father—he would have had to embrace me . . ." (T 49). In this distinction between a "real" or true father who is absent, and a false and "alien" father who is present, resides a dualistic structure which closely corresponds to the Gnostic concept of divinity. To be sure, here it still appears in the biographical-psychological framework of the realist convention of fiction, and it receives biographical corroboration from Kafka's "Letter to his Father." Kafka discerns a very similar incongruity in his own father, who, Kafka claims, never adhered to the commandments he himself had laid down:

> When I was a child everything you commanded was practically a commandment from Heaven for me. I never forgot it. It remained the most important means for judging the world and especially for judging you; and there you were found wanting utterly. . . . You, the immeasurably important lawgiver, did not adhere to the commandments you yourself had imposed on me. (H 172–73)

Kafka's language alludes to the close connection, typical of him, between the autobiographical-psychological and the religious sphere. His metaphors import heaven and the Decalogue into the family dining room of his childhood. The "jokes" about his father, exchanged between Kafka and his sister Ottla, he calls "jokes of the kind one spreads about gods and kings" (H 81). His mythologizing of his father points toward a dualism which also inheres in the Gnostic concept of the divine.

If there is anything all Gnostic sects and religions hold in common, it is the doctrine of the two Gods, the true God and the false one, or the upper and the lower, the pure and the fallen aspect of divinity. The heavenly commandment of Kafka's father corresponds to the true and supreme God of the Gnostics. Kafka sees this heavenly commandment as an absolute which makes it possible for him to judge his actual father's failure to live up to himself and his own law. We find here a close analogy to the Gnostic division of divinity into a true and supreme spirit of pure luminosity, whom some Gnostic texts call "the Father," and into the inferior powers that have made this world of imperfection and rule over it. The Gnostic is enabled to judge and reject the inadequacy of cosmic reality because he possesses the knowledge, the gnosis, of the true "father," who is the substance of light and spirit, and the absolute measuring yard for all else. Thus we find in Kafka's view of the paternal figure of his life and in the Gnostic concept of divinity a closely parallel structure of contradiction between essence and actuality. The actuality of this life flies in the face of what the "essence" or the law, the heavenly commandment of the true "father," makes his creature, respectively his son, expect. The Gnostic imagination holds divine perfection contradicted and mocked by the way things are. Instead of attributing the discrepancy, in the manner of the mainstream Judeo-Christian tradition, to human sin and the Fall of man, the Gnostic separates the two aspects of God—perfection and power—and distributes them over two radically different gods or groups of divine beings. Kafka's image of his father and the Gnostic idea of divinity have this in common: in both cases the power that rules the actual world is false or has fallen away from itself, while that which is true has become remote from and ineffectual in actual life.

This Gnostic duality can be demonstrated in all the father figures as well as those of power and authority in Kafka's works and constitutes an essential feature of it. Three years before the aphorisms of the Zürau period, Kafka gave one of the most memorable poetic formulations to it in the doorkeeper parable, "Before the Law," which he inserted into his novel *The Trial.* The law, the highest goal of human yearning, corresponds to the supreme divinity which the Gnostics call "the father" and equate with the substance of light. This connection can be seen in Kafka's parable in "the radiance that streams inextinguishably from the door of the Law." The doorkeeper of Kafka's parable, on the other hand, stands in a direct line of descent from his archetype whom we first encounter in Gnostic texts,[11] and then, under the strong influence of Gnostic sources, in Jewish Merkaba mysticism (Politzer 182–83). He belongs to the so-called Archontes or Aeons, or "Powers" that have created the sensory world and keep it enslaved. They block man's access to his true home and destination. If man wishes to reach the true God, he must see through the works of the powers and doorkeepers, and overcome them.

The Gnostic duality of law and doorkeeper becomes in Kafka's aphorisms and meditations of the Zürau period an aporia of the divine. On the one hand, God is here identical with the "spiritual world" to which man's essence, the indestructible core in him, also belongs. Thus God is essentially identical with the core of man. On the other hand, Kafka speaks of God's "raging against the human family." Obviously, Kafka's idea of God in the aphorisms is not unitary, and the strange contradiction in it closely corresponds to Gnostic dualism.

In the Coptic-Gnostic text, "Treatise without a Title," man's expulsion from Paradise is caused by the jealous "powers" of the cosmos who feel threatened by Adam. They wish to keep him from the tree of life because his eating from it would make him immortal and thus equal to them.[12] Analogously Kafka says about the Fall: "Why do we lament original sin [*Sündenfall*]? We have not been driven out of Paradise because of it, but because of the tree of life so that we should not eat of it" (H 99). Like the Gnostics, Kafka, in this aphorism, pronounces man free of guilt for his loss of Paradise. Not because of his sin did man lose Paradise, but because he was to be kept from the tree of life. The implication is that God begrudges man eternal life. He keeps man from life as the doorkeeper in the parable keeps the man from the country from entering the law. As in Gnosticism, man appears here as a guiltless victim of a power that is intent on keeping its monopoly.

Both Kafka and the Gnostic text derive their heterodox interpretation of the Fall directly from Genesis. God drives Adam from Paradise with this argument: "Behold the man is become as one of us, to know good and evil; and now, lest he put forth his hand, and take also of the tree of life, and eat, and live for ever: Therefore the Lord God sent him forth from the garden of Eden, to till the ground from whence he was taken" (Genesis 3.22).

The Gnostics cannot reconcile their exalted idea of true divinity with such petty jealousy and fear of rivalry. Therefore they divorce the true and highest God from Jehovah's behavior and motivation and attribute these to lower divinities, the "Archontes" or "powers." In fact, the Gnostics interpret man's expulsion from Paradise as a hostile act of the cosmic "powers" against the true God. The true God stands on man's side and encourages him to acquire knowledge.

Kafka's dualism appears as a duality in God Himself. God's true nature may be infinitely good; however, He has bad moods. In a conversation that was recorded by Max Brod, Kafka said that ". . . our world is only a bad mood of God, a bad day of his" (Benjamin 116). He continued, "[there is] plenty of hope, an infinite amount of hope—but not for us." From the context of this conversation, it appears that Kafka's dualism is not essentially different from that of the Gnostics of whom Brod was immediately reminded. To be sure, Kafka denies that his view of the world as one of the "nihilistic thoughts, the suicidal thoughts that come into God's head" was to be equated with the "Gnostic view of life," in which God is "the evil Demiurge" and "the world [is] his Fall." Kafka denies the permanence of God's fall and emphasizes the temporary character of His self-defection. There is "infinite hope" for God, who will pass again from His bad to His good mood. However, from the human perspective, the result is as dismal as though God had permanently fallen. There is no hope "for us," no hope for this temporal universe that, as an emanation of God's self-destructiveness, can never free itself from that evil which forms its essence. In the finite time that is our cosmos, God's destructive and self-hating side is all we get to know.

As for the Gnostics, there exists for Kafka another God who is completely different from the tyrant who rages against the human family. This God is not a ruler. He is no doorkeeper, no power figure excluding man from entering his sphere. He is the indestructible in man himself, man's real God, who is one with man as Oskar, the hero of Kafka's early fragment, "Urban World," thinks himself to be one with his "real" father, whom he cannot recognize in his accuser.

The essential identity between God and man, which connects Valentinian Gnosticism[13] with Hegelian philosophy, also forms the best base from which to approach this aspect of Kafka's idea of God as it appears in the Octave notebooks: "We are separated from God on two sides. The fall separates us from Him; the tree of life separates Him from us" (H 101). But the life which separates God from us is also in us. Kafka makes it very clear that this God is not a superhuman person different from man's essence: "Man cannot live without a permanent trust in something indestructible in himself. But both the indestructible and his trust in it may be permanently hidden from him. One of the ways by which this concealment is expressed is belief in a personal God" (H 44). Belief in a personal God is man's blindness to the indestructible in himself. We cannot think of this God as an individual, even as we cannot think of the indestructible within man as identical with the individual soul: "The indestructible is one; it is each single human being and, at the same time, it is common to all men; from it follows the uniquely inseparable connectedness of human beings" (H 47).

Kafka's thought seems to suggest a startling resemblance to the atheistic anthropology of the Hegelian Ludwig Feuerbach. Faith in a personal God masks our true belief in the unity and divinity of mankind. But such an equation of Kafka with Feuerbach would distort Kafka's thought. For Kafka's faith in the indestructible is not the faith of left Hegelian humanism in the unique value of mankind's "species being." Rather, it is trust in man's participation in that eternity which is the indestructible, and in that indivisibility which Kafka calls "truth." Again the analogy with Gnosticism may help us to understand Kafka's thought. According to Valentinian Gnosticism, God's self-estrangement fragmented Him into innumerable individual sparks of spirit or "pneuma." These "pneumatic" sparks are imprisoned in the visible walls of the flesh of human beings and the invisible walls which enclose and isolate each psyche. But the imprisoned sparks of pneuma hidden in human beings are fallen particles of God, literally one with Him, and thus with each other. They are scattered, isolated fragments of the unitary and divine substance.[14] To recognize them in ourselves is to recognize our own indestructible essence and, at the same time, to discover the essential oneness of all spiritual life.

Like Valentinian Gnosticism, Kafka believes in the fundamental oneness of spiritual existence. Such a faith differs radically from the biblical belief in the personhood of God and the creatureliness of man. Biblical faith sees man and God as different from each other as the creature is different from its creator. There cannot be identity between God and man; there can only be bonds relating separate individuals to each other through obedience, partnership, judgment, love. Kafka, like Valentinian Gnosticism, by contrast, sees the multiplicity of the sensory world not as the fruit of creativeness, but as the result of delusion. Individuated existence follows the self-estrangement of original unity. Individual man is "the failure" of the divine.

The idea of divine self-estrangement explains the contradiction in Kafka's concept of God. God in His fallen state, God divided from His own law and essence, appears as the anxious and arbitrary ruler who, like an Oedipal father, fears man as his rival and cuts him off from eternal life. But God, in His true being, is this eternal life. He is the indestructible unity which embraces man, in which man is one with God. These two aspects of God seem so radically different that nothing appears to be able to reconcile them.

So far I have dealt with only one side of a dichotomy. Next to Gnostic Dualism, there is in Kafka an equally, or perhaps even more profound and powerful, component of something much closer to traditional Judaism—something corresponding to the "earthly chain" of the literal "double-bind" with which we began our discussion. At no time, not even in the "Meditations" of the Zürau period, in which Kafka's Gnostic sensibility seems to assume absolute ascendancy, is Jehovah's demand on the earthly, historical, ethnic, and ethical existence of the individual Jew completely absent. What connects Kafka with traditional Judaism is also that which, in important respects, sets him apart from Gnosticism. In two factors above all can we see a fundamentally anti-Gnostic, traditionally Judaic side of Kafka: in his radical devaluation of knowledge— *Erkenntnis* or gnosis—which causes him to interpret the Fall in some aphorisms in a much more traditional manner than in the aphorisms we have discussed here; and in his conviction that action alone can realize and indeed redeem knowledge. In other words, gnosis or the cognitive is for Kafka subordinate to the practical, moral, and existential dimension of man. Space does not permit elaboration of these distinctions here; such an elaboration must be postponed for subsequent exploration.*

NOTES

1. This article was delivered as a lecture at the 1983 SAMLA Convention on 29 October.

Kafka's works will be referred to by the following abbreviations: H = *Hochzeitsvorbereitungen;* T = *Tagebücher;* B = *Beschreibung.* All translations from Kafka's works are my own.

2. For the most detailed treatment of Kafka's encounter with the Warsaw Yiddish Theater, see Beck.

3. On the Jewish foundations of Gnosticism, see particularly Wilson, especially 71–75 and 123; see also Quispel, "Der gnostische Anthropos," 195–97. The discoveries of the Coptic-Gnostic texts at Nag Hammadi are of supreme importance for the illumination of the indebtedness of Gnosticism to Judaism. See Rudolph 40–57. Because of the rich documentary yield of these excavations, "the part played by Jewish tradition and ideas in the genesis of gnosticism . . . can be shown even more clearly and persuasively [than before]" (Rudolph 157).

4. See the important and informative study by Hoffmann, who investigates the influence of Jewish mysticism on Kafka's aphorisms and arrives at many illuminating results. However, he ignores the fact that the closeness of Kafka's writings to Jewish mysticism lies in precisely those areas where Jewish mysticism in turn is profoundly marked by Gnostic thought. Hoffmann's neglect of this connection results in his underestimation of the continuity and consistency in Kafka's work and thought which, apart from all influence, Kafka's extreme predisposition toward the Gnostic cast of mind establishes.

5. Foulkes, as well as Kurz, emphasizes a nihilistically or existentially interpreted pessimism in Kafka, and tends to neglect his dualistic cast of thought.

*This essay was originally published in the *South Atlantic Review,* 50 (1985), pp. 3–22, and is reprinted here with permission.

6. For this perspectivist dualism, to be sure, no equivalent can be found in Gnosticism.

7. The only parallel in Gnosticism to Kafka's experimental dualism can be found in the view held by many Gnostics of an unbridgeable gulf between themselves, "the knowing ones," and the masses who are incapable of ever perceiving the truth. See Wilson 132–33. On the spiritual elitism of the Gnostics, see also Rudolph 63.

8. See Kafka's extremely important aphorism on allusion as the sole way in which language is able to refer to "anything outside the sensory world" (H 45).

9. See the excellent dissertation by Gray.

10. Hoffmann 116 sees "a break in Kafka's existence with the onset of his tuberculosis" and divides Kafka's writing into an earlier phase, in which he sees a "justification of existence," and a subsequent phase which he calls "meditation on ultimate things." However, such a division contradicts the powerful diachronic unity of Kafka's entire *oeuvre*. An examination of Kafka's Gnostic predisposition makes this unity most apparent.

11. See *Origenis contra Celsum libri octo,* quoted by Rudolph 186.

12. See *Nag Hammadi Codex* II, S, quoted by Rudolph 117.

13. See Jonas 123–24 in regard to the Mandaeans; and 174–75 in regard to the Valentinians. See also Rudolph 165.

REFERENCES

Auerbach, Erich. *Mimesis: The Representation of Reality in Western Literature.* 1946. Trans. Willard Trask. New York: Doubleday Anchor Book, 1957.

Bateson, Gregory, et al. "Toward a Theory of Schizophrenia." *Behavioral Science* 1.4 (1956): 251–64.

Beck, Evelyn Torton. *Kafka and the Yiddish Theater: Its Impact on His Work.* Madison: University of Wisconsin Press, 1971.

Benjamin, Walter. *Illuminations.* Ed. and introd. Hannah Arendt, trans. Harry Zohn. New York: Schocken, 1969.

Bergmann, Samuel Hugo. "Erinnerungen an Franz Kafka." *Universitas* 27.7 (1972): 739–50.

Bloom, Harold. Rev. of *Zhakor: Jewish History and Jewish Memory,* by Yosef Hayim Yerushalmi. *New York Review of Books* 17 Feb. 1983: 23–24.

Bloom, Harold. Rev. of *Ancient Evenings,* by Norman Mailer. *New York Review of Books* 28 April 1983: 3–6.

Foulkes, A. P. *The Reluctant Pessimist: A Study of Franz Kafka.* The Hague: Mouton, 1967.

Gray, Richard Terrence. "Aphorism and Metaphorism: The Aphoristic Tradition and the Aphorisms of Franz Kafka," Dissertation, University of Virginia, 1981.

von Harnack, Adolph. *Marcion: Das Evangelium vom fremden Gott. Neue Studien zu Marcion.* Leipzig: Hinrichs, 1924.

Hegel, Georg Wilhelm Friedrich. "Die Kunst-Religion." *Phänomenologie des Geistes.* Ed. Johannes Hoffmeister. 6th ed. Berlin: Meiner, 1952. 490–520.

Heller, Erich. *The Disinherited Mind.* Cleveland: Meridian Books, World Publishing, 1959.

Hoffmann, Werner. *Kafkas Aphorismen.* Bern: Francke, 1975.

Jonas, Hans. "Epilogue. Gnosticism, Existentialism, and Nihilism." *The Gnostic Religion: The Message of the Alien God and the Beginnings of Christianity.* 2nd ed. Boston: Beacon Press, 1963.

Kafka, Franz. *Beschreibung eines Kampfes: Novellen, Skizzen, Aphorismen aus dem Nachlass.* Vol. 5 of *Gesammelte Schriften.* Ed. Max Brod. New York: Schocken, 1946.

Kafka, Franz. *Hochzeitsvorbereitungen auf dem Lande und andere Prosa aus dem Nachlass.* Gesammelte Werke. Ed. Max Brod. New York: Schocken, 1946.

Kafka, Franz. *Tagebücher 1910–1923.* Gesammelte Werke. Ed. Max Brod. New York: Schocken, 1948.

Kurz, Gerhard. *Traum-Schrecken: Kafkas literarische Existenzanalyse.* Stuttgart: Metzler, 1980.

Politzer, Heinz. *Franz Kafka: Parable and Paradox.* Ithaca, NY: Cornell University Press, 1962.

Quispel, Gilles. "Hesse, Jung und die Gnosis: Die 'Septem sermones ad mortuos' und 'Basilides'." *Gnostic Studies.* 1970. Publications de l'Institut historique et archeologique néerlandais de Stamboul 34.2. Istambul: Nederlands historisch-archeologisch Instituut te Istambul, 1975. 2:241–58.

Quispel, Gilles. "Der gnostische Anthropos und die jüdische Tradition." *Eranos Jahrbuch* 22 (1953): 195–234.

Rudolph, Kurt. *Die Gnosis: Wesen und Geschichte einer spätantiken Religion.* Göttingen: Vandenhoeck & Ruprecht, 1977.

Scholem, Gershom. *Major Trends in Jewish Mysticism.* New York: Schocken, 1961.

Sokel, Walter H. "Kafka's Poetics of the Inner Self." *Modern Austrian Literature* 11.3–4 (1978): 37–58.

Sokel, Walter H. "Freud and the Magic of Kafka's Writing." *The World of Franz Kafka.* Ed. J. P. Stern. London: Weidenfeld & Nicholson, 1980. 145–58.

Wagenbach, Klaus. *Franz Kafka: Eine Biographie seiner Jugend, 1883–1912.* Bern: Francke, 1958.

Wilson, R. McLachlan. *The Gnostic Problem: A Study of the Relations Between Hellenistic Judaism and the Gnostic Heresy.* 1958. London: Mowbray, 1964.

[12]

LEAVING HOME: A GNOSTIC NOTE IN THE LIVES OF C. G. JUNG AND T. S. ELIOT

Daniel A. Lindley

IN this essay I propose a connection between Gnosticism and the abandonment of a familiar world for an unknown one. My purpose is to consider Gnosticism not as a set of beliefs but as a response to the experience of *leaving home* in both the literal and the metaphoric sense. By "home" I mean an established order, a "right" way of thinking and doing, a fixed set of customs and rules. Specifically, I propose that Gnosticism is one response to the loss of belief in such order. This essay is essentially clinical rather than philosophical or theological. The "clinical material" consists of fragments of biographical material from the lives of C. G. Jung and T. S. Eliot. But first, a bit of conceptual scaffolding.

The natural course of growing up is a three-stage progression: from the known, the security of home (its certainty, whether comfortable or painful), to an adventure into the unknown (as represented, say, in a good teacher, in some of one's friends, or in a journey) and finally, to a stable adult role in work or family. This progression is a variant of Joseph Campbell's paradigm in *The Hero with a Thousand Faces* (1968, p. 245), where there is a call to adventure, which, if accepted, leads to the crossing of the threshold between the known and the unknown. Home, adventure, adult role: three stages, with the middle stage—adventure—often shadow for parents. "Shadow" is Jung's term for the denied and consequently the unknown in ourselves. Shadow is "everything we would least like to be." So it is not only unknown; it is also threatening and repellent. This is precisely how parents often view the adventurings of their adolescent children, with the result that adolescents are often encouraged to stay children ("Just Say No") until they take on a profession or a family of their own. The mother of one of my colleagues in the Chicago Jungian community told him, as he was about to go away to college: "Work hard, learn a lot, but *don't change.*"

There is such obvious security in a place with known rituals and familiar ways that any alternative can seem at the least frivolous and even evil. Gnosticism is such an alternative. Historically, the Catholic Church was the secure, familiar home. The "old forms," as Elaine Pagels (1981, pp. 144–45) states, were represented by the established institution of the Church. Gnosticism offered a new, unknown world. I turn now to the experience of "leaving home" in the lives of Jung and Eliot.

C. G. JUNG

The theme of leaving home pervades the first half of C. G. Jung's life. In his autobiography (Jung 1963) Jung describes what we today would call a dysfunctional and abusive family. His mother was both strange and strained, and she engendered a mother imago (the representation of mother that formed in Jung's psyche) which was dramatically threatening to Jung the small boy. Early in his book Jung describes his childhood fear that either Jesus or the Jesuits would take away small children like him. Then he tells us his famous dream of the phallus in the cave. In that dream his mother—that is, the mother imago—speaks. She identifies the phallus as "the man-eater," an identification that Jung found terrifying because of its ambiguity: was the phallus Jesus and the Jesuits or the devourer itself? Yet there was a deeper terror in this dream which Jung does not acknowledge: that the mother *knew* something arcane which she announced but then, cruelly, did not explain. The dreaming child was left alone in his terror.

And to the sadistic mother we must add a defeated, defeating father, a pastor who never knew faith and who therefore could not keep up with his inquiring son. The Swiss middle-class life, with its pieties and forms, was an empty, frightening void for Jung as a child. It is remarkable that he escaped from it. It is notable that Jung's doctoral dissertation was a study of the one member of his family who seemed to be open to a more mysterious and clearly numinous world, one created within the psyche. For Jung, this study may have been a gesture of revenge, however unconscious.

Given this kind of home, Jung's psychic leaving of it might have seemed both natural and necessary. Leaving home, however, is difficult no matter what home is like. Consider how many people remain, often for years, in abusive relationships. It is as Hamlet says: we would rather bear those ills we have than fly to others that we know not of.

Jung's early career provided worldly success: he did acclaimed research (the word-association studies), married wealth, and set up a private practice. Had his life continued in this way, he would have perhaps replicated the same unexamined yet haunted life that he had experienced in his own family. Obviously nothing of the kind happened. The early and intense association with Freud changed everything, and it was the breakup of this relationship, far more than his estrangement from his parents, that was Jung's experience of "leaving home." After he broke with Freud, and was therefore completely on his own, he plunged into his own unconscious. That extraordinary inner exploration was the seed of his Gnosticism. Jung's adventure involved an active imagination reflecting death and rebirth, then an archetypal dream, and then another active imagination in which the figures of Elijah and Salome appeared to him as guides. Elijah then changed into a figure whom Jung named Philemon, "a pagan . . . with a Gnostic coloration" (Jung 1963, p. 182). Soon after, Jung experienced a crowd of "The Dead":

> The whole house was filled as if there were a crowd present, crammed full of spirits. They were packed deep right up to the door, and the air was so thick it was scarcely possible to breathe. As for myself, I was all a-quiver with the question: "For God's sake, what in the world is this?" Then they cried out in chorus, "We have come back from Jerusalem where we found not what we sought." (Jung 1963, pp. 190–91)

Fittingly, Jung's encounter with the dead inspired the composition of his own Gnostic myth, the "Seven Sermons to the Dead." I suggest that these dead people were Jung's projection of his traditional, heroic ego: the outer, bourgeois "heroism" of the successful doctor and the prosperous family; the world of form covering feeling; the outer world of his childhood and of his house at 228 Seestrasse in Zurich. The dead are a crowd, representing an ego identified with the conventional collective. Such an ego ventures forth on what is supposed to be a victorious quest but returns transformed—returns as the dead. The whole outer world is dead. Even Jung's following Freud was following convention—that of like-minded analysts. The ego-as-crowd, the ego as ordinary, went to Jerusalem, a symbol for an established order.

The ego, composed of unexamined assumptions, habits, and manners, typically goes off seeking a mirror of its own ordinariness. It seeks the world created in children by parents, who are full of "oughts" and "shoulds," who tell misbehaving children that they should "know better." Imagine a child crying in the supermarket. The parent tells the child to stop crying. Not only does this ignore the child's pain, but it is said entirely in the parent's interest: all this parent wants is that the child stop embarrassing him or her in public.

This is a humble example, but the underlying issue is a very serious matter. The world the dead sought was, and is, an unattainable utopia where children never cry. It is the shadow-free and conflict-free world of Dick and Jane, of Sunday lunch at the golf club. More generally, it is a world ruled by form and unexamined custom: Jerusalem imagined through unthinking sentimentality. It is the world of Protestant fundamentalism of the sort that finds all necessary knowledge in Scripture and nowhere else, especially not in secular education or the nightly news. It is the world of people who fear change and resist it. It is also the world many adolescents think their parents live in. But it is a world *not to be found,* as the dead discovered.

Not only did the dead not find what they sought; they did not find anything at all. Jung, in the person of Basilides, his favorite Gnostic authority, must therefore teach Gnosticism to "the dead"—to this deprived, conventional, collective ego. This ego thought that the truth was to be found in the world of conventions, of customs, a world with the motto "Everything will be all right." To start from such a set of positive givens is a fallacy. Instead, we must start, as the Gnostics did, with paradox. Basilides's own advocacy of this position is, of course, Jung's own advocacy of it for himself. In this dialogue between the failed heroic ego and a new consciousness lies the origin of the Gnostic vision. I suggest that here Jung, through Basilides, is cheering himself up. This is not a trivial thing to do: the alternatives could be despair, depression, suicide.

T. S. ELIOT

Lyndall Gordon, in her trenchant biography of T. S. Eliot, after describing the somewhat puritanical atmosphere of Eliot's family, quotes Eliot himself: "The Arts insist that a man shall dispose of all he has, even his family tree, and follow art alone. For they demand that a man be not a member of a family or a caste or of a party or of a coterie, but simply and solely himself" (1977, p. 11). Jung scientifically explored his subjective experience and made this exploration his life's work. His inner voice told him that what he was doing was art. Eliot was not so fortunate: he could never be "simply and solely himself." He was a puritan and a banker as well as a poet, and his external life was uneasy, even tragic. Like Jung, he had his breakdown (1921). Like Jung, he chose to leave home. And like Jung, he experienced overwhelming, numinous otherness:

> About the same time that Eliot graduated from Harvard College, while walking one day in Boston, he saw the streets suddenly shrink and divide. His everyday preoccupations, his past, all the claims of the future fell away and he was enfolded in a great silence. In June 1910 he wrote a poem he never published called "Silence," his first and perhaps most lucid description of the timeless moment. . . . At the age of twenty-one Eliot had one of those experiences which, he said, many have had once or twice in their lives and have never been able to put into words. "You may call it communion with the Divine or you may call it temporary crystallization of the mind," he said on another occasion. For some, such a moment is part of an orthodox religious life, for others—like Emerson—it is terminal, sufficient in itself, and gratefully received. For Eliot, however, the memory of bliss was to remain a kind of torment, a mocking reminder through the years that followed that there was an area of experience just beyond his grasp, which contemporary images of life could not compass. (Gordon 1977, p. 15)

As with Jung, we have the questioning of the everyday world by an experience of something beyond it. Consider, in the light of both Jung's experience and Eliot's, the opening of "The Love Song of J. Alfred Prufrock": "Let us go then, you and I,/When the evening is spread out against the sky/Like a patient etherized upon a table . . . " (Eliot 1952, p. 3)."

Here, in one of the most memorable images in modern poetry, is the equivalent of Jung's crowd of the dead: the evening as etherized patient. The impending surgery is an image of the inner journey, an image for turning away from the outer world of form and deed: the "body" of the evening is to be opened and explored, but as we journey into it with Prufrock we encounter fog, lonely men in shirt sleeves, women talking of Michelangelo, a crab scuttling under the sea—a jumble of images and sensations. We wander through streets that lead to "an overwhelming question," but we never hear the question, let alone an answer. The whole of "Prufrock" is a description of an aging man ("Shall I part my hair behind? Do I dare to eat a peach?/I shall wear white flannel trousers, and walk upon the beach.")—an aging man who can no longer connect with the shallow outer world but who has not yet connected with any inner life. "I have heard the mermaids singing, each to each./I do not think that they will sing to me." Like Jung's dead, Prufrock is tragically lost. Unlike the dead, he has no Basilides to guide him. Prufrock knows that there is a quest, but he has no knowledge, no gnosis, to aid him. All he can do ("Let us go then, you and I") is to ask us to join him.

Yet the author of "Prufrock" is not in fact an old man who has given up. This poem was written by Eliot when he was twenty-three years old. The rest of Eliot's life and work can be read as the quest of a person who has lost the old forms and is struggling to find new ones.

Gnosticism, as Jung saw, was a response to that very struggle. Jung's background was such that the church was not hard to give up. For Eliot, this was far more difficult: he was as much caught in form (language, manners) as free to explore. He did not, like Jung, develop a new vision; but he did, like Jung, struggle.

Both Jung and Eliot faced the void that opens up when old ways fail. It is at this moment that Gnosticism may "form" in the psyche. Whether it does is up to us. We must each choose whether to resign ourselves to a world where the unknown is shadow and change itself the enemy or to seek out a world in which the unknown thrusts change upon us. Jung and Eliot help us, in their distinct but analogous ways, to make the Gnostic choice.

REFERENCES

Campbell, Joseph. 1968 [1949]. *The Hero with a Thousand Faces.* Princeton, NJ: Princeton University Press.

Eliot, T. S. 1952. *The Complete Poems and Plays.* New York: Harcourt, Brace.

Gordon, Lyndall. 1977. *Eliot's Early Years.* Oxford and New York: Oxford University Press.

Jung, C. G. 1963 [1961]. *Memories, Dreams, Reflections,* ed. Aniela Jaffé, trs. Richard and Clara Winston. New York: Pantheon Books.

Pagels, Elaine. 1981 [1979]. *The Gnostic Gospels.* New York: Vintage Books.

[13]

BUDDHISM AND GNOSIS

Edward Conze

THE topic of my paper has a fairly long ancestry. Already in 1828 Isaac Jacob Schmidt, a German living in Russia, published a pamphlet entitled "Über die Verwandtschaft der gnostisch-theosophischen Lehren mit den Religionssystemen des Orients, vorzüglich dem Buddhaismus,"[1] which Arthur Schopenhauer in his collected works recommended no fewer than three times. Much has been learned in the intervening 138 years, and today a German living in England will try to outline briefly the present state of the question as he sees it.

By "Buddhism" I mean in this context the Mahāyāna form of that religion which developed as a distinctive trend from about 100 B.C. onwards, and had its greatest creative period in the first centuries of the Christian era. Not all the doctrines I shall adduce in this paper are, however, *exclusively* mahāyānistic. Some of them can also be found in the "Hīnayāna," either because they represent an earlier tradition accepted by all Buddhists, or because the "Hīnayānists" had at some time or other absorbed the new doctrines. For the Mahāyāna has in the main four components: (1) ancient Buddhist teachings which had been neglected and now receive greater emphasis, (2) logical deductions which had not previously been made, (3) reactions to non-Indian thinking, and (4) absorption of the customs and thought-forms of popular piety.

This Buddhism I propose to compare with "Gnosis" rather than "the Gnostics," because the connotation of the latter term is still so uncertain that this Congress has been specially convened for the purpose of defining it. The adherents of Gnosis in my view are those who share the eight assumptions which I will outline in my paper and which can be found in varying degrees in most forms of Hellenistic mysticism and its offshoots.[2] All these traditions are one in spirit, and while the differences between them must seem important to the Near Eastern specialist, for comparative purposes they are of a fairly minor order. Some doctrines are, of course, nearer to Buddhism than others. For instance, a Buddhist who had to take sides on the question whether the world (*kosmos*) is irremediably evil (*kakon*), would on principle have to decide against Plotinus[3] (because to him all conditioned things would be *duḥkha,* ill). The brevity of this paper forces me to concentrate on essentials.

Now I will describe the eight basic similarities between Gnosis and Mahāyāna Buddhism:

(1) (a) *Salvation* takes place through *gnōsis* or *jñāna,* and nothing else can finally achieve it. Both words are etymologically derived from the same Indo-European root. Their meaning also is quite similar. "Not Baptism alone sets us free, but gnosis—who we were, what we have become; where we were, whereinto we have been thrown; whither we hasten, whence we are redeemed; what is birth and what rebirth"—so the *Excerpta ex Theodoto.*[4] Buddhism in its turn claims that the cognition of conditioned co-production, which the Buddha attained shortly before his enlightenment, dispels all misconceptions on precisely the points enumerated in the Valentinian statement.[5] In both cases the mere insight into the origination and nature of the world liberates us from it, and effects some kind of re-union with the transcendental One, which is identical with our true Self.

(b) As a negative corollary to this, Buddhism teaches that *ignorance* (*avidyā*) is the root evil and the starting point of the chain of causation. This ignorance is in part blindness to the true facts of existence, and in part a self-deception which, misdirecting our attention towards a manufactured world of our own making, conceals the true reality to which wisdom, the highest form of gnosis, alone can penetrate.[6] In the Mahāyāna it means that fictitious beings indulge in a multiplicity of vain and baseless imaginings which cover up the ultimate One. Likewise some, though not perhaps all, Gnostic systems explicitly declare ignorance to be the basic fault[7] which has alienated us from true reality.

(c) This Gnostic knowledge is derived solely from revelation,[8] although each one has to experience it within himself.

(2) We secondly consider the teaching concerning the *levels of spiritual attainment,* and that under three headings:

(a) There is a very sharp division between the aristocracy of the *perfecti* or Elect, and the ordinary run of the *auditores.*[9] To it corresponds in Buddhism that between the *āryas* ("holy" or "noble" men) and the "foolish common people" (*bālapṛthagianā*), who occupy two distinct planes of existence, respectively known as the "wordly" and the "supramundane." Ordinary people are entirely absorbed in the pursuit of sensory objects, or the flight from them, while the saints have undergone a spiritual rebirth, have turned away from this world to the world of the spirit, and have won sufficient detachment from conditioned things to effectively turn to the Path which leads to Nirvāṇa.[10]

(b) There is a *qualitative* difference between the highest ranks of the spiritually awakened and the ordinary run of mankind. They have attained a positively superhuman stature and no common bond of humanity unites them with the rest of us. They have conquered death and become immortal;[11] they have become divine, equal to God,[12] and deserve to be worshipped; the Tathāgatas are absolutely pure, completely omniscient,[13] and omnipresent. The process of salvation is based on the kinship (*syngéneia*) of saviour and saved, because both have a divine origin. The doctrine of the divine spark, which is our true Self,[14] is indeed fundamental in both systems. For the Mahāyāna the intimate essence of man's being is "the celestial nature itself, purest light, *bodhicittam prakṛtiprabhāsvaram.*"[15] In salvation the god within has united with the god outside.[16]

(c) The division between the "saints" and the "foolish worldlings" is found in all Buddhist sects and must go back for a long time. It is only after about A.D. 200 that some Mahāyānists superimposed upon it another division which distinguishes three classes (*gotra* or *rāśi*) of people, i.e. those destined for salvation (*samyaktva-niyata*), those destined for perdition (*mithyātva-niyata*) and those whose destiny is not fixed either way (*aniyata*).[17] This classification, as Tucci has pointed out,[18] corresponds to the well-known Gnostic division into those who possess the divine essence (*spermatikoi*), those who, devoid of the divine Self, can by their very material nature not be saved (*hylikoi*), and those who may or may not be saved according to the circumstances (*psychikoi*). Tucci assumes a Gnostic influence, and I am prepared to agree with him. First of all, those who were excluded from salvation, as being destitute of the Buddha-nature, became sometimes known as *icchantika.* So far no one has found a convincing etymological derivation for this term, and everything said about it is guesswork or belongs to the realm of Volksetymologie.[19] Secondly, it is hard to see how the determinist and almost Calvinistic postulate that these people are permanently damned, because totally without merit,[20] could possibly be derived by logical steps within Buddhism itself from its own presuppositions. And, thirdly, within the Mahāyāna it is clearly a foreign body and in direct conflict with its basic teaching that the Absolute, or the "Buddha-nature," is the same in all conditioned dharmas and therefore also in all beings. In consequence, this concept became the subject of prolonged discussions,[21] also in China, and numerous attempts were made to abolish it and to find some loophole by which the force of supernatural compassion could somehow redeem these people.

(3) Our third point concerns the crucial role which *Wisdom* plays in both systems. We will consider wisdom under three headings: (a) as a kind of archetype, (b) in her cosmogonic function, and (c) as a feminine deity.

(a) As to the first, I may well be said to be stretching a point by introducing some of the "Wisdom Books" of the Old Testament. But they obviously belong to the same religious complex, and were the work of the immediate predecessors of the Gnostics as well as a source of inspiration to many of them. It seems to me remarkable that during the same period of time—i.e. from ca. 200 B.C. onwards —two distinct civilizations, one in the Mediterranean, the other in India, should have constructed a closely analogous set of ideas concerning "Wisdom," each one apparently independently, from its own cultural antecedents. Here are some of the similarities between Chochma[22] and Sophia on the one side and the Prajñāpāramitā on the other:[23] both are feminine, and called "mothers" and "nurses." They are equated with the Law (tōrā and *Dharma*), have existed from all times, are the equivalent of God or the Buddha, the consort of Jahve or Vajradhara,[24] extremely elusive, respectively a gift of God or due to the Buddha's might, dispense the waters of knowledge and the food of life, are extremely pure, related to the sky or ether, connected with trees and compared to light. We are urged to "lean on" them and to accept their chastisement. They are vitally important to kings and will disappear in the chaos of the last days.

(b) The *cosmogonic function* of Sophia is quite pronounced in many Gnostic systems. Until a few years ago every Buddhist scholar would have asserted categorically that *Prajñā* (even in a debased or fallen form, if such a thing were conceivable) could not possibly have anything to do with the creation of the world, being entirely occupied with its removal. Then in 1959 we had the first critical edition of a Buddhist Tantra, and there, in the *Hevajra Tantra*,[25] we unmistakeably read that *"Prajñā* is called Mother, because she gives birth to the world." Dr. Snellgrove, the editor, stresses the presence in this text of "notions that are not Buddhist, in the sense that they are not properly assimilated, and seem to exist in contradiction with the wider context."[26] This particular idea about *Prajñā* is so much at variance with what is possible within the orbit of Buddhist thinking that it must have come from the outside, and the Gnostics seem the most likely source. If we bear in mind that there are literally thousands of Tantras which have never yet been critically investigated by Europeans, many more surprises are likely to be in store for us.

(c) Perhaps the most radical innovation of the Mahāyāna was the introduction of *feminine* deities. As usually the dates are none too certain, but by A.D. 400 female deities, among them the *Prajñāpāramitā,* were definite cult objects. Much earlier the *Prajñāpāramitā* had been proclaimed as the Mother of the Buddhas.[27] To cut it short, if it gives sense to distinguish between "matriarchal" and "patriarchal" religions, then surely the Mahāyāna and Gnosticism are more "matriarchal"[28] than, say, the "Hīnayāna" and Protestant Christianity. Later on, in the Tantras, the consorts of the Buddhas and Bodhisattvas, and by implication the girls involved in ritual intercourse with the Tantric *siddhas,* were known as *prajñās* and *vidyās.*[29] It is a noteworthy coincidence that a few centuries before their time Sophia should have been described as suitable for sexual intercourse[30] and that a bit later the Gnostic Simon should have called his consort Helene, a harlot[31] he had found in a brothel in Tyre, by the names of "Sophia" (= *prajñā*) or "Ennoia" (= *vidyā*).[32]

(4) Both Mahāyāna and Gnostics are indifferent to *historical facts* and tend to replace them by *myths.* This shows itself in at least two ways:

(a) A *docetistic* interpretation of the Founder's life. It would be unsuitable for me to tell this audience about the Docetism of the Gnostics.[33] In the Mahāyāna it takes the form of asserting that the Buddha's physical body, his human and earthly life, his birth, enlightenment and death, were not really real, but a mere show conjured up to teach and awaken people. To quote *The Lotus of the Good Law:* "Although the Tathāgata has not actually entered Nirvāna, he makes a show of doing so, for the sake of those who have to be educated."[34] The real Buddha should not be mistaken for the historical Buddha, who is no more than a phantom body displayed by Him.

(b) The scriptural tradition is authenticated by reference to persons and events which have often no clearly defined place within the framework of observable and verifiable human history, and their initial revelation normally takes place neither on earth nor among men,[35] and often at the beginning of time. The *Pistis Sophia* is the teaching of the Risen Christ, another text is ascribed to "Poimandres, the Nous of the Absolute Power,"[36] the Manichean *Kephalaia* have been revealed by "the Living Paraclete"[37] and the Hermetic tradition dates back to Hermes Trismegistos, who is identified with Thoth. Just so all Mahāyāna scriptures were inspired and compiled by mythological personages, such as Maitreya, Amitābha, Avalokiteśvara, or Mañjuśrī.[38] The lineage of the *Guhyasamāja,* for instance, gives first the Buddha Vajradhara and the Bodhisattva Vajrapāni, and only then a number of historical names.[39] The Hermetists were in the habit of unearthing books hidden away by godlike sages in the remote past (*exemásteuse* is the technical term), and likewise the Tibetan Nyingmapas and Kahgyutpas put their faith in the *gter-ma,* or buried texts, which were hidden by Buddhas or Saints (esp. Padmasambhava) and later on recovered by predestined persons, often with the help of the *ḍākinīs,* or "sky-walkers."[40]

(5) A tendency towards *antinomianism* is inherent in both systems. This ticklish theme can be discussed on the plane of either theory or practice. As far as *theory* is concerned, there is no difficulty. The exalted spiritual condition generated in the perfect by the power of full understanding must of necessity cause a certain disdain for the puny demands of conventional morality. In consequence some Gnostic sects taught that once a man has gained salvation, he is free to disregard moral obligations.[41] Likewise some Mahāyānists were so intoxicated by the heights to which the perfection of wisdom had carried them that they regarded the practice of morality as unworthy of their attention, while others went out of their way to demonstrate their spiritual freedom by deliberately breaking all the moral precepts intended only for the lesser breed.[42] As for the actual *practice,* the case is different. How far did sexual symbolism imply sexual activity? Did these saintly men ever commit any of the abominations which they so freely commended in words? The answer is, I suppose, that while some did and some did not, their opponents would make the most of those who did. The Fathers of the Church were most eloquent about the misdeeds of the Gnostics, but the books recently found in Chenoboskion hardly bear them out. This is all that need be said, and a closer scrutiny of the actual behaviour of these people would only serve to gratify a vulgar and prurient curiosity.

(6) As distinct from the theistic religions, both Mahāyāna and Gnosis differentiate between the still and quiescent *godhead,* and the

active *creator god,* who is placed at a lower level. Of the first, the Hermetists said that "of him no words can tell, no tongue can speak, silence only can declare Him."[43] And so the Buddhists on countless occasions about the Absolute which they identified with Nirvāna, the Buddha, the Realm of Dharma, Suchness, etc. The Demiurge, in his turn, is a secondary divine being who, himself a proud, ambitious and impure spirit, has created this most unsatisfactory world.[44] His Buddhist counterpart is to some extent the Hindu god Brahmā, who in his stupidity boasts about having created this cosmos,[45] when in fact it is the automatic product of cycles of evolution and involution going on over the ages. But, however the world may have come about, at present it is, in any case, the domain of an evil force, of Satan or of Māra the Evil One.[46]

(7) Both systems despise easy popularity, and their writings aim at initiates and exclude the multitude. In consequence there is everywhere a predilection for the mysterious, the secret, the enigmatic, the hidden, the esoteric. In Buddhism it increased as time went on. The first step was, about A.D. 300, the largely Yogācārin concept of *samdhābhāsya,* according to which words had both an obvious and a hidden meaning, and works composed under Yogācārin influence made much of this "hidden meaning."[47] The second step was the wholesale adoption of an esoteric terminology which was unintelligible without the oral explanations of a *guru,* and thus tended to conceal rather than reveal the message conveyed. Many Tantras, and also some Ch'an works,[48] were composed in this fashion.

(8) Last, but not least, both systems adopted a metaphysics which is *monistic* in the sense that it enjoins an intellectual, emotional and volitional revulsion from multiple things, and advocates, more or less explicitly, a re-union with a One which transcends the multiple world.[49] Occasionally both systems also adopt a dialectical critique of all thought-constructions which shows them to be untenable and self-contradictory figments of the imagination which have to be paradoxically both discarded and somehow preserved for the vision of the ineffable One to become possible.[50]

These are my eight chief points. There is no room for the discussion of numerous minor analogies. In any case, if these are the similarities, what then are the *differences?* They are, I think, basically threefold. (1) The intellectual categories in which these theories are clothed are indigenous and therefore in one case taken from the Abhidharma, in the other from Greek philosophy; and also the mythological figures vary accordingly. (2) Compared with the Mahāyāna, some Gnostics seem guilty of excessive myth-mongering, though I feel that some Christian authors, both ancient and modern, have somewhat exaggerated its importance. From this point of view Prof. F. R. Hamm was right when he argued against me that "der Tenor" of Gnostic Sophia literature is essentially different from that of the Buddhist wisdom books.[51] (3) Assuming that man has fallen into this world from a more perfect condition, the Gnostics expended much ingenuity on trying to describe the process which brought about this fall. Classical Buddhism shows no interest in what may have preceded ignorance. All one wanted to know was how salvation can be achieved, and not how it became necessary. But there is the proviso that the later Yogācārins, particularly in China, devoted much attention to the stages by which the world is derived from an originally pure "store-consciousness" (ālayavijñāna).

Making allowance for the differences, I still think that the similarities between Gnosticism and Mahāyāna Buddhism are remarkably close, and do not concern only fortuitous details, but the essential structure itself.[52]

Here are a few more apparent, and at least possible similarities:

(1) Both systems are fond of Serpents (nāgas) as being connected with wisdom (J 93–95, 228);

(2) both hold astrology in high esteem (J 157, 254–65); the principal Buddhist literary source is the late Kālacakratantra, but the actual practices are almost universal in Buddhist countries;

(3) both rely on the power of secret formulas, mantras or spells;

(4) both place great emphasis on Light (phōs and āloka);

(5) both show a tendency towards syncretism, borrow from ancient mythologies and revive the most archaic ideas. In this connection I must refer to U. Bianchi's "Le problème des origines du gnosticisme et l'histoire des religions," Numen xii, 1965, 161–78, who has well shown not only that Gnosticism as a "complexe idéologique" is foreshadowed already in Orphism, but also that many of its basic ideas are of great antiquity and that some can be traced back to prehistoric times. Bianchi has also seen the affinity with Buddhism in "Initiation, Mystères, Gnose," Initiation, ed. C. Bleeker, 1965, pp. 167–69. His views are confirmed by R. Crahay's paper in the Colloquio;

(6) in both the perfect can demonstrate their high degree of spirituality by the display of wonderworking powers; there is indeed a close affinity between some of the later Neoplatonists, such as Proclus (see A. J. Festugière's paper in the Colloquio) and the later Tantric professors at Nālandā University in the 8th century, in that

both combine (1) a sober and perfectly rational philosophical dialectic with (2) a yearning for union with the One and (3) a cultivation of magical prowesses of various kinds (for parallels to Festugière from the Mahāyāna see my *A Short History of Buddhism,* 1960, p. 63);

(7) the more philosophical authors and the *Prajñāpāramitā* texts show many verbal coincidences; here Sophia as the *oikía* of the wise, there the P.P. as their *vihāra* (dwelling); the epithet *phōsphóros* corresponds to *ālokakarī* (Light-bringer), *achrántos* to *anupalipta* (immaculate), etc. etc. The *Heart Sūtra,* both in structure and content, shows much similarity to Dionysius Areopagita's *Divine Theology* (I 2, II 1, III 1, IV–V), and in general the "negative theology" (J 268) uses the same approach as the *Prajñāpāramitā* Sūtras, which employ negations to such an extent that their philosophical exegesis by the Mādhyamikas consists largely in clarifying the logic of negative propositions. Some attempts are made in both systems to somehow mediate between the absolutely transcendental One and the completely incommensurable conditioned world. So in the "Questions of Maitreya" in the *Pañcaviṃśatisāhasrikā prajñāpāramitā* (fol. 580 no. 31) we read: "But if the inexpressible realm were quite other than the entity which is the sign of something conditioned, then even just now that sign could not be apprehended through which there would be a penetration into this inexpressible realm." This statement may, or may not, be connected with what Proclus (*The Elements of Theology,* ed. E. R. Dodds, 1933) says (pp. 109–11, prop. 123), i.e. "All that is divine is itself ineffable and unknowable by any secondary being because of its supra-existential unity, but it may be apprehended and known from the existents which participate in it";

(8) there may be some relation between the "Counterfeit Spirit" (J 92, 205, 226) and the *prativarṇikā prajñāpāramitā* (e.g. *Aṣṭasāhasrikā prajñāpāramitā,* ed. R. Mitra, 1888, v 112–13) or the "Counterfeit Dharma" of Chinese Buddhist tradition;

(9) the figure of Yama, god of death, seems to be inspired by Gnosticism (J 87);

(10) the Gnostics attach importance to "Seals" (J 119–20) and in later Buddhism the term *mudrā* is increasingly used;

(11) some sub-sects give allegiance to persons violently repudiated by the main tradition, e.g. to Cain (J 95) and Devadatta;

(12) the formula "because this is so, therefore this is so" (J 310) looks very much like the famous *evaṃ sati idaṃ hoti;*

(13) both show fondness for sexual imagery;

(14) salvation is likened to an "awakening" (J 80 sq.), and in consequence there is a tendency to regard this world, as it appears, as a dream (J 70), wholly unsubstantial (J 84) and "a Nothing" (J 184 n.); see also R. Crahay's paper on pp. 10–11;

(15) in both systems sexual intercourse (J 72) and coarse food (J 114) played a decisive part in the gradual deterioration of mankind (for the Buddhists see e.g. *Buddhist Texts,* ed. E. Conze, 1954, no. 206); and likewise in both cases the size of people corresponds to their spiritual stature (see Böhlig's paper p. 21);

(16) there is also a striking similarity between some of the similes used as well as the conclusions drawn from them. One may compare: "As gold sunk in filth will not lose its beauty but preserve its own nature, and the filth will be unable to impair the gold, etc." (J 271) with *Ratnagotravibhāga:* "Supposing that gold belonging to a man on his travels had fallen into a place full of stinking dirt. As it is indestructible by nature, it would stay there for many hundreds of years", etc. up to verse 110 (*Buddhist Texts,* 1954, pp. 182–83)—and in both cases this is a simile for the divine spark in man;

(17) Hyppolytos' *Philosophumena* (ca. 250) refer to a Bactrian (= Bamian, Serae Parthorum) Gnostic doctrine according to which the son of God was not incarnated (born) for the first time in Bethlehem, but was incarnated before and will be incarnated again in the future (A. Lloyd, *Mitteilungen,* p. 396).

A few further points concern the *Manicheans* in particular, e.g.:

(18) there is strong resemblance between the descriptions of a messenger (J 108, 230) and a Mahāyāna Bodhisattva;

(19) The loving contemplation of the repulsiveness of the body (J 227–28) surely owes something to the Buddhist meditations on *aśubha* (see E. Conze, *Buddhist Meditation,* 1956, pp. 95–107);

(20) the emphasis on Peace, self-sacrifice and *ahiṃsā* (J 215–16, 232; *Buddhist Texts,* p. 169) unites them both;

(21) Jonas (232) says of the "Elect" that they "must have led a monastic life of extraordinary asceticism, perhaps modelled on Buddhist monasticism";

(22) the Pentads of the Manicheans (J 217–18) are closely analogous to those of the Vajrayāna (H. Hoffmann, *Die Religionen Tibets,* 1956, pp. 40–42);

(23) the Buddha's triple body corresponds to the triple Jesus of Mani. The three forms of Jesus are: (1) transcendental, corresponding to the *dharmakāya;* (2) historical, who only apparently underwent the Passion, corresponding to the *nirmāṇakāya;* (3) *Jesus*

patibilis (P 82–83, J 228–29), who is not at all dissimilar to the Buddha's intermediary body (*saṃbhogakāya,* etc.) in its more cosmic interpretations: *iti kāritra-vaipulyād buddho vyāpī nirucyate* (*Abhisamayālaṅkāra* VIII 11). "From the abundance of his activity the Buddha is thus described as 'all-pervading'." It is true that the Buddhists speak of the Buddha's "activity" and the Manicheans of the "passion" of Jesus, but on closer consideration this difference will be found to be mainly a verbal one.

These are some of the points which may be worth following up.

How then can we account for the facts? There are, as far as I can see, only three hypotheses, all equally unattractive:

(1) The kinship may be due to *mutual borrowing.* We now have abundant evidence of the close contact between the Buddhist and the Hellenistic world,[53] and many instances of borrowing by one or the other side have come to light.[54] Nevertheless, even if there was a large-scale exchange of ideas, the mode of their transmission remains obscure. It is a fact that both the Mahāyāna and the Tantras developed in the border regions of India which were exposed to the impact of Roman-Hellenistic, Iranian and Chinese civilizations,[55] and we also know that the Buddhists were in contact with the Thomas Christians in South India and the Manicheans in Central Asia. But that is about all. And it is indeed remarkable that Gnostic texts often invoke Jewish, Babylonian, Iranian, Egyptian, etc. authorities, but very rarely Buddhist ones.[56]

Alternatively we may have to deal with either a (2) *joint* or a (3) *parallel* development. (2) In the first case one may assume that both Asia and Europe form one unit in which a parallel rhythm assures a fairly uniform development from age to age. This hypothesis works better for some periods than for others, and somewhat lacks in a respectable rational foundation.[57] (3) In the second case one may assume that Gnosticism is one of the basic types of human religiosity and therefore likely to reproduce itself at any period. Its self-consistent theoretical statements would then spring from a common mentality and from common spiritual experiences, and occur whenever certain men feel not only totally alienated from the world around them[58] but also in contact with a living spiritual tradition.[59] In that case one would still have to explain why it reached such prominence just when it did, both in India and the Mediterranean at the same time.

All I can say is that there is here a definite problem, but as yet no definite solution. And what, of course, still remains to be seen is whether my alleged parallels will stand up to the scrutiny of the experts!*

NOTES

1. Leipzig, IV + 25 pages, 4to.—I. J. Schmidt said "dass die Gnostiker ihre Ideen aus den Religionssystemen des Orients geschöpft haben" (p. iii; also p. 16) and on p. 20 he says that "diese Lehrsätze (of the Gnostics) fast genau so klingen als wären sie wörtlich aus den buddhaistischen Schriften vorgetragen oder abgeschrieben." These were the views of a period which had "die Überzeugung, dass alle Cultur, die sich in Europa zu eigenem Leben zu entfalten Raum fand und deren Früchte wir jetzt geniessen, ihren Ursprung aus Asien hat" (*Über einige Grundlehren des Buddhaismus,* 1829, p. 2). (In 1952 Widengren described Gnosis as "a principally Indo-Iranian movement"). I. J. Schmidt's description of Buddhism, which he had derived from its "geachtetsten Religionsschriften" (p. 13 n. 4) concerns naturally the Mahāyāna in its Lamaist form with which alone, as a resident of Russia, he could at that time be familiar.—Another person who has worked on this subject is A. Lloyd, a missionary in Japan. His book *The Creed of Half Japan* (1911) and his article *Kirchenväter und Mahayanismus* in *Mitteilungen der deutschen Gesellschaft für Natur- und Völkerkunde Ostasiens,* vol. XI, Tokyo 1909, contain many hopeful suggestions, but it is not always easy to separate the wheat from the tares.

2. I.e. the Hermetic tradition, the Christian Gnostics, the more spiritual mystery religions (J 38), the neo-Pythagoreans, neo-Platonists, Mandeans, and Manicheans (P 69-72). For the convenience of my fellow Buddhologues I have documented the principal Gnostic tenets from two easily accessible books, i.e. H. Jonas, *The Gnostic Religion,* 1963 (abbreviated as J) and H.-C. Puech, *Le Manichéisme,* 1949 (abbreviated as P).

3. *Enn.* II 9. Though, of course, some of the views of the Gnōstikoi would be none too palatable either.

4. 78:2. For parallels see P n. 279.

5. E.g. Buddhaghosa, *Visuddhimagga,* ed. H. C. Warren, 1950, xvii 112-9.—A good collection of Buddhist descriptions of *jñāna* in *Hōbōgirin,* s.v. Chi.—J 34-7, 284-5.—Also R. Bultmann's (*Theologie des Neuen Testaments,* 1958, p. 168) definition of *gnōsis* as "das Wissen um die himmlische Herkunft des Selbst" would fit the Mahāyāna quite well.

6. For more details see my *Buddhist Meditation,* 1956, p. 153, which is based on the *Visuddhimagga.*

---

*This essay was originally published in *Le Origini dello Gnosticismo,* ed. Ugo Bianchi (Leiden: Brill, 1970), pp. 651-67, and is reprinted here with permission. The footnotes have been changed to endnotes and renumbered consecutively.

7. E.g. Hermetics x:8. The Valentinian *Gospel of Truth* ascribes creation to Error personified (J 76).—The world is bad,—under the control of evil, ignorance or nothingness. The Manicheans: "L'âme s'oublia elle-même; elle oublia sa demeure primitive, son centre véritable, son existence éternelle," quot. P 156.—J 63, 71, 127, 131, 174–5, 183, 194, 197, 201, 254.—See Bultmann (pp. 169–70) about the "Anfang des Dramas, das tragische Ereignis der Urzeit." For the Christian Gnostics see also ibid. p. 180.

8. *Buddhism and Culture.* Suzuki Commemorative Volume, ed. S. Yamagucchi, 1960, p. 30.—*Buddhist Thought in India,* 1962, pp. 28–30.—J 45.—For a masterly survey of the modes of revelation see Le R. P. Festugière, *La révélation d'Hermès Trismégiste,* I, 1950, pp. 59–60, 309–354.

9. The two classes are "wesenhaft verschieden", Reitzenstein quot. in H. Jonas, *Gnosis und spätantiker Geist,* I, 1934, p. 212; cf. ibid. 212–4 for the two, respectively three, classes of men.—P 88–9, n. 374; 91, n. 393; J 232–3, P 86–7 and n. 362 about the Manichean hierarchy.

10. For further information see my *Buddhist Wisdom Books,* 1958, pp. 38–9.

11. E.g. Apuleius in book XI describes a rite of deification which purges man of his mortality, reconstructs him as an immortal being, and fills him with divine power.

12. Hermetists: In his essential being man is *nous,* which is divine, "wherefore some men (who know their true nature) are divine, and their humanity is nigh unto divinity" (xii:1). "If thou canst not make thyself equal to God, thou canst not know God" (xi:20). *Manichaeus qui se mira superbia adsumptum a gemino suo, hoc est spiritu sancto, esse gloriatur.* P 44. U. Bianchi 165. J 45, 107, 153, 166, 296–7.

13. E.g. *Saddharmapuṇḍarīka,* ed. U. Wogihara, 1958, II p. 29.

14. J 44, 122–3, 263–4, 271; P 71, 85, n. 275.

15. G. Tucci, *Tibetan Painted Scrolls,* I, 1949, p. 211. The "self-luminous thought" which is at the centre of our being and has been overlaid by "adventitious defilements" (*āgantukehi upakkilesehi*) becomes in the Mahāyāna "the embryo of the Tathāgata" (for some documentation see E. Lamotte, *L'enseignement de Vimalakīrti,* 1962, pp. 52–6). To see through to one's own "Buddha-self" became the chief preoccupation of the Zen sect. The Manicheans likewise speak of "our original luminous nature" (J 123), "those around Basilides are in the habit of calling the passions 'append-ages'" (J 159) and "in the *Poimandres* the ascent is described as a series of progressive subtractions which leaves the 'naked' true self" (J 166).

16. E.g. *Buddhist Texts,* 1954, n. 185. A good explanation in E. Obermiller, *Analysis of the Abhisamayālaṅkāra,* 1933, pp. 86–94.

17. E.g. *Aṣṭādaśasāhasrikā prajñāpāramitā,* ed. E Conze, 1962, pp. 141–2.

18. *Jñānamuktāvalī. Commemorative volume in honour of J. Nobel,* New Delhi, 1959, p. 226.

19. See F. Edgerton, *Buddhist Hybrid Sanskrit Dictionary,* 1953, s.v.—D. T. Suzuki, *Studies in the Lankavatara Sutra,* 1957, p. 219 n.

20. Lit. "they have lost all merit", *sarvakuśalamūlotsarga. Lankāvatāra Sūtra,* ed. B. Nanjio, 1923, p. 66, 1.

21. The Manicheans also were divided on this issue. P 85.

22. For my information about the Hebrew side I rely on H. Ringgren, *Word and Wisdom,* 1947.

23. The references can be found in *Oriental Art,* I, 4, 1948, pp. 196–7.

24. Likewise the Valentinians spoke of the marriage of Sophia and Jesus.

25. Ed. D. L. Snellgrove, 1959, I, v. 16: *Jananī bhanyate prajñā janayati yasmāj jagat.* For my further comments on this passage see BLSOAS xxiii 3, 1960, p. 604. In Irenaeus, *adv. haer.* I, 23, 2 the Helene of Simon is called *mater omnium.*

26. P. 7; cf. pp. 11, 18.—J. 306: The different versions of the *Apocryphon of John* "show the ease with which heterogeneous material was accepted into gnostic compositions of well established literary identity."

27. For the *Ratnaguṇasaṃcayagāthā* see *Suzuki Commemorative Volume,* 1960, pp. 25–6.

28. For the Gnostics see e.g. E. O. James, *The cult of the mother goddess,* 1959, pp. 192–4.—In greater detail see *Gnosis und spätantiker Geist,* I, 1934, where H. Jonas distinguishes a "männliche Gruppe" (335–51) and a "weibliche Gruppe" (351–75); p. 352: "dass z.B. die spekulativ zentrale weibliche Gottheit von der Gestalt einer syrisch-phönizisch-ägyptischen Mond-, Mutter- und Geschlechtsgöttin hergeleitet ist, hat Bousset nachgewiesen."

29. The term *śakti* is exclusively Hindu and never used by Buddhists.

30. Ringgren, p. 119; cf. p. 106.

31. In the Mahāyāna, by contrast, the Bodhisattvas Samantabhadra (D. T. Suzuki, *Essays in Zen Buddhism,* III, 1934, p. 372) and Avalokiteśvara (F. Sierksma, *The gods as we shape them,* 1960, pl. 28) manifest themselves as harlots.

32. J. 104, 107.

33. J 78, 128, 133, 195.

34. *Buddhist Texts through the Ages,* ed. E. Conze, 1954, no. 135.

35. E. Lamotte, *Sur la formation du Mahāyāna,* in *Asiatica,* Festschrift Friedrich Weller, 1954, pp. 381–6. The Mahāyāna scriptures are said to have been compiled on Vimalasvabhāva, a mythical mountain, by a council composed of Bodhisattvas, presided by Samantabhadra,—Mañjuśrī reciting the Abhidharma, Maitreya the Vinaya and Vajrapāṇi the Sūtras. They were miraculously preserved for five centuries in hidden places, such as the palace of the king of the Gandharvas, or of the king of Nāgas, etc. Some of the scriptures were also due to Mahāyāna saints going up into the Tushita heaven and being there instructed by the Bodhisattva Maitreya. Tucci p. 210: "Some Tantras were spoken on Sumeru, to an assembly of bodhisattvas, or of divine

beings. Others in the Akaniṣṭha paradise, others among the Śuddhāvāsa gods and so on."

36. J 148.

37. J 208.

38. E. Lamotte, *Manjuśrī*, in *T'oung Pao*, XLVIII, 1960, pp. 5–8, 40–48. Alternatively Maitreya descends on earth to recite Sūtras, or "one sees the face of Manjuśrī" and learns from him. See note 8.

39. A. Wayman in JAOS 75, 1955, p. 258.

40. Le R. P. Festugière, *La révélation d'Hermès Trismégiste*, I, 1950, pp. 76, 78, 319–24; H. Hoffmann, *Die Religionen Tibets*, 1956, pp. 45, 49, 54, 175; W. Y. Evans-Wentz, *The Tibetan Book of the Dead*, 1957, LIV–LV, 73–7.

41. For a very fine account of Gnostic antinomianism see J 266–77; also J 46, 110, 136.

42. Śantideva, *Śikṣāsamuccaya*, ed. C. Bendall, 1902, p. 97 and *Suzuki Commemorative Volume* pp 38–9; D. L. Snellgrove, *The Hevajra Tantra*, I, 1959, pp. 8–9, 18, 42–4, 81; E. Conze, *Buddhism*, 1951, pp. 177–8, 195–7; S. B. Dasgupta, *Introduction to Tāntric Buddhism*, 1950, pp. 113–8, 198–211. For a fairly early statement see *Kāśyapaparivarta*, ed. A. von Stael-Holstein, 1926, par. 103.

43. I:31.—In both systems immense efforts were made to guard the transcendental character of the ultimate reality. J 251: "The true God . . . is the Unknown, the totally Other, unknowable in terms of any worldly analogies." This might have been said of Nirvāna. So also J 42, 288–9. Or J 142: "There is no trace in all nature from which even his (the true God's) existence could be suspected." He is altogether "Beyond" (J 51), and *pāram* is one of the keywords of Buddhism.

44. J xiii, 109–10, 134–6, 191 n., 295–8; P 71 and n. 274.

45. *Dīgha Nikāya* I 18. In popular belief he is "Victor, Unvanquished, All-seeing, Controller, Lord, Maker, Creator, Chief, Disposer, Master, Father of all that have become and will be".

46. T. O. Ling, *Buddhism and the Mythology of Evil*, 1962, pp. 58–9, 86. J 211, 224. Bultmann, p. 173. For the Mandean Ruha see J 72.

47. For a definition see Asanga, *Mahāyānasamgraha*, in E. Lamotte, *La Somme du grand Véhicule*, II 1, 1938, pp. 129–132, with further literature at 23*, and for examples see *Suzuki Commemorative Volume*, 1960, pp. 40–1. An early example is *Dhammapada* 294–5, unless these two verses foreshadow the later antinomianism.—Likewise the Valentinians in "their pneumatic exegesis of Scripture stressed the difference between the manifest meaning open to the 'psychics' and the hidden one accessible to themselves" (J 206).

48. E.g. "The Stories of the founders of the five Ch'an sects." See my review in *The Middle Way*, xxxvi, 1961, pp. 136–7.

49. For both Buddhists and Gnostics the world of divine freedom is strictly *transcosmical*. Nirvāṇa is defined as the place "where do water, earth and fire,—where does air no footing find," or "where these four great elements

cease to exist without leaving any trace of them." *Dīgha Nikāya* I 222, in F. L. Woodward, *Some Sayings of the Buddha,* 1925, p. 321.—About Gnostic Monism see J 60–1.

50. R. Gnoli in *La Parola del Passato,* LXXVII 1961, pp. 155–8 about Damaskios and Nāgārjuna.

51. OLZ 58, 1963, p. 188.

52. See also G. Tucci, p. 210: "The Tantras may in fact be best defined as the expression of Indian gnosis"; p. 211, "Gnosis was born in India a little later than in the West and Iran," but in spite of all contacts Tucci regards it as "a spontaneous germination of India" (p. 212).

53. See e.g. H. De Lubac, *La rencontre du Bouddhisme et de l'occident,* 1952, pp. 9–32 (période hellénistique). S. Radhakrishnan, *Eastern religions and Western thought,* 1940. E. Lamotte, *Les premières relations entre l'Inde et l'Occident,* in *La Nouvelle Clio,* V, 1953, pp. 83–118. M. Wheeler, *Rome beyond the imperial frontiers,* 1955, pp. 141–202.

54. See e.g. M. Eliade, *Yoga,* 1958, pp. 202, 431–2. E. Conze in BLSOAS xiv, 1952, pp. 252–3.

55. E. Conze in *The Concise Encyclopedia of Living Faiths,* ed. R. C. Zaehner, 1959, pp. 296–7; G. Tucci pp. 210, 212–6.

56. An exception is, of course, Mani. See P 23, 31, 42, 44, 59, 61, 144–5, 147 n. 249, 149. The references to "Nirvāṇa" in the Central Asian documents (P 86, n. 359), as well as the designation of Mani as a "Buddha" (P 28, 45, n. 250) are, however, later accommodations to a largely Buddhist environment.

57. I have discussed it in some detail in *Oriental Art,* I 3, 1948, pp. 148–9.

58. J 49–50, 65–8, 237, 251; P pp. 70–1, nn., 273, 278.—The rather startling paper of G. Lanczkowski about the Gnostic elements in ancient American religions has led me to think of a *fourth* possibility. Perhaps the basic ideas were thought out in some prehistoric period as a kind of *philosophia perennis,* at a time before Europeans, Asians and Americans dispersed into their respective continents. In the same way we infer from the similarities between the various Indo-European languages that the ancestors of those who now use them once lived together in the same part of the world.

59. This is what differentiates the Buddhists and Gnostics from most modern existentialists. H. Jonas in his otherwise very instructive article on *Gnosis und moderner Nihilismus,* in *Kerygma und Dogma,* 1960, pp. 155–171 seems to overlook this vital point, and I cannot agree with his thesis that the Gnostics, and for that matter the Buddhists, are "nihilistic" in the sense in which our post-Nietzschean existentialists are. At one point (p. 167) Jonas concedes that "Ein entscheidender Unterschied allerdings zu den modernen Parallelen ist der: obwohl geworfen in die Zeitlichkeit haben wir der gnostischen Formel gemäss: unseren Ursprung in der Ewigkeit. Dies stellt den innerweltlichen Nihilismus in einen metaphysischen Horizont, der dem modernen Gegenstück fehlt". I would suggest that it is more than a matter of "metaphysical horizon," that the *spiritual practices* which corre-

spond to the conviction that "we had an origin in eternity, and so also have an aim in eternity" (so the English version at J 335) make life far from meaningless, that to describe the renunciation of the world by mystics and ascetics as "inner-weltlichen Nihilismus" is a misuse of words, and that Jonas (J 239) is wrong in emphasizing the "non-traditional" character of Gnosticism. It is true that without the "Beyond" "we should have nothing but a hopeless worldly pessimism" (J 261). But it is precisely this Beyond which is the lifeblood of both Gnosis and the Mahāyāna. As I put it ten years ago: "What then is the subject matter" of the *Prajñāpāramitā* Sutras? It is just the Unconditioned, nothing but the Absolute, over and over again." "Out of the abundance of the heart the mouth speaketh. The lengthy writings on Perfect Wisdom are one long declamation in praise of the Absolute" (*Selected Sayings form the Perfection of Wisdom,* 1955, pp. 18–9). For a fuller discussion of this important topic see also what I have said in "Philosophy East and West," xiii, 1963, 111–3 and in the Suzuki Commemorative Volume pp. 38–9. My point is, I think, very well borne out by R. Crahay's paper on p. 14. In modern existentialism we find plenty about la séparation, la descente, la chute, l'exil, l'obscurcissement, la captivité, la souillure, la peur. But when ever do we hear about le rappel, la confiance, la purification, la libération, l'illumination, le repatriement, la remontée, l'union?

[14]

PARALLELS TO GNOSTICISM IN PURE LAND BUDDHISM

Kenneth O'Neill

THE history of Gnosticism remains a shrouded, fascinating mystery. Although Gnosticism is generally identified with only the ancient Near East, its influence may have spread throughout the ancient world. Expanded inquiry into the origins of Gnosticism would extend research throughout the Middle East, India, and possibly even to Central Asia. Several scholars have shown correspondences, including the diffusion and exchange of ideas, between Buddhism and Gnosticism. As Elaine Pagels puts it: "What we call Eastern and Western religions, and tend to regard as separate streams, were not clearly differentiated 2,000 years ago" (Pagels 1979, p. xxi).

The suggestion of connections between Gnosticism and Indian Buddhism, perhaps even resulting in the emergence of so-called Mahayana Buddhism, remains speculative. We know with certainty that trade routes connected the Indian, Chinese, Middle Eastern, and Mediterranean worlds. The fates of shifting political boundaries reflect the coming and going of various empires. The Buddha began his teaching in the fifth century B.C., followed in short time by the foreign conquest of India. Buddhism was carried throughout Central Asia and China by merchants using the Silk Road, with monks accompanying caravans to ensure successful journeys and to guard against evil. Three kings whose empires included major parts of India helped spread Buddhism to other parts of the ancient world.

Ashoka Mauriya (ca. 268–232 B.C.) effected the largest political unification of ancient India through conquest. Repentant over bloodletting and sorrow inflicted by his campaigns, he became a lay

Buddhist. Early Buddhist writings result from his conversion, consisting of bilingual inscriptions in Aramaic and Greek celebrating his virtuous reign. Along with patronizing the construction of Buddhist architectural sites, Ashoka sent Buddhist teachers throughout the known world. He dispatched teachers to the West, including Macedonia and Egypt. Alexandria was the site of one such mission. Thus he opened the way for cross-cultural diffusion by Buddhist teachers traveling beyond India.

Menander (ca. 125–95 B.C.) ruled a Greek military state, including Bactria and the entire Indus Valley, where Hellenistic and Buddhist influences commingled. A Buddhist text tells of his debates concerning two hundred sixty-two questions with the Buddhist monk Nagasena. The text ends with Nagasena's victory and the conversion of the Greek king, whose patronage ensured further diffusion (see Rhys-Davids 1890, 1894).

Kanisha (ca. 78?–123? A.D., or 120?–162? A.D.) inherited the Kushan Empire, an extensive state that included most of Central Asia, Afghanistan, parts of the Bactrian and Persian empires, and much of India. Many hold that Mahayana Buddhism originated in the mixture of people and ideas of this Buddhist king's reign. Of significance is the vast territorial influence of that empire. A convert to Buddhism, Kanisha, too, was a lavish patron of monks and of the arts engaged in by the lay community. The earliest mythic texts of Bodhisattva Buddhism are believed to have been written under his patronage.

Direct connections cannot yet be established between an emerging proto-Gnosticism and Mahayana Buddhism. We cannot ignore the development of an eclectic civilization arising from Alexander's conquest of the Persian Empire to Northern India. After that, varieties of Hellenistic, Persian, and Indian spirituality were open to one another. In time, Roman, Christian, and Manichean influence crossed over those same established routes.

My interest in connections between Buddhism and Gnosticism grew from Edward Conze. His contributions shed light on the ancient period of Gnosticism and Buddhism. He enumerated correspondences between the two, even showing textual cross-pollination. [See Conze's essay in this volume.] Straddling the two very different worlds of Western academic Buddhist studies and Buddhist traditions, my work gives special attention to the primary archetypal image of Buddhism: that of the *bodhisattva* (person of awakening).

When examined for theological content, Gnosticism does not

have doctrines so much as a complex of contradictory ideas and myths. What unites the various strands of Gnosticism is the quest for salvation through personal spiritual knowledge. So it is, too, for Mahayana Buddhism.

I became interested in Western Gnostic traditions through William Gray's *An Outlook on Our Inner Western Ways* (1980). His thesis applies the "East is East, West is West" theme to spirituality. Yet I found that each would-be distinctively Western example of his argument in fact has a counterpart in Buddhist and other Asian traditions. From Gray, I learned of certain Western Gnostic traditions closely matching Buddhism, including a ready-made language of gnosis. That revelation solved my long-standing frustration with the standard translations and interpretations of Buddhism, which typically come from normative Christian perspectives: having studied Chinese and Sanskrit texts as part of my traditional Buddhist training, I knew very well that standard Western approaches misunderstand Buddhism. The most pervasive form of Buddhism, the so-called "Pure Land" variety, remains popularly thought of as a religion of faith in a transcendental savior akin to Lutheran theology. In actuality, the Gnostic character of Buddhism is evident in its primary emphasis on the attainment of individual spiritual awakening through knowledge.

PESSIMISTIC BUDDHISM

Buddhism derives from the spiritual awakening of its historical originator, Gautama (ca. fifth century B.C.). His teachings were originally transmitted at great annual gatherings and only centuries later were set down in writing. Those teachings are a constellation of ideas instead of a central doctrine. Hundreds of scriptures record his responses to questions put to him by persons from all walks of life, and his responses are said to vary with the capacity of the listener to understand his teaching. Still, the teaching of liberation is always emphasized. The goal is to give persons a knowledge that will free them from this world.

Early Buddhism expresses a pessimistic, radically dualistic outlook akin to that of ancient Gnosticism. This world is one of suffering and sorrow. Named *samsara* (literally "going around in circles"), ordinary life is regarded as the realm of "dis-ease" (*duhkha*). Early Buddhists sought release through the attainment of *nirvana,* meaning the "blowing out of a flame consuming itself." The pain and sorrow of *samsara* come from three mental poisons afflicting one's perception of life: greed, hate, and delusion. These poisons in turn arise from blindness (*avidya*). A late version of early Buddhism survives today as the Theravada tradition found in Sri Lankha, Burma, and Thailand. The initial Western impression of Buddhism came from the encounter of British and German colonialists with Theravada, which was found to be nihilistic and world-rejecting.

OPTIMISTIC BUDDHISM

Mahayana, or more properly Bodhisattva, Buddhism is of uncertain origin. In contrast to Theravada, it is optimistic in outlook. Mahayana shifts the emphasis from the attainment of nirvana to the emulation of the *bodhisattva*.[1] Instead of seeking emancipation from this world, the *bodhisattva* gains liberation from the suffering associated with a misunderstanding of this world. *Bodhisattvas* continue to live in this world, but with an enlightened perspective. By seeing through and rising above the conventional illusions that are the source of suffering, they are freed to be in the world but not of it. Bodhisattva Buddhism introduces a wide range of methods for attaining understanding.

Bodhisattvas are sometimes confused with saints. In fact, the rich complex of *bodhisattva* stories have but one point: how to come to live a life of maturing enlightenment. *Bodhisattvas* are known to take on any form to assist those seeking liberation from liberation.

The *bodhisattva* outlook is said to be made of *bodhicitta* (Sanskrit, *bodaishin* in Japanese), which is usually translated as "the thought of enlightenment." *Bodhicitta* is anything but passive thought. Indeed, the arising of *bodhi* (gnosis, or awakening) involves a psychic intrusion that disengages one from normal, habitual consciousness (*samsara,* the world of going around in circles) and reveals how awakened beings (buddhas) experience the world free of "thought-coverings" (*acittavarana*). The difference between an ordinary, unregenerate person and a *bodhisattva* lies precisely in the *bodhisattva*'s experience of awakening (*bodhicitta*). That experience is called a "turning about in the seat of consciousness (*ashrayaparavrtti*)," reverberating in a vow to become fully awakened.

Long ago in mythic time, a young prince chanced to meet Lokesvararaja (a variant of Avalokitesvara, the lord looking down on the world with both wisdom and compassion). The mere presence of one so "above it all" yet so compassionate spoke for itself, awakening the desire for illumination within the young man. On the spot, he vowed from the depth of his heart to become a Buddha. He added another vow unique to his character, declaring that he would establish conditions for a realm of awakening, a Buddha land, instantly available to all beings who had only to call his name wholeheartedly in order to gain rebirth to that land. Awakening the wholehearted desire for spiritual liberation in the presence of a Buddha was itself the attainment of *bodhicitta.*

Our story, which comes from the *Sukhavativvha Sutra,* encapsulates Pure Land Buddhism. There developed various Pure Land traditions in Tibet, China, Korea, and Japan. Of the several Pure Land movements that arose in Japan, Jodoshinsu, or Shin, Buddhism became the largest school of Japanese Buddhism.[2] Its reliance on a force from outside of this world to effect liberation looks suspiciously like a Protestant version of salvation through Christ. Indeed, most Western treatments of Shin deem Mahayana Buddhism a religion of faith in a savior. In actuality, Shin, like Pure Land and indeed Mahayana Buddhism in general, stresses individual knowledge rather than faith in a savior. In this respect it is akin to Gnosticism—its optimism aside.

Further akin to Gnosticism, Mahayana Buddhism maintains that this world of sorrowful alienation arises from ignorance, the corrective for which is therefore knowledge. Those caught up in the habitual psychic re-creation of the world in every moment of life's unfolding are not on a path (*marga*) leading somewhere. They are simply the victimized subjects of the Lord of the World in his two aspects as *Mara* and *Yama.* A liberating divine spark resides within all sentient beings, a dormant "awake nature" (*busshin,* usually rendered "buddha nature").

SHIN BUDDHISM

Shin Buddhism sees human nature as composed of two opposing forces at play. More than other varieties of Buddhism, Shin calls attention to the limiting, seemingly inexhaustible nature of self-centeredness. Self-centeredness (Sanskrit, *ahamkara,* self-making; Japanese *jiriki,* selfish force) is the internal locus of the work and the worship of the Lord of the World, who is the Lord of the Dead. *Jiriki* personifies karma, or blind actions. Some persons are obsessed with discussing their karma, or their "past lives." From the Buddhist perspective, a preoccupation with past lives is tantamount to bragging about one's stupid, deeply entrenched obsessions, a misplaced idolatry. Blinded by passions rooted in ignorance and fear of death, one's nature desperately seeks to perpetuate its small-minded world.

Yet stirring deep within and deep without is a second force, known as the "other power" (*tariki*). It is designated as "other," because it lies outside self-centeredness. Even the location of *tariki* is mysterious because our habitual perspective is so dominated by self-centered awareness. Because self-centeredness is thoroughly made of passion and desire informed by ignorance, any desire it might harbor for illuminating liberation is also an epiphany of selfishness. The origin of spiritual experience is thus outside of oneself. Just as you cannot bite your own teeth, *jiriki* cannot cause *tariki*.

An outlook based on absolute polarities typically fosters a "top dog, under dog" outlook. By transcending all opposites, Shin pulls the carpet out from any attempt to gain superiority resting on egotism. True ego strength is evidenced not in authoritarian dominant/submissive behavior but in the transcendence of polarities. We recognize that we are angel and devil at once, *jiriki* and *tariki*.

If you were to read those tired, standard English translations of Mahayana reiterated for over a century now, you would have a very different conception of its teachings. The Sanskrit and Chinese Pure Land scriptures are written in a deliberate language of ecstatic celebration, of participation in the life of the world. They inform us how to let go of our blind strivings in favor of creative participation rooted in gratitude. Shin's famous clarification of the Chinese Buddhist statement *bonno soku bodai,* "the passions themselves are illumination," points to the heart of rebirth. Liberation of the passions does not result in antinomian or libertine license. Instead, balance is achieved with utmost value placed on the freedom of all beings. The major source of heresy (*i-anjin*, unsettled heart) in Shin history has been "licensed evil," or antinomianism.

The Pure Land tradition rests on the image of spiritual liberation from an alien world presided over by an alien god (*Mara/Yama*). From beyond that world the androgynous Immeasurably Awakened (Amitabha Buddha) enters the world drama, manifesting itself as the historic Shakyamuni Buddha of our era, and as the Buddhas of all times and places, in order to show the way to Enlightenment. Behind all practices and expressions resides the vow to save others. You need only call from out of the depths of alienated despair, with whole-hearted intent, to be *liberated from* this world of darkness.

CERTAINTY BORN OF GNOSIS

Central to Shin is the experience of spiritual rebirth, which Western works consistently misrender as "faith." Shinjin is a spiritual experience of knowledge, not blind faith. The term *shinjin* is therefore better translated as "certainty." One is removed from the psychological world of *samsara,* reborn in the perspective of all Buddhas for a momentary duration. After *shinjin,* certain insightful realizations occur. Of those, the most important is that of one's twofold nature. Prior to *shinjin,* the "truth" of Buddhism was merely part of the world of illusion. Before *shinjin,* conventional truth was one's sole reality. With *shinjin,* truth beyond this world enters, bringing resolution and a sense of the heart's being settled. In *shinjin,* opposites are transcended. The contrast between conventional and ultimate truth is known from personal experience. One is certain of the difference between self-centeredness and self-transcendence.

Shin, along with the Zen and Nichiren teachings, emerged at a time of crisis and at the end of three centuries of a Japanese Buddhist renaissance. In those three centuries Chinese and Indian forms of Buddhism came to Japan and died, replaced by a distinctively Japanese Buddhism. Japanese Buddhism came after an obsession with ritual and superstition gave way to renewed concern with gnosis. Shin did away with the distinctions between monastic and lay classes. Shin teachers and students are "neither monk nor laity" but are instead fellow followers on pilgrimage to liberation. Like Gnostic Hermeticism, it falls into Frances Yates's category of "optimistic gnosis" (Yates 1964, p. 22ff.). The visible token of attaining *shinjin* is gratitude and thanksgiving, expressed as participation in life. Such gratitude hinges on recognition of the interconnected, interdependent nature of all life: breaking free of self-centeredness (*satkaya drsti,* the false view of isolated self), one recognizes that one is not in this life all alone.

Western Gnosticism exists primarily in literary fragments and archaeological ruins, a suppressed teaching reconstructed through research. By contrast, Shin provides an instructive example of a living Gnostic culture. Shin's unique secular adaptation of the *bodhisattva* as lotus-born *myokonin* (Japanese for "good, simple persons") evinces the life of naturalness. Shin crosses all layers of Japan's rigidly stratified society. *Myokonin* are usually semiliterate, often "untouchables," yet are revered for their wisdom.

Despite the popular stereotype that Zen accounts for nearly all of Japanese culture, other Buddhist traditions contribute to it as well.

Shin and Zen are complementary expressions of gnosis and are engaged in the same cultural traditions. Cultural arts—the *do*'s, or *Tao*'s—provide a path to the development of character and to the spontaneous expression of individuality. The calligraphy brush, tea ceremony, flower arranging, and incense ceremony exist as refined, spiritually aesthetic subcultures. More than crafts to entertain, escape boredom, or manage stress, these activities heighten creativity. Elaine Pagels observes that ancient Gnostics held the visible token of gnosis to be creativity (Pagels 1979, p. 22). Japan's traditional arts offer a living example of creativity.

Eastern Gnosticism clearly has had an advantage over that of the West because its traditions have enjoyed the freedom to develop openly, above ground. They may therefore offer a maturity that the disrupted, discontinuous underground traditions of the West have never developed. In sum, Arnold Toynbee's prediction that the outcome of the twentieth century would be determined by the coming together of Mahayana Buddhism and Christianity might best occur on Gnostic grounds.

NOTES

1. My work in process, *Stealing Enlightenment—The Bodhisattva's Way,* offers the first interpretation of bodhisattva Buddhism, shifting the emphasis from Mahayana as philosophy to the guiding myth and symbolism of its living liberative tradition: the *bodhisattva.*

2. Hundreds of books and articles on Shin Buddhism have been published in the past century. Of them, the works of Alfred Bloom, Mokusen Miyuki, D. T. Suzuki, and Dennis Hirota are the most reliable guides, although they differ considerably from one another. Bloom's career reopened the case of Shin interpretation, resulting in a steady blossoming of academic studies since the late 1970s.

REFERENCES

Conze, Edward. 1970. "Buddhism and Gnosis." In *Le Origini dello Gnosticismo,* ed. Ugo Bianchi, Studies in the History of Religions (Supplements to *Numen*), Vol. XII (Leiden: Brill), pp. 651–67.

Gray, William. 1980. *An Outlook on Our Inner Western Way.* New York: Samuel Weiser.

Pagels, Elaine. 1979. *The Gnostic Gospels.* New York: Random House.

Rhys-Davids, T. W., tr. 1890, 1894. *The Questions of King Milinda.* In

Sacred Books of the East, vols. XXXV and XXXVI, Oxford: Clarendon Press.

Robinson, James M., ed. 1977. *The Nag Hammadi Library in English.* San Francisco: Harper & Row.

Yates, Frances A. 1964. *Giordano Bruno and the Hermetic Tradition.* Chicago: University of Chicago Press.

[15]

THE EXPERIENCE OF GNOSIS

Rosamonde Miller

NEARLY sixteen hundred years ago, a band of men and women carrying sealed jars made a secret journey into the desert. They dug as deeply as they could and buried the body of their recorded knowledge and experience in the protective arms of the land. Only since the discovery of the Nag Hammadi texts in 1945 have we been able to study the teachings of the early Gnostics from their own writings instead of from those of their detractors.

Study alone, however, is far removed from the experience of gnosis. We can learn sophisticated images and mythologies from the experiences of others. But once we ourselves have been brushed by the eternal, everything else remains unsatisfying.

I cannot say that I first came to conscious awareness of gnosis through a glimpse of light in the darkness. Rather, it happened through the loss of light and descent into darkness.

Originally, gnosis was there, as close as my own heartbeat and as naturally a part of me as breathing. I was not, however, conscious of it because I had never been apart from it. My awareness was of an extraordinary Presence that sometimes was much stronger than at other times. And then, suddenly, it was gone.

I was nineteen years old when I first experienced in my own flesh the cruelty of the world. Living with my family in Castro's Cuba, I was taken a political prisoner at a secret police headquarters, where I was repeatedly beaten and brutally tortured. I was raped by I don't know how many soldiers. It seemed like one hundred but may have been only twelve or fifteen. That was when I lost it! That was when I lost that sense of the Presence. That loss was worse than all the torture, rape, and other cruelties. It was an experience of something that was like a reverse cosmic consciousness. A sense of aloneness. The absence of that Presence. There was no joy, no hope, no life.

Some days later I was returned to my cell after more beatings and torture. It was then, sitting alone in agony, that I had a staggering experience. I overheard a conversation between two of the soldiers. One of them was the officer in charge. He had never smiled. Some of the others would smile sarcastically or tauntingly and chide me, but this one never did. He never touched me, but he was the one who would give the orders to the others of what was to be done. He frightened me the most. He was the most terrifying individual I had ever encountered. He embodied all the dark images of the Catholic Satan. He was a monster. For the first time in my life I saw something that seemed totally evil. Until then I had never believed in total evil.

One day I heard this monster speaking very enthusiastically—the first time he had ever been so animated. I looked out of my cell at him, and he had the brightest smile on his face. That made me very curious. This monster can smile? He can speak with enthusiasm? He was talking about how he had gotten a puppy for his daughter and how excited he was to be giving it to her. He was full of love and enthusiasm in anticipating his little girl's joy at seeing that puppy. I thought, Can he have a little girl? Does he love a little girl?

Then I saw that light aspect of him, his capability of loving his child just like any human parent, of loving a dog just as I would love my dog. That was a horrifying experience for me. For it meant that the man was not so utterly different from me, that he could love like me, that even he had some light inside him. Even worse, it meant that his darkness, his horror, must also exist potentially in me. So while we had different inclinations, we were still made of the same cloth.

All of my life until then I had devoted to God. Having considered spending my life in a convent, I had offered myself as a bargaining tool to God for the sake of humanity, offering myself as a sacrifice to compensate for the pain of the world. The realization that came to me in a Cuban jail annihilated this onesided view of my tormentor. Humanity no longer existed as a set of opposites but was more like a fabric interwoven of light and dark threads. I could no longer leave the darkness behind. Once I accepted the wholeness of life, once I accepted darkness as an integral part of humanity, my prayer for all of life without rejection exploded within me. Hopelessness ended, and I was totally possessed by joy. The Presence once again filled my being. Pain was still there, but suffering was not. This time I did not take the experience of the Presence to be as common and natural as breathing. I now recognized it as wholly Other. It infused every atom of my humanity, yet it remained distinct from me.

I had many questions after it all happened, such as, What brings this extraordinary state about? Why and how do we lose it? How can we bring it back? These questions I explored solely on my own, without teachers or authorities on the matter. However, I listened for the voice of the wholly Other, the Beloved, in all the sounds I heard. The Beloved instructed me through every eye that looked at me. Not all of those eyes were human eyes. I remember a cat I had. I was looking at her eyes when all of a sudden a look crossed her pupils from beyond her little cat brain. Something immeasurable was there, alien yet so familiar, so different from me yet so much a part of me. With my body and my psyche as my laboratory and test tube, I was guided to gnosis again and again, solely by the silent prompting of that wholly Other resounding in my heart.

In spite of having lived in constant communion with that Presence for nineteen years, I was certain I had lost it. In reality, I had barely reached the early stages of gnosis, as I term it now. Through the subsequent years of observing the phenomenon coming and leaving to return again, I can say that we experience gnosis in varying degrees of intensity and permanence. Not that the Other itself comes and goes or is of different levels or degrees. What fluctuates is not the nature of what is experienced but the nature of those who experience it. As we mature in gnosis, we acquire a "knack" for surrendering our whole being. The external world is thereby silenced. In inner emptiness we become a vessel for the Eternal.

In the preliminary stages of gnosis we feel touched by grace and love. We are permeated by a sense of trust that no matter what happens, everything is in order with God and the universe. Everything seems ultimately good. Later on, the Gnostic is hit by the duality of the world in a very dramatic manner and is no longer capable of denying the world's capacity for cruelty. There is pain and death everywhere.

If we go no further, we may think that we know it all, that this is the truth of existence. It makes us bitter or resigned. But if we accept suffering as simply a part of life and continue, we can advance to deeper stages of gnosis.

As the vision unfolds, the lens of our mind opens wider to encompass a numinous Presence that is totally beyond even words such as "love" and "God." We cross an abyss by the end of which fear and judgment vanish and all human logic and knowledge crumble. All theologies, philosophies, and beliefs dissolve, as if they had never been. Finally, we ourselves dissolve into the Presence.

And then the lens slowly narrows. It narrows enough to permit us to move within that Presence yet still be capable of functioning on a day-to-day basis. We accept the world as it is: the ugliness together with the beauty. We can't help but try to improve the condition of the world, but we are always conscious that suffering remains alongside happiness. The individual is now poised between two worlds, the physical and the Eternal.

That which we call "I" wants to keep this experience in memory so that it can be relished later, but there is no clear memory or understanding of the event itself. The experience paralyzes our capacity for thought. Our finite brains cannot capture it, cannot examine it, cannot explain it, cannot form it into a concept. We know only that something incredible happened and left a lingering taste in the mouth for more. Gnosis is like nothing else. Trying to describe it is like trying to describe the taste of a mango. No matter what comparisons we make, we don't know what a mango tastes like until we bite into its flesh and let the taste wash over the inside of our mouth and down our throat. We can never speak of its essence. We can only speak of our reaction to the experience.

All of these ideas must never be confused with the experience itself. They are just words poorly describing a few of my many reactions to it. Intellect is desperate to enfold and to control the experience, but it cannot. If we are in the early stages of gnosis, we try to do many things to regulate it. Some may look for a guru to initiate them or seek ordination themselves. Others may run to libraries and bookstores to see what others have done. We can fast, pray, renounce the world, wallow in it, follow all sorts of laws and disciplines, and pretend that there is something that we can do in this world that may affect that which is totally alien to it. Only nothing works. We come then to the realization that what we seek is beyond our efforts—but yet so close!

It has been my experience that when reality as we have known it finally crashes against truth and utterly crumbles, if we can avoid escaping into insanity or finding new games to keep the dark away, we may find ourselves at the fulcrum of a revolution within us. This moment mandates our total attention, energy, and passion. We must eliminate any expectations—either recollections of the past or speculations about the future. The second that we start looking at the past with relief or regret or start wondering about the future, the moment is gone. In that silence of the mind, we enter into the more advanced stages of gnosis. The timeless breaks through time and fuses with our soul.

The Gnostic is neither an ascetic nor a theologian and need not even be particularly religious in the conventional way. The Gnostic is an artist. The Gnostic's brushes, colors, and canvasses are her own body, his own psyche. The Gnostic's technique is one of living and observing life and recognizing it for what it is, without illusions of security, glamor, or despair. The Gnostic continually explores, always seeking the core of the nature of things. But gnosis, like art, cannot be taught. The flame of living gnosis awakens and rises of its own accord. All we can provide is a nest within our heart, a sanctuary of repose where the breath of the Infinite may whisper its secrets.

In the words of the Gnostic poet William Blake,

> He who binds to himself a joy
> Does its winged life destroy
> But he who kisses the joy as it flies
> Lives in eternity's sunrise.

[16]

THE REVIVAL OF ANCIENT GNOSIS

Richard Smith

But if the Gnostics were destroyed, the Gnosis, *based on the secret science of sciences, still lives* (Blavatsky 1877, p. 38).

THE ECCLESIA GNOSTICA

ON Hollywood Boulevard, by a sharp corner where the boulevard dead-ends at Sunset, is a small store front. Within a few blocks are major centers of the Self-Realization Fellowship and of Scientology, as well as an assortment of shops, foreign movie theaters, and adult movie theaters. These distracting features of New Age Babylon do not concern us. We are visiting the modest store front home of the Ecclesia Gnostica. It is Sunday morning. Stephan Hoeller, Presiding Bishop of the Ecclesia, is celebrating the Gnostic Holy Eucharist. He is dressed in brocade vestments. Incense is smoking, candles are burning, and bells are ringing. "We invoke thee, O Light of Lights, who art above every power of the Father, Thou Who art called Light and Spirit and Life: for Thou hast reigned in our bodies for evermore." Close by, deacons are serving at the altar, and a handful of congregants are prepared to commune "with the Indwelling and Cosmic Christ" (Hoeller 1972, pp. 12, 17).

This group, like ancient Gnostic groups, has blended several disparate traditions and may therefore be described as syncretistic. Its syncretism frustrates a simple description of the Ecclesia Gnostica. I have introduced this sect by focusing on a moment that is central to its existence: the celebration, with high formality, of the Eucharist. The reasons that this modern Gnostic group performs sacraments that resemble those of the Roman Catholic Church are the result of an historical development. Tracing the development of the streams that now mingle in the Gnostic chalice illuminates the beliefs and practices of this eclectic group. We need not look to the first century for the origins of this gnosis, but to the last one.

Let us examine the invocation just quoted. It does indeed come from an actual ancient Gnostic ritual (Irenaeus 1981, p. 356). Its immediate source, however, and its translation are from G. R. S. Mead's *Fragments of a Faith Forgotten* (1960, p. 380), a book first published in 1900. Mead was an officer in the Theosophical Society and a friend of H. P. Blavatsky. Madame Blavatsky had stimulated a renewal of Gnosticism through her writings and by founding the Theosophical Society in 1875. Both of these activities promoted on a popular level the study of comparative, especially esoteric, religions. Her first great work, *Isis Unveiled,* presented Gnosticism as the secret truth behind Christianity. Gnosticism, in turn, was an "offshoot of Buddhism" (1877, p. 158), which was, in turn, the source of all esoteric truth. Blavatsky did not figure this out for herself. She read it in a book. The book was one of the few English-language studies of Gnosticism in her time: *The Gnostics and Their Remains* by C. W. King. King theorized that Gnosticism had borrowed much from Buddhism as a result of missionaries sent from India to Egypt during the Hellenistic period (1982, pp. 50–51, 390). From the beginning, then, Theosophy had an affinity with Gnosticism.

In the teens of this century another fusion was made. This time, Theosophy was blended with the traditional Catholic sacraments. Two Theosophists, James T. Wedgwood and Charles W. Leadbeater, obtained Holy Orders and founded, in 1918, the Liberal Catholic Church. They were supported in this by Annie Besant, a leader of one branch of the Theosophical Society. In a series of visions from the astral plane, she learned that the crucifixion of the mystical Christ is the extension throughout matter of the Logos, the divine spark in human beings. Leadbeater also had visions, especially during the Mass, of a large spiritual bubble rising like a dome over the chapel and of colorful rays streaming forth from the Eucharistic elements (1920). Such "superstitions" raised the anger of Katherine Tingly, the leader of yet a third branch of the Theosophical Society. She tried, unsuccessfully, to drive the Liberal Catholics out of the Society.

Perhaps a few words are appropriate regarding the Holy Orders that are administered by the Liberal Catholic Church. Obviously the Roman Church would not lay its hands on these activities. The Roman Church had, however, a few times in its history, driven small groups out of its ranks. In the eighteenth century over the Jansenist

controversy, and in the nineteenth over the issue of papal infallibili-
ty, churches split from Rome and retained tangential lines of
apostolic succession. These churches, today known generally as the
Old Catholic Movement, have been a haven for independent
churches wishing to develop idiosyncratic theologies or lifestyles. It
was from independent bishops of this movement that Wedgwood
and Leadbeater obtained their orders (Anson 1964, pp. 342–53).

Let us now look at another Theosophist, James Morgan Pryse.
Pryse, like Leadbeater and Mead, was an officer in the Theosophical
Society. In the 1920s he moved to Los Angeles, where he was a leader
of a local Theosophical lodge. On Friday evenings a group met in the
house which Pryse shared with his brother, John. The group listened
to chamber music and discussed Pryse's special interest, Gnosticism.
The group was incorporated in 1939 as the Gnostic Society. Pryse
wrote and his brother printed several books claiming to be Gnostic
interpretations of Christian scriptures (Pryse 1925). In the late 1940s
the Pryse brothers died, the Society's activities declined, and the
corporate entity fell into the hands of a young Theosophist named
Arthur Fronius. And now the stage is set for the revival of the ancient
gnosis.

In 1952, displaced from his family home in Eastern Europe by the
Second World War, Stephan A. Hoeller arrived in the United States
and in 1954, at the age of twenty-three, came to Los Angeles. Brought
up as a Roman Catholic, he had a deep love for the Church's rituals;
but he also had an interest in the occult and was a Theosophist. In
Europe he had developed an interest in the psychology of C. G. Jung.
In Los Angeles he linked up with local Theosophists, with Liberal
Catholics, and, through Fronius, with the Gnostic Society. Hoeller
was ordained a priest in 1958. The following year he began an
affiliation with the Order of the Pleroma, a Gnostic group formed in
London in 1953 by Ronald Powell, who styled himself Richard, Duc
de Palatine. De Palatine was also a Theosophist as well as an
Independent Catholic Bishop. In 1967 Hoeller himself was consecrated a bishop.[1] De Palatine moved to Los Angeles in 1970. There
were differences, a schism, and a bitter feud that lasted until de
Palatine's death in 1977.[2]

Bishop Hoeller and his Ecclesia Gnostica do not continue to
promote themselves as Theosophists or Liberal Catholics, yet the
traditions I have traced are central to them (Ellwood 1973, pp.
114–18; Pruter and Melton 1983, pp. 91–100, 211). Hoeller is a
popular lecturer on the Theosophical Society's lecture circuit, he is a
frequent contributor to the *American Theosophist,* and his books are

published by the Theosophical Publishing House (1975, 1982, 1989). The Gnostic Eucharist is the liturgy of the Liberal Catholic Church with minor revisions. The Ecclesia Gnostica describes itself, however, as "an association of persons, who value Gnostic sacramental practice in addition to theory. It practices the seven Christian mysteries, or sacraments, and possesses an apostolic succession recognized as valid by mainstream sacramental Christendom." The Gnostic Society has been relegated to the church's "associated lay organization" (Perala 1984).

The relation between the Ecclesia Gnostica and ancient Gnosticism is loose. Bishop Hoeller, who views himself with a refreshing levelheadedness and an engaging sense of humor, does *not* claim to be practicing or teaching ancient Gnosticism. The Gnosticism of the first few centuries, he admits, was crushed by the orthodox church: "It did not continue under its own name . . . rather, it took a variety of embodiments throughout history . . . alchemy, kabbala, ceremonial magic, heterodox Christian mysticism, the Rosicrucian mystery, Tarot cards," and so forth (Hoeller 1981). On Friday evenings at eight, one is more likely to hear a lecture on one of these topics than on Gnosticism proper.

Yet these various subjects have in common with Gnosticism "an essential message . . . the conviction that direct personal and absolute knowledge of the authentic truths of existence are accessible to human beings" (Hoeller 1981). But more than "rational knowledge," it is a "knowing that arises in the heart in an intuitive and mysterious manner and therefore is called in the *Gospel of Truth* the *gnosis kardias,* the knowledge of the heart" (Hoeller 1983, pp. 11, 202).[3] This gnosis is of the indwelling god, a god which is none other than the collective unconscious of Jungian psychology (Hoeller 1982, p. 118). Jung provided the overarching scheme that synthesizes these diverse esoteric traditions into a new gnosis. Indeed, modern Gnosticism, for Hoeller and his group, *is* Jungian psychology. Jung discovered the great secret of which the ancients were largely unaware: that the Gnostic systems were psychological, that they were symbolic of self-realization, or the reintegration of the archetypes of the unconscious with consciousness toward the goal of wholeness (Hoeller 1982, pp. 31, 101, 128, 151; 1989, pp. 192, 245).

For Hoeller, academic scholars of ancient Gnosticism, with their historical approach, "are totally lacking in any serious appreciation of psychology." They are "quibblers over Coptic words" (Hoeller 1982, pp. 17–18; 1989, p. xviii). Hoeller prides himself, with his psychological interpretation of Gnosticism, on having rescued it from the ivory towers of antiquarianism. Indeed, according to him, "Jung's influence is almost solely responsible for . . . the publication of the Nag Hammadi Library" (1982, pp. 18, 33).[4]

Nevertheless, because his interpretation was already in place, Hoeller has not seriously reckoned with the Gnostic texts from Nag Hammadi. When they were first being translated, he told *Los Angeles Times* religion writer John Dart that he was not very interested in the new discovery, saying "we feel we know enough about Gnosticism to be able to apply overall principles of Gnosis to life" (Dart 1973). In his 1982 book, published five years after the entire Nag Hammadi Library became generally available, Hoeller quoted from only three Gnostic texts, and in his latest book (1989) he discusses only four at any length. Actual Gnostic texts serve him not as inspiration but, where they seem to fit, as proof texts for the psychological method. For example, the *Gospel of Thomas* declares that "If you bring forth what is within you, what you bring forth will save you," which proves "psychological insight and contact with the unconscious" (Hoeller 1982, p. 155).

Is it appropriate, then, to compare the Ecclesia Gnostica with ancient Gnosticism? Probably, for Jung was in a sense correct in his psychological reading of the old Gnostics. They frequently claimed that divinity lies, knowable, within the self. For the second-century teacher Valentinus, Gnostics were "saved by nature" (Clement 1983, p. 349), and salvation was a process of self-discovery, not faith in an external savior. For ancient Gnostics, however, the rescue of this indwelling fragment of divinity was not achieved, as for Jung and Hoeller, by the integration into consciousness of the total contents of the unconscious. Rather, it was achieved by freeing this divine particle from painful suffering, from the body, from the entire world, so that it could escape and return to its true home with the transcendent God. As Valentinus tells it, the entire material universe was formed out of the emotional grief of the fallen Goddess Sophia by evil powers who themselves arose out of her sufferings. Christ came to earth as a demonstration that the spirit has nothing to do with matter and with suffering (Irenaeus 1981, pp. 317–25).

By internalizing this entire cosmic myth within the human psyche (Hoeller 1989, pp. 99–116), the Jungian interpretation departs radically from classical Gnosticism. Hoeller quotes with approval Jung's statement that "all darkness is expressly lacking" in the orthodox figure of Christ, whereas the Gnostic Christ is a symbol of wholeness which integrates, not rejects, evil. For Jung, the evil Gnostic creators of the world are really psychological forces that need to be consciously acknowledged (Hoeller 1982, pp. 83, 88, 129). But ancient Gnostics would have disagreed. Valentinus, for example, wanted "the expulsion of every evil from the heart" (Clement 1983, p. 372).

The Ecclesia Gnostica frequently refers to historical Gnosticism yet disengages itself from the anti-cosmic dualism basic to any theology claiming to be Gnostic.[5] It "is not the case," Hoeller claims, "that the Gnostics were world haters" (1981). They "were accused of 'dualism' by their opponents." What Gnostics really believed in, he argues, was "duality," a "conflict of light and dark . . . spirit and flesh as a troublesome but ultimately beneficent process." This process strives for the reconciliation of the opposites, a gnosis envisioned by such men as Valentinus as the experience of totality or wholeness." Far from being dualists, Hoeller's ancient Gnostics loved nature and this world because "God lives in it" (1982, pp. 106, 135, 151, 160).

In disagreement with this optimistic interpretation stand the actual Valentinian texts from Nag Hammadi, which condemn nature as "death." These texts identify salvation with leaving the body and getting out of the flesh into the spirit, out of the physical into the angelic (Robinson 1988, pp. 54, 56, 488). It is difficult to find a single ancient passage that, upon close examination, justifies the view that the Gnostics promoted a world-embracing outlook. Such a conclusion does not say anything, of course, about the validity or invalidity of Jungian ideas. With regard to historical Gnosticism, however, Jungianism is more a matter of interpretive appropriation than of analogy.

If Jungian psychology provides a tenuous link with ancient Gnosticism, sacramentalism provides a closer affinity. Valentinus and his followers, to whom Bishop Hoeller frequently refers, were one of the earliest Christian sects to develop a sacramental system. A famous passage in the *Gospel of Philip* (Robinson 1988, p. 150) mentions five mysteries, or sacraments: baptism, chrism, eucharist, redemption, and the enigmatic ritual of the bridal chamber. Also from Nag Hammadi are some short Valentinian tracts on three of these sacraments, including the eucharist. Patristic sources provide us with descriptions of sacramental rituals practiced by Valentinian and related groups. Gnostics were divided over the efficacy of these practices, however. Some felt that a transcendent deity beyond sensible perception cannot possibly be communed with by means of material objects. *Knowledge* of this deity, gnosis itself, is enough to effect redemption (Irenaeus 1981, p. 346).

As for such sacraments being performed by a clergy ordained within an apostolic succession, there is no such thing among the ancient Gnostics. On the contrary, the institutionalization of the apostolic succession was developed by the orthodox church specifically to combat and discredit Gnosticism. The Church Fathers, in combatting the Gnostics, held up the apostolic tradition as a shield against the crazy barrage of ideas issuing from the heretics. The orthodox "church received their doctrine from the apostles, the apostles from Christ and Christ from God; . . . all other doctrine," accuses Tertullian, "is ipso facto false" (1980b, p. 252). The Gnostics, knowing God without intermediaries, received their teachings directly out of the blue. It was this revelation *de caelo* and the resultant anarchy that drove the church to establish its authority by means of an institutionalized tradition.

It is most surprising, therefore, to see the Ecclesia Gnostica boast about its apostolic ordinations performed by a valid bishop.[6] The purpose, of course, is not to be a church in the same fashion as the Roman church. It is not a church in the sense of a group of believers. Nor is the bishop an overseer of the group. Although the outward form is traditionally Catholic, the intent is to have a mystery religion, and the Holy Orders given are grades of personal initiation (Hoeller 1973, p. 34; 1989, pp. 202–16). For the Ecclesia Gnostica, the sacraments are personal experiences of transformation, as indeed they were for some ancient Gnostics.

THE GNOSTIC ASSOCIATION

Within a couple of miles geographically from the Ecclesia Gnostica, but aeons removed in its understanding of ancient traditions, another organization teaches Gnosticism. The Gnostic Center, on Melrose Avenue near Western, is the English-language branch of the Associacion Gnostica de Estudios Anthropologicos y Culturales (The Gnostic Association of Anthropological and Cultural Studies). South and East of this Center, in the largely Latino districts of Los Angeles, are a dozen more centers that offer the teachings in Spanish. These are the local branches of a growing international movement. There are perhaps at least eight million members throughout the world, mostly in Latin America, but with large memberships also in Japan, Quebec, France, and several other countries. In the United States, centers are located in New York, Miami, Houston, Omaha, San Francisco, and, for the past fifteen years, Los Angeles. Every few years at least a thousand delegates gather from all over the world at conferences that have been held in Mexico, Spain, Paris, Vienna, and Montreal.

The group was formed in 1962 by a native of Columbia, Samael Aun Weor, "Master Samael." For years, Master Samael had searched in many esoteric traditions for the single truth that would enable him to understand the purpose of human existence. He pursued Theosophy, Rosicrucianism, Freemasonry, Spiritualism, and the teachings of the Russian mystics G. I. Gurdjieff and P. D. Ouspensky. Finally, he encountered the Rosicrucian Gnostic, Arnoldo Krumm-Heller. Krumm-Heller was from a family of Germans who had emigrated to Mexico. In the early years of this century he was a prolific writer, in both German and Spanish, of books on historical, medical, and occult subjects. He headed an organization called the Fraternitas Rosicruciana Antigua. For Master Samael, his Rosicrucian-Gnostic teachings were a revelation which enabled him to put together "the Synthesis of all Religions, Schools and Sects." In 1961, in a book titled *The Perfect Marriage,* Samael Aun Weor unveiled the secret that had purportedly been passed down through the ages by means of occult symbols: "He who wants to become a God, should not ejaculate the semen" (xviii).

There is, of course, more to the secret than the idea of seminal retention. This idea is simply the central doctrine of a vast system of teachings about humankind and the universe. These teachings, referred to as "The Gnostic Philosophy," or simply "The Gnosis," have been promulgated since Master Samael's death in 1977 through different means. Many of Master Samael's books have now been translated from Spanish into other languages. Each of the centers presents lectures on the Gnostic Philosophy. In Los Angeles, courses are taught on Monday evenings by José and Florence Gonzalez. They have come to Los Angeles from Belize to help spread the Gnostic Philosophy. José Gonzalez has a friendly, take-it-or-leave-it attitude and asks his audience "neither to accept nor reject the material until after it has been investigated. The Gnostic Philosophy offers techniques and methods of investigation for verifying the theories" presented in the lectures. The topics the students are invited to investigate include "Astral Travel," "The Age of Aquarius," "The Seven Root Races and the Seven Sub-Races," and "Infra, Normal, and Supra-sexuality." The courses usually include guided meditations so that the material can be investigated on a personal level. These public courses are part of the group's "exoteric level, the first chamber." A mesoteric level and then an esoteric third chamber follow, during which the presentation of the material progresses from the theoretical to the practical. The practical work is alchemical and psychological, but not according to the common understanding of these terms. Regarding psychology, Freud seems to be discussed more often than Jung.

A great deal of the Gnostic Philosophy is standard occult lore. The cosmology and anthropology, for instance, owe much to the influential Madame Blavatsky. This may not be the place to investigate all of these theories. A comparison between the Gnostic Association and ancient Gnosticism may best be made by limiting the discussion to the modern group's central doctrine of seminal retention. The group teaches neither asceticism nor libertinism but the proper use of sexuality: the transmutation of the sexual energy to bring about the regeneration of the human being. This is accomplished through "la sexo-yoga," translated from Master Samael's writings into English as "Sex Magic."

> If a man and woman know how to retire without the spasm; if they would have in those moments of delightful enjoyment will power to control the Animal Ego and if then they would retire from the act without ejaculating the semen, neither inside nor outside the womb, neither inside of it nor to the side of it, nor in any place, they would have performed an act of Sex Magic. (1961, p. 7)

The beliefs that lead to such an unusual practice are not dissimilar to beliefs held by ancient Gnostics. This is so even though the writings and teachings of the Gnostic Philosophy show little knowledge of historical Gnosticism.[7] First of all, according to the Gnostic Philosophy, we have a "multiplicity of egos" within us which we falsely assume to be our self. These multiple egos are like several brains—intellectual, emotional, instinctive, sexual, and so on. These false "I's," thousands of them, determine our behavior and make us like machines because they are subject to the on-off switch of stimulus and response. When one of these "I's" is active, we think it is our self, but we are wrong. This "pluralized self" is "a mass of devils" (Weor n.d., pp. 77, 133).

This is proper Gnostic teaching. In the middle of the second century the Alexandrian Gnostics Basilides and Valentinus taught the very same thing. Basilides "called the passions appendages." They were not part of us but were wicked spirits attached to our souls. A person, he said, was like the Trojan horse, containing "in one body a host of different spirits." Valentinus likewise compared our insides with an inn where many demons camped.

Both of these ancient teachers called for a house cleaning of these forces by a higher, divine power (Clement 1983, p. 372). The Gnostic Association claims, in our own age, to "teach the 'Modus Operandi' in which one can be helped by such powers superior to the mind." It is, Master Samael writes, "a flammiferous power . . . capable by itself to disintegrate the aberrations that we carry in our psychological interior" (n.d., pp. 94, 159–60). "Fortunately," he adds, "this serpentine power exists in ourselves. This fantastic fire that the old alchemists called Stella Maris, the Isis of the Egyptians, the Tonantzin of the Aztecs . . . Mother God always symbolized in our interior by the holy snake of the Great Mysteries" (n.d., p. 159; 1961, p. 159). Primarily, this internal snake is the Kundalini of Indian Tantric Yoga, "the solar fire enclosed in the seminal atoms" (1961, pp. 32, 136–39).

The importance of the Gnostic Philosophy's central doctrine should now be clear. There are, says Master Samael, two kinds of Sex Magic: Black and White. "Those who practice White Sex Magic never ejaculate the semen. Those who practice Black Sex Magic always ejaculate the semen." A great battle is going on in the universe, the outcome of which is influenced by these two opposite practices. It is the battle between "the tempting serpent of Eden and the brazen serpent which healed the Israelites. . . . When the serpent ascends, we become Angels, when it descends, Demons" (1961, p. 17). Semen, or more exactly the hormonal energy produced in the endocrine system (1961, p. 146), can transmute us when it is turned around and raised inwardly.

This mystery was known in bygone times, in Lemuria, where sex was a sacrament performed without seminal ejaculation. The Lemurians were, alas, taught ejaculation by the Dark Lucifers (1961, p. 24). Their history is allegorized in the Bible by the trees of good and evil. Adam and Eve were an entire race, and original sin consisted in ejaculating the semen. Next came the Atlanteans, who also knew the mystery, abused it, and likewise sank to the bottom of the sea. Each time, some advanced folk escaped to teach the next race. Hence the story of Noah, an allegory of the Atlantean race.[8] Some members of our present race have known this mystery. Read Leviticus 15.

Scholars frequently divide ancient Gnostics into two camps: ascetic and libertine. One side of the dualist argument denies the flesh; the opposite says, "What difference does it make?" This is a misleading taxonomy. It assumes that sexual activity among Gnostics, when it took place, was wild merrymaking. Since the early centuries, sex has been depicted with a leering attention to detail. In the fourth century Epiphanius, a bishop from Cyprus, wrote the following: The Gnostics hold "a feast; and they serve up lavish helpings of meat and wine. Then when they have had their drinking party, they give themselves over to . . . the passion of fornication." The account then describes an appallingly sexual eucharistic meal (Foerster 1972, p. 319).

It may be useful to compare this account with one of the first descriptions by an outsider of a Hindu tantric ritual. According to H. H. Wilson, who wrote a decade after the coronation of Queen Victoria,

> The Shakti (that is, the power of the divine in action) is personated by a naked female, to whom meat and wine are offered, and then distributed amongst the assistants, the recitation of various *Mantras* and texts, and the performance of the *Mudra,* or gesticulations with the fingers, accompanying the different stages of the ceremony, and it is terminated with the most scandalous orgies amongst the votaries. (1846, pp. 257–58)

Our own century has treated the tantric practices of Hinduism with more reverence. Today, Western scholars such as Agehananda Bharati (1970, pp. 228–78) describe tantric rituals from the inside, as learned apologists.

It is unfortunate that the extant accounts of Gnostic sexuality parallel those of the Victorians observing the Hindus. What hints we do have regarding these matters from the pens of the Gnostics point not to orgies but to a pious, sacramental sexuality. This is certainly the case with the contemporary Gnostic Association:

> The homes of the Gnostic Initiates should have a background of happiness, music and ineffable kisses. . . . Love and Wisdom should alone reign . . . to practice Sex Magic, the Initiate unites sexually *only* with his wife. . . . It is necessary that there be no animal desire during the practice. Remember that Desire is diabolical. The 'I' is Desire. The 'I' is diabolical. Where Desire exists there cannot be Love. . . . Love is a flow from heart to heart, from Soul to Soul. . . . Love is the best Religion man can come to profess. (Weor 1961, pp. 49, 71, 144)

Among the ancient Gnostics, similar distinctions were drawn between wrongful and spiritual sexual intercourse. The Valentinians said that "Whosoever being *in* this world does not so love a woman as to obtain possession of her, is not of the truth, nor shall attain to the truth. But whosoever being *of* this world has intercourse with a woman shall not attain to the truth because he has so acted under the power of concupiscence" (Irenaeus 1981, pp. 324–25). Animal conduct, they said, leads nowhere. The goal is the perfection of the spiritual seed.

Seed, the male seed, was a numinous substance for many ancient Gnostics. The Naassenes, a serpent-worshiping sect attacked by the Church Father Hippolytus in the late second century, associated seed with the divine light and with the creative word (1981, pp. 47–64). When it is employed in earthly intercourse, seed leads to birth and so to death. The flow of that spiritual seed should be reversed, as Joshua turned around the Jordan River, and be made to flow upwards to heaven. Whether this Hellenistic Gnostic sect practiced kundalini yoga is nearly inconceivable, but consider the following: Hippolytus claims that the Naassenes drew a correspondence between a seven-fold heaven and a sevenfold arrangement of our interior anatomy. He claims that they taught that the descent of the spiritual seed into matter and its rising into the heavens is paralleled inside of us by a spiritual current flowing up and down our spinal column between our genitals and the pineal gland at the front of our brain. Further-more, this saving energy that propels the seed up the spine was portrayed by the Gnostics as a serpent (1981, pp. 46, 64). Master Samael, with no apparent knowledge of this most interesting passage in Hippolytus, argues forcefully that none of the ancient mysteries can be understood apart from kundalini yoga (1981, p. 139). All ancient symbolism, properly expounded, is about the raising of this powerful snake, the Kundalini of the tantrics, up through the seven centers, or chakras, along our spine to purge our being of the false, demonic egos that possess us.[9]

Can such striking parallels between Indian Tantric and Mediterra-nean Gnostic mysteries be the result of direct contact? Master Samael makes no attempt to produce a documented argument, and even C. W. King's claims remained speculative. There was frequent trade between the two regions from the time of Alexander the Great through the early Roman Empire, at first overland and later by ship through the Red Sea. Indians were seen at Alexandria, and a few curious Westerners are known to have gone off to look at India. Scholars of Hellenistic religions have seen this more as an exchange of merchandise than as an exchange of ideas or practices, but scholars of Indian religions have been less conservative. Giuseppe Tucci speculated that the tantras, which arose in the northwestern frontier of India, could have borrowed from Gnosticism (1949, p. 212). And the Buddhist scholar Edward Conze argued repeatedly that "India received many Gnostic ideas from Alexandria and Asia Minor" (1967, pp. 651–67; 1977, p. 71).

Meanwhile, whatever the ancient connections between tantric and Gnostic beliefs, what are we to make of Master Samael's claim that a continuing occult tradition has been passed down in the West, especially a tradition of sex magic? This tradition can certainly be traced to the nineteenth century, when India was full of Europeans who discovered, among other things, the Tantras. Apart from the scholars who translated the texts, the following personalities are important to the tradition received by Master Samael. First, Karl Kellner, an Austrian businessman and Freemason, was perhaps initiated into tantric sexual practices in India. He founded the Ordo Templi Orientis (O.T.O.) in Germany. The British magician Aleister Crowley was initiated into this group in 1914. O.T.O. groups throughout England and the United States still celebrate the Gnostic Mass, full of heavy-handed sexual imagery, that Crowley composed (1929, pp. 345–61). As well as sex magic and kundalini yoga, there are many identities between the O.T.O. and Master Samael's Gnostic Association, although the O.T.O. does not practice *coitus reservatus.* Also important in the introduction of these practices to the West was the American Pascal Beverly Randolph. Randolph read Eastern texts and may have been initiated. During the 1860s he taught sex magic throughout America and Europe, and he wrote two books: *Eulis! The History of Love* and *Magia Sexualis.* He was involved in Germany with Kellner and through him to Krumm-Heller and then to Master Samael.

Tantric yogic practice, however, does not result in our spiritual perfection. According to the Gnostic Association, it is merely our psychological preparation. Here the group departs from the teachings of the groups from which it is immediately derived to align itself even more strongly with ancient Gnostic ideas. Following this preparatory work, according to the group's teachings, the true person can develop. With Kundalini, our feminine snake, raised within us and our inner being cleansed, we are ready to receive our true essence, our soul, which comes down to us from the stars. This true self, which is masculine, consummates its incarnation in us with a marriage to the feminine power we have raised to meet it. An ancient Gnostic text, the *Exegesis on the Soul* (Robinson 1988, pp. 192–98), graphically describes just such a marriage. In this text a female soul turns herself from outside to within. When she was external, she had lustful sex with the world. By turning herself inward, she is able to receive, as a womb, her heavenly bridegroom. She is then regenerated and saved. The ancient sacrament of the bridal chamber may have been an enactment of this inner marriage with our true heavenly counterpart (Irenaeus 1981, p. 334).

For the modern Gnostic Association, Jesus is our role model for this doctrine. The Association separates, as did the ancient Gnostics, Jesus the human being from Christ the divine self that came upon him. Master Samael informs us that "Jesus studied in Egypt and practiced sex magic inside one of the pyramids. . . . That is how he prepared himself to incarnate the Christ in the Jordan" (1961, pp. 55, 223).

The idea that we receive a new name at this spiritual rebirth is found in ancient times. A Gnostic scribe signs his name at the end of the *Gospel of the Egyptians* as "Eugnostos, the beloved in the Spirit with my fellow lights in incorruptibility, in the flesh my name is Gongessos" (Robinson 1988, pp. 218–19). He therefore has two names, his worldly name and the name of his true self which is known to his spiritual companions. A Columbian occultist named Victor Manuel Gomez incarnated Samael, the angel of the planet Mars,[10] and thus received the name of his higher self, "Master Samael Aun Weor."

Reality, for Master Samael and his students, is somewhere quite other than where our demonic egos tend to locate it. It is in another dimension, the astral, the source of our true essence, the plane of all real experience and our hope for immortality. "The Gnostic Church," we are told, "exists in the Higher Worlds: it is the Cathedral of the Soul." Leave the physical body, "and go in the Astral body to the Gnostic Church." Every night, as one goes to sleep, one must pray, thousands of times, "I believe in Christ. I believe in Oguara. Please take me out of bed . . . take me to the Gnostic Church" (Weor 1961, p. 74).

Many, many years ago, a Gnostic heroine named Norea prayed for rescue from the rulers of this dark world, wicked powers who were trying to rape her. In answer to her prayer, now found in an old Coptic text from Egypt, an angel descended. The angel told Norea that these dark powers could not defile her, for her true home was superior to the world: "You . . . are from the primeval father, from above, out of the imperishable Light" (Robinson 1988, p. 169). This is what Gnosticism, both ancient and modern, teaches.

There are some differences. The physiological literalness attributed to the saving seed is consistent with some ancient beliefs, but the practice of retaining the seed is not. That practice is tantric (Bharati 1970, p. 179). The literalism creates an ambiguity about regeneration. Both the physical[11] and the astral body are regenerated. An ancient Gnostic would not have appreciated this concern with the physical body. The centrality of this doctrine distinguishes this modern movement from ancient Gnosticism. There are, neverthe-

less, many other correspondences. Students of the Gnostic Philosophy are provided the solution, in a complete and consistent manner,
to the same eternal and quintessential questions that Gnostics have
worried over since Theodotus the Valentinian first posed them in the
second century: "Who are we? Where do we come from? Where are
we going? From what are we delivered? What is birth, and what is
rebirth?" (Foerster 1972, p. 230).

Both of these groups, the Ecclesia Gnostica and the Gnostic
Association, claim to be Gnostic. They differ, on many points, from
ancient Gnosticism as well as from each other. The Ecclesia
Gnostica, although having greater familiarity with ancient sources,
ignores many of the hard dualistic doctrines of the ancient Gnostics.
In an attempt to speak to the modern audience, the Ecclesia Gnostica
has softened the tradition toward psychological reductionism. The
Gnostic Association has less of a grasp on the ancient sources. It has
nevertheless constructed a religious system which shows close affinity to the ancient Gnostic myth.[12]

The literature and lectures of both groups avoid the term "Gnosticism," preferring to speak of "gnosis." This shift in terms has also
been promoted among some scholars of Gnosticism.[13] The shift to
"gnosis" allows the inclusion of several diverse mystical traditions.
For these modern groups, an appeal to "gnosis" justifies beliefs and
practices that are linked only secondarily with ancient Gnosticism
and are primarily tied to traditions that entered our culture only
within the last century.

NOTES

I want to thank Chris Farmer for his assistance with this essay.

1.   There are currently well over six hundred Independent Old Catholic
bishops active in the United States, or about twice as many as Roman
Catholic bishops!

2.   A few members of de Palatine's group continue in Los Angeles as the
Pre-Nicene Ekklesia. Other groups have subsequently splintered from
Hoeller, especially the Ecclesia Gnostica Mysteriorum in Palo Alto, California. Under the leadership of Bishop Rosamonde Miller, this church practices
rites preserved by a secret succession of women, the Holy Order of Mary
Magdalene (Miller 1984a, 1984b). The schismatic proclivities of these
groups parallel at least two aspects of ancient Gnosticism: first, the diversity
of our primary sources (Robinson 1988, p. 1); second, the movement's
ultimately suicidal sectarianism. Tertullian, describing the second generation of Valentinians, could point to only one follower who held true to the

teachings of the movement's founder (1980a, p. 505). The great church did not need to divide the Gnostics in order to conquer. It simply kept chanting the mantra "one" (for example, Clement 1983, p. 555).

3. These Greek words do not, however, appear in the Coptic text of the *Gospel of Truth,* nor is "knowledge of the heart" a correct translation of the Coptic phrase that does appear. Better is MacRae's translation "interior knowledge" (Robinson 1988, p. 46). The difficulty with "knowledge of the heart" is that "heart" meant something different to the ancients than it does to us. We feel with our hearts and think with our heads. They sensed with their heads, felt with their guts, and thought with their hearts. Thus a proper translation of the Greek word *kardia* is often "mind."

4. "Jung's long-time friend and collaborator Professor Gilles Quispel took the lead, . . . acquired one of the codices, . . . and it was from this portion of the great library that most of the early translations were made, thus shaming the scholarly community into speeding up its long-delayed work" (Hoeller 1982, p. 19). Statements such as this are so distant from the facts that they do a disservice to Jung and Professor Quispel as well as libel many other scholars. The Jung Institute purchased Codex I of the Nag Hammadi Library in 1952. An edition and translation of one of the five tractates contained in the codex was brought out in 1956. The same year a photographic facsimile of three and a half tractates from Codex II was published in Cairo. All these texts were translated and published by "the scholarly community"—two East German scholars—in 1958–59, years before the Jung Codex team brought out their second volume in 1963. The rest of the library of thirteen codices was simply unavailable to scholars, as it was held by the Egyptian authorities. In 1970 a UNESCO committee with James M. Robinson as secretary was formed to publish facsimile plates of the entire library. Seven years later, an American team under the direction of Robinson published translations of the entire library (45 tractates). In 1975, after twenty-three years, the Jung Codex team published the last of its five tractates (Robinson 1984, pp. 88–95).

5. For definitions of Gnosticism see Yamauchi (1983, pp. 13–19, 188–89). For further discussions of Jung and Gnosticism see Segal (1992) and Smith (1988a).

6. "The Ecclesia celebrates the seven mysteries known as Sacraments in the Roman and other Catholic churches which are administered by priests and priestesses ordained within an Apostolic Succession that is recognized as ancient and valid by Catholic authorities" (Hoeller 1981–82, p. 8). Roman Catholic canon law nevertheless regards such orders as illicit and invalid. Tertullian does tell a story about Valentinus's being rejected as a candidate for Bishop of Rome (1980, p. 505), but this story is hardly believable (Pagels 1979, p. 39).

7. Weor's writings confound ancient Gnosticism with primitive Christianity: "The Primitive Christian Church was the true esoteric trunk, today's Roman Sect is only a derivation . . . to the Primitive Catholic Christian

Gnostic Church belonged: Saturnine of Antioch, Simon Magus, Harpocrates, Marcion De Ponto, St. Thomas, Valentine, St. Augustine, Tertullian, St. Ambrose, Irenaeus, Hippolytus, Epiphanius, Clement of Alexandria, Mark, Cerdon, Empedocles, St. Geronimo . . ." (1961, pp. 71–72). This list contains more opponents than practitioners of historical Gnosticism (and one stray pre-Socratic philosopher).

8. The legend of Atlantis was first written down by Plato in the *Timaeus* but is said by him to have been narrated in Egypt. Lemuria, now an article of faith among occultists, was unheard of until the 1850s. To account for the peculiar distribution of lemurs, Darwinists posited a sunken continent and named it Lemuria.

9. Hippolytus, in Book V of his *Refutation,* discusses several related sects. The specific group that associated serpent-seed-spine was the Peratae. Edmund Meltzer has drawn my attention to an article which claims that the ancient Egyptians made the same associations (Schwabe et al., 1982). For a lengthy discussion of ancient Gnostic interpretations of semen, see Smith (1988b).

10. Samael is called "the angel of Mars" by the nineteenth-century French occultist Eliphas Levi (1910, p. 78). Many of the illustrations reproduced by Weor, especially the pentagram (1961, p. 196) frequently printed on brochures of the Gnostic Association, are from Levi's book.

11. The Gnostic Association cites the example of the French physician Charles Edward Brown-Séquard. In 1899, at the age of seventy-two, Brown-Séquard announced that he had rejuvenated himself through the injection of extracts taken from the testicles of animals.

12. Leaders of both groups kindly responded to a preliminary version of this paper. Bishop Hoeller pointed out that my discussion of him as a Liberal Catholic was in error. I have made some revisions in accordance with his wishes. José Gonzalez pointed out a methodological problem with my analysis of Master Samael's immediate historical background: "Gnosis is not based on books or organizations, but on Samael's research in superior planes of consciousness."

13. Robert McL. Wilson, especially, has encouraged the use of the term "gnosis" (1968). The discussion was advanced by Rudolph (1983).

REFERENCES

Anson, Peter F. 1964. *Bishops at Large.* London: Faber and Faber.

Bharati, Agehananda. 1970 [1965]. *The Tantric Tradition.* Garden City, NY: Doubleday.

Blavatsky, H. P. 1877. *Isis Unveiled.* 2 vols. Adyar, India: Theosophical Publishing House.

———. 1888. *The Secret Doctrine.* 2 vols. Adyar, India: Theosophical Publishing House.

Clement of Alexandria. 1983. *The Stromata,* tr. William Wilson. In *The Ante-Nicene Fathers,* eds. Alexander Roberts and James Donaldson, Vol. II (Grand Rapids, MI: Eerdmans), pp. 299–568.

Conze, Edward. 1967. "Buddhism and Gnosis." In *Le Origini dello Gnosticismo,* ed. Ugo Bianchi, Studies in the History of Religions (Supplements to *Numen*), Vol. XII (Leiden: Brill), pp. 651–67.

———. 1979. *The Memoirs of a Modern Gnostic.* Part I. Sherborne, Eng.: Samizdat.

Crowley, Aleister. [1929]. *Magic in Theory and Practice.* New York: Castle Books. (Undated reprint of the Paris private edition)

Dart, John. 1973. "L.A. Gnostics Stress Psychology of Religion." *Los Angeles Times,* September 9, Part II, p. 2.

Duc de Palatine, Richard. 1973. *The Gnostic Forum,* I, No. 3. Sherman Oaks, CA: Privately printed.

Ellwood, Robert S. 1973. *Religious and Spiritual Groups in Modern America.* Englewood Cliffs, NJ: Prentice-Hall.

Foerster, Werner, ed. 1972. *Gnosis,* tr. R. McL. Wilson. Vol. I. London: Oxford University Press.

Hoeller, Stephan A. 1972. *The Gnostic Holy Eucharist.* Hollywood, CA: Privately printed.

———. 1973. *The Mystery and Magic of the Eucharist.* Hollywood, CA: Privately printed.

———. 1975. *The Royal Road: A Manual of Kabalistic Meditations on the Tarot.* Wheaton, IL: Theosophical Publishing House.

———. 1976. "Sophia, the Gnostic Archetype of Feminine Soul-Wisdom." *American Theosophist* 64:123–29.

———. 1977. "Gnostic Rituals: Early Sacramental Techniques of Ecstasy." *American Theosophist* 65:133–38.

———. 1981. "What on Earth are Gnostics?" Lecture delivered December 4, 1981. Cassette #GN1, The Gnostic Society, 4516 Hollywood Boulevard, Los Angeles, CA 90027.

———. 1981–82. *The Gnostic Society Winter Quarter Activities: Practical Studies in Gnosticism, Jungian Psychology, Kabbala, Sacrament and the Tarot Through Lectures, Classes and Recordings by Dr. Stephan Hoeller.* Hollywood, CA: Privately printed.

———. 1982. *The Gnostic Jung and the Seven Sermons to the Dead.* Wheaton, IL: Theosophical Publishing House.

———. 1989. *Jung and the Lost Gospels.* Wheaton, IL: Theosophical Publishing House.

Hippolytus. 1981. *The Refutation of All Heresies,* tr. J. H. MacMahon. In *The Ante-Nicene Fathers,* eds. Alexander Roberts and James Donaldson, Vol. II (Grand Rapids, MI: Eerdmans), pp. 299–568.

Irenaeus. 1981. *Against Heresies,* trs. Alexander Roberts and others. In *The Ante-Nicene Fathers,* eds. Alexander Roberts and James Donaldson, Vol. I (Grand Rapids, MI: Eerdmans), pp. 309–567.

King, C. W. 1982 [1887]. *The Gnostics and Their Remains.* 2nd ed. San Diego: Wizards Bookshelf.

Leadbeater, Charles Webster. 1920. *The Science of the Sacraments.* Los Angeles: St. Alban Press.

Lévi, Eliphas. 1910 [1855–56]. *Transcendental Magic,* tr. Arthur Edward Waite. Chicago: Occult Publishing House.

Mead, G. R. S. 1960 [1906]. *Fragments of a Faith Forgotten.* 2nd ed. New Hyde Park, NY: University Books.

Miller, Rosamonde. 1984a. *The Gnostic Holy Eucharist.* Palo Alto, CA: Privately printed.

———. 1984b. *The Gnostic* (newsletter). Palo Alto, CA: Privately printed.

Pagels, Elaine. 1979. *The Gnostic Gospels.* New York: Random House.

Perala, Nestor O., ed. 1984. *Abraxas 84.* Hollywood, CA: Privately printed.

Pruter, Karl, and J. Gordon Melton, eds. 1983. *The Old Catholic Sourcebook.* New York: Garland.

Pryse, James M. 1925a. *The Apocalypse Unsealed.* Los Angeles: John M. Pryse.

———. 1925b. *The Restored New Testament.* Los Angeles: John M. Pryse.

Robinson, James M., ed. 1984. *The Facsimile Edition of The Nag Hammadi Codices: Introduction.* Leiden: Brill.

———, ed. 1988. *The Nag Hammadi Library in English.* 3rd ed. San Francisco: Harper & Row.

Rudolph, Kurt. 1983. "'Gnosis' and 'Gnosticism'." In *The New Testament and Gnosis,* eds. A. H. B. Logan and A. J. M. Wedderburn (Edinburgh: T. & T. Clark), pp. 21–37.

Schwade, Calvin W., Joyce Adams, and Carlton T. Hodge. 1982. "Egyptian Beliefs About the Bull's Spine: An Anatomical Origin for Ankh." *Anthropological Linguistics* 24:445–79.

Segal, Robert A., ed. 1992. *The Gnostic Jung.* Princeton, NJ: Princeton University Press.

Smith, Richard. 1988a. "Afterword: The Modern Relevance of Gnosticism." In Robinson (1988), pp. 532–49.

———. "Sex Education in Gnostic Schools." In *Images of the Feminine in Gnosticism,* ed. Karen L. King (Philadelphia: Fortress), pp. 345–60.

Tertullian. 1980a. *Against the Valentinians,* tr. Alexander Roberts. In *The Ante-Nicene Fathers,* eds. Alexander Roberts and James Donaldson, Vol. III (Grand Rapids, MI: Eerdmans), pp. 503–20.

———. 1980b. *The Prescription Against Heretics,* tr. Peter Holmes. In *The Ante-Nicene Fathers,* eds. Alexander Roberts and James Donaldson, Vol. III (Grand Rapids, MI: Eerdmans), pp. 243–67.

Tucci, Giuseppe. 1949. *Tibetan Painted Scrolls.* Rome: La Libreria dello Stato.

(Wedgwood, James Ingal). 1924. *The Liturgy According to the Use of the Liberal Catholic Church.* London: St. Alban Press.

Weor, Samael Aun. 1961. *The Perfect Marriage.* Mexico: Privately printed.

————. 1983. *Glosario Esoterico Gnostico.* Mexico: Privately printed.

————. n.d. *Treatise on Esoterical and Revolutionary Psychology.* San Salvador: Logos Solar.

Wilson, R[obert] McL. 1968. *Gnosis and the New Testament.* Philadelphia: Fortress.

Yamauchi, Edwin M. 1983. *Pre-Christian Gnosticism.* 2nd ed. Grand Rapids, MI: Baker Book House.

INDEX

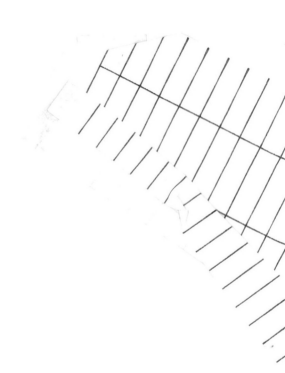